The devil in modern philosophy

***

Ernest Gellner

edited with a preface by I. C. Jarvie
and Joseph Agassi

Routledge & Kegan Paul
London and Boston

First published in 1974
by Routledge & Kegan Paul Ltd
Broadway House, 68–74 Carter Lane,
London EC4V 5EL and
9 Park Street,
Boston, Mass. 02108, U.S.A.
Printed in Great Britain by
Richard Clay (The Chaucer Press) Ltd
Bungay, Suffolk
© Ernest Gellner 1974

ISBN 0 7100 7886 2
Library of Congress Catalog Card No. 73–93636

Contents

Preface

Ernest Gellner became a philosopher at a bad time: the dominant stream of philosophy in this country—'Oxford' philosophy or 'linguistic' philosophy—was boring. Not only was it boring—indeed it made a virtue of being boring—it was pointless. Not only was it pointless—indeed it made a virtue of being pointless—it was self-serving. It even made a virtue of being self-serving. Anyone interested in Gellner and his philosophical ideas has to take these as premisses. Although Gellner has long since become a professionally qualified and published anthropologist; although he teaches in a sociology department and doubtless thinks of himself as something of a sociologist (perhaps an amateur but no dilettante); he remains above all a philosopher. The problems which preoccupy him, the things he has to say, are directly philosophical.

Coming of age at a time when philosophy was supposed to naturally have no problems, or at worst to have had them and to be engaged in making them go away (dissolve); at a time when philosophers were not supposed to be so vulgar as to have something to *say* about these problems (as opposed to something to *do*); at such a time a genuine philosopher had to break out to breathe. This aspect of Gellner's career, which brought him his original fame (for some, notoriety for others), the struggle for the freedom to philosophize, is hardly touched upon in this volume. We have rigorously excluded papers that were precursors of, or spin-offs from, his devastating act of breaking out, *Words and Things* (1959). Doubtless, when Ph.D. theses are written about the dispute over Oxford linguistic philosophy in Britain in the 1950s, these papers will be anthologized—by others. Our purpose, in collecting papers spread over twenty years of philosophical reflection, is to show how Gellner's break-out was not just that. It led him to conclude that philosophical movements and fashions could not be adequately explained solely by philosophical means. This in turn led him into explorations of English intellectual culture, with a critical detachment and insight all the more remarkable because in this case the anthropologist is a member of the tribe.

Gellner's systematic philosophy, if he has one, is also not expounded here. Again, the books *Thought and Change* (1965) and *The Legitimation of Belief* (1974) speak for themselves. What is to be found here are chapters on specific philosophical problems, and others on specific people with interesting philosophical ideas (not all of them philosophers). Despite wide differences on many matters, on one very profound point about philosophy Popper and Gellner are at one against Oxford linguistic philosophy: for both of them, philosophy is not a detached and free-floating activity for specialists; it cannot be separated out from people's common-or-garden beliefs and day-to-day lives. Everyone has, however implicit, attitudes towards the basic philosophical quests of man, regarding his place in nature and society, regarding the meaning of life and of history. Philosophy is being critical about these questions, and proposing new solutions to them. Gellner is a philosopher who tries to contribute to this ambitious and magnificent tradition. And, in that tradition, each formulation, each statement, each view, is just another approximation, another speech in the continuing dialogue. Appropriately enough, the volume ends with the author's homage to another ambitious thinker, Noam Chomsky, in whom he senses a similar quest and to whom he looks hopefully for further enlightenment.

I. C. J.
J. A.

Acknowledgments

The editors met Ernest Gellner in the 1950s at the London School of Economics when they were students, whom he treated as colleagues. Their appreciation of his work has grown since then, and they were glad to receive permission to edit his work. The editors wish to thank the publishers and editors of the different papers here republished. They take joint and equal responsibility for the selection, arrangement, and preface. Most of the technical work in preparing the volume for the press and seeing it through to publication was done by Jarvie, who wishes to thank his research assistant, Mr Michael Burchak. Agassi takes the blame for the flamboyant subject index.

York University, Toronto   I. C. J.
Boston University and *Tel Aviv University*   J. A.

Part one   Philosophy in general

Chapter 1   The devil in modern philosophy

Modern philosophy, from Descartes onwards and including the present generation of philosophers, can be *defined* as belief in the devil. What gives post-Cartesian philosophy unity is the daemon. Descartes invented him, but all the others believe in him.

Why and how did Descartes invent him? As is well known, Descartes, surveying the chaos of past errors, and noticing that even the greatest absurdities were believed by someone, hoped that reason could lift itself by its own bootstraps and liberate itself from all possible error. But to do that one had to start from scratch. Now, if you want to start from scratch the main difficulty is to find the scratch; to find that firm point from which the totally new but safe departure is to be made. This is where the *assumption* of the devil comes in. Assume an evil-minded and all-powerful devil whose aim is to frustrate you, and above all to frustrate you in attempts to know anything about the world.

Now try, just try really seriously to make this assumption and see which of your convictions stand up to it: very few, if any. Still, there might be some convictions that survived. There may be some convictions which even on the assumption of the malignant daemon who interferes with us, must still remain indubitably true. If indeed there are such, then *they* constitute the scratch. They must be the bedrock, the firm and truly reliable base, the foundation of a new edifice. Now just this was the function in Descartes of the *assumption* of the devil: to use it as an acid test, as a means of isolating that which is really certain, from that which only appears so. Note that for this it is quite unnecessary for the devil really to exist; only the assumption, not the reality, is required. And as a matter of historical fact, Descartes did not believe in his existence. On the contrary, he believed that the truth of rigorous thinking was underwritten by a benevolent God.

The particular firm base that Descartes managed to locate by his device is well known: I think, therefore I am. I may doubt everything, but the doubt itself is a case of thinking, and therefore I exist.

Whatever can be doubted, whatever may be suspect as a possible *front* of the devil, one's own existence cannot. This argument can be interpreted in (at least) three ways: as what contemporary philosophers would call a pragmatic paradox, as hinging on the fact that the occurrence of a doubt is itself an instance of thinking, and hence the existence of thought is proved by the very doubt itself. Or it can be interpreted as an argument from the certainty and indubitability of the immediate data of consciousness. Or again, it may be interpreted as the argument that an activity entails an agent, a manifestation entails a substance of which it is the manifestation. Whichever of these interpretations we adopt, the arguments conveyed have interesting subsequent histories. Just what Descartes did with his bedrock when he found it doesn't concern us now.

For most philosophers after Descartes, the devil was far from fictitious. They did not *assume* his existence, whilst remaining quite confident that he did not exist. No, on the contrary, they firmly believe that he exists. Subsequent philosophers can be classified according to how they identified him.

The first theory was that the devil was our own mind. It was our own mind which organized the systematic misrepresentation which Descartes feared but did not really think went on. It is our own mind which makes us believe in the existence of things which are not truly there, or obscures the existence of those which are. There are many variations on this theme. For instance, it may be held that our mind misleads us by trusting the senses too much; but it has also been supposed that it misleads us through indulgence in abstract thought.

The second major theory is that the devil is *history*. This theory grew very naturally from the earlier identification of the daemon with mind. Thinkers such as Locke or Hume thought they were carrying out their investigations into *the* human understanding, or human nature as such; that by dissecting the mind they would be able to tell us enough about the habits of this one daemon, so that anyone anywhere could be forewarned. Not that Hume, for instance, was unaware of something that we may call cultural relativism; still, basically it was the same mind everywhere, the same devil.

The transition from identifying the daemon with mind to identifying him with history came after Kant, and was perhaps implicit in some of his views. If for Kant truth was still unique, error was not random. Error as much as truth reflected the structure of the mind (perhaps more so); such basic errors as exist are external manifestations of something essential in us, and they will for that very reason tend to appear in certain patterns. The errors that we find on looking back at the history of thought are not like the random dispersal round the bull's eye, a tedious record of trial and error with more error than daemon. The daemon was held to be invincible to the extent that we could not do without him, or break his habits, but he was not invincible to the extent of being able to hide his tricks; at least not after Kant had uncovered them for us. We had to go on living with them, but at least we knew what they were. The more pernicious ones, those tempting us into wild-goose chases, could be neutralized if not extirpated. And in one sphere, Kant deified the daemon; by equating morality with rationality, he equated moral truth with what the mind imposed.

Those who collaborate with the devil often justify it by giving him a good character. There is the sociological theory which makes out deceit to be important for the sake of social cohesion. A man will in some sense subscribe to beliefs which he does not really consider true because they are in his view the devices of a benevolent daemon, even if no longer an all-powerful one. Thus men may subscribe to mythologies which have, they think, desirable political or social functions. This is truly a case of helping a poor devil who can no longer deceive but who pleads good intentions.

Contemporary philosophy in this country has in the recent decades started out from an outlook which intended to outwit the devil by means of a perfect language and logic; these were intended as a kind of holy water that could keep him at bay. Any time the sulphur of metaphysics or of a seemingly insoluble problem was smelt, the incantation of a reduction of the problem in good logical grammar would restore order. Since then, however, whilst the devil continues to be identified with language, there has been an almost complete swing over to deifying him. Thus whatever language does is *ipso facto* O.K. The main school, the Oxonians, stand for the enthusiastic restoration of *Oldspeak*. At present they are such enthusiastic collaborators that their main joy is hunting out resisters caught with some of the old logical weapons still in their hands.

The most recent version of the linguistic devil is interesting in that the sphere in which the devil must be fought has shrunk very much indeed. All the common activities, scientific or ordinary, are fairly free from undesirable machinations. It is only past philosophical theories, whether metaphysical or positivist, that reveal his doings. A curious reversal! In the past, ordinary unreflective experience and thought were sometimes considered as the veil past which the philosopher must penetrate to find true reality. According to the new school, it is the veil which is reality; the doctrine *that it is the veil* is an illusion, and the only one. Descartes started a new philosophy by doubting virtually everything. This new school has started another by systematically doubting *nothing*. (This is known as Common Sense or respect for ordinary usage.) Or to use another parable; philosophy is still seen in terms of Plato's cave, but the philosopher's job is now said to be to lead us back *into the cave*.   1958

Chapter 2   The crisis in the humanities and the mainstream of philosophy

The state of England

Assume that a nuclear war destroys Britain. The only surviving collection of documents is the library of a philosopher of the recently fashionable linguistic school who, perhaps emulating the legendary self-exile of the Master in Norway, settled on a lonely island in the Outer Hebrides. This linguo-hermit, we shall assume, was one of those who divested himself of all old works of thought, somewhat ashamed of having ever owned them,[1] so that this sole extant library consists of linguo-philosophic works only.

Imagine some archaeologist/historian from another planet discovering this library and reconstructing the history of Britain from it. After much pain, our extra-terrestrial investigator has deciphered the script and come to understand written English. Let us also suppose that he knows, from outside surviving sources, that during the middle of the twentieth century Britain was frequently in economic difficulties.

One can all too easily visualize the history of Britain written by our archaeologist in possession of the linguo-philosophic library. It might run something as follows:

> In the middle of the twentieth century, the British economy was stagnant. It is not clear why this was so, given that strong evidence exists that in an earlier period this island was the premier industrial and commercial power. One must assume that a new wave of immigrants, with a social organization and ethos wholly different from the previous industrially and commercially enterprising population, had come in and subdued or expelled the proto-inhabitants, bringing a new set of *mores* with them.
>
> One must assume, from the fact that they conquered and replaced the earlier inhabitants, that their values and practices contained a military element. Few indices of this, however, survive. The extant literature, on the contrary, contains constant

allusions to metaphysical rather than martial preoccupations. Hence one must assume that, rather as in the case of the Indian caste system, a priestly or intellectual class was placed above the warrior class, and that the relative esteem accorded to the latter was so small that the literature was preoccupied exclusively with the concerns of the former.

The preoccupation of metaphysics, both favourable and hostile, must have been very considerable, judging from the very great frequency of allusions to it. Happily we possess a surviving file of a document known as the *Radio Times*, which gives us a list of the broadcasts of the period. On the so-called Third Programme, devoted to serious matters, a quite outstandingly large proportion of time was given to many and various series of talks expounding the views of the Anti-metaphysical school. As is well known, moralists and thinkers do not preach against vices which do not tempt their listeners: hence the amount of energy and time—far greater than that accorded to any other theme—bears eloquent testimony to the pervasiveness of metaphysical inclinations amongst the people. Given that we know from other sources that this was a period of economic difficulty and decline, it is reasonable to conclude that the other-worldly preoccupations, particularly with metaphysics, of the priestly caste and of the population under its sway (presumably associated with a prohibition of trade), paralysed economic life.

The picture which life on the island presented must have been a curious, even an inspiring, one. A whole population was apparently preoccupied with abstruse issues such as the reality of time or the reality of the external world, or even the reality of each other, and in the hot debate of these issues neglected more mundane tasks.

This trend was not left unchallenged. Appalled by the economic and other consequences of this universal immersion in metaphysics, an anti-metaphysical reformist movement arose as indicated, which attempted to cure this preoccupation by teaching, broadcasting, writing, etc., and to turn the attention of their citizens to more useful concerns. They endeavoured to explain to their fellow-citizens that their abstruse and abstract concerns were but a pathological misuse, a dislocation, of the words and ideas that had once played a proper and useful role in their lives and language. The available evidence does not, unfortunately, make clear whether this movement was led by surviving members of the earlier inhabitants of Britain, or by deviant individuals from amongst the metaphysical invaders.

One must assume that the metaphysical befuddlement was

well-nigh universal amongst the population, for the works
which have been unearthed amongst the Hebridean MSS show
that the members of the reform movement were concerned with
virtually nothing else. As, clearly, there must have been other
intellectual problems facing the society of the time, one can
only conclude that the fight with metaphysics had absolute
priority, and this it could only have had in view of the
deplorable hold metaphysics had over the minds and hearts of
the citizens. A curious land, in which work and play were
neglected for transcendent reasoning and contemplation!

The brave reformers, of course, offended the prejudices, and
the vested interests, of the venomous metaphysical priests.
Hence they were maligned, abused, caricatured, and
misrepresented, in various scurrilous works and even, it appears,
in the national press. Though as a historian one must deplore
the loss of any document, nevertheless one cannot but rejoice
that no copy of those nasty, abusive works has survived . . . etc.,
etc.

Of course, if our hypothetical archaeologist or historian had
nothing but linguo-philosophical documents to go by, one might
well forgive him if he concluded that metaphysics and preoccupation
with the transcendent, etc., had gripped the whole population of
Britain to a dangerous extent, and hence that in his reconstructed
picture of the twentieth century Britain was something like an exaggerated version of India—an economically backward country ham-
pered by an other-worldly culture or outlook. He might well be
moved and saddened by the story of those brave reformers who
tried to oppose the creeping metaphysical disease, and become
angered, justly angered, even across the distance of space and time,
by those scurrilous, abusive, malevolent, intemperate attacks which
their intellectual daring and integrity had provoked from lesser and
jealous men.

This is precisely the image of recently fashionable philosophy
which one would indeed obtain, if one went by its own pronouncements. This is also the image which, by and large, is left with the
general public: a picture of a movement of tough-minded anti-
metaphysicians.[2] This is the image which, basically, they like to
present. They say in effect: we offer no World-pictures. We do not
legislate about the nature of the world, of nature, man, morals,
society. We clear up muddles, conceptual confusions, springing up
from misunderstandings of how language really works. In particular, we liberate you from the frightful heritage of past philosophers,
who, by their bombastic and presumptuous claims, and above all by
their rash tendency to jump to general theories (rather than attend-

ing, as we have learnt to do, to the detailed intricacies of our use of language), have left behind a heritage of theory so confused, yet so ingrained, that it is almost beyond sorting out. Better far to turn to new areas] (Mr Geoffrey Warnock, in 'J. L. Austin: a Remarkable Philospher', *Listener*, 7 April 1960, 617):

> Around the usual, and particularly the more imposing, topics of philosophy, the air is already thick with philosophical theories, and the ground, in Austin's words, is 'trodden into bogs and tracks' by generations of philosophers. . . . We flounder in the bogs . . . extreme measures are called for. The escape . . . from the magnetic fields of Plato, or Aristotle, or Kant . . . it may be salutary to place a moratorium on discussion of the state, or virtue, or the moral law, and consider instead . . . the difference between kindness and kindliness, or exactly what it is to be tactless and inconsiderate.

Or again (Professor Gilbert Ryle, *Dilemmas*, Cambridge, 1954, p.13):

> I daresay that my title has aroused the expectation . . . that I should be discussing . . . the feud . . . between Idealists and Realists, . . . between Empiricists and Rationalists. But I shall not try to interest you in these . . . I am not interested in them myself. They do not matter.

There is a number of things a bit wrong with this picture. One: this anti-metaphysical ardour is less than passionate. After all, 'metaphysics' in the pejorative sense need not own up to this name —why should it? 'Metaphysics', in the sense of loose and woolly language, the peddling of unwarranted factual claims and moral injunctions, claims of access to hidden realms, and all such dogmatism, camouflaged by shifts of meaning or lack of meaning altogether —all this *does* exist in this society in some measure. But it exists most plentifully, and in most influential form, in places such as 'literary criticism', or the writings of some psycho-analytic authors, in left-wing theology, on either of the two possible interpretations of the phrase,[3] and various other 'lay' forms of philosophy. (Consider the metaphysics of 'life', 'anti-life', 'life-enhancing', 'quality of experience', etc., practised by a school of 'literary criticism', for instance. When John Stuart Mill concerned himself with the differences in the *quality* of our experiences, he felt obliged to defend any claims to the ability to distinguish between higher and lower quality, by careful, conscientious, and perhaps unsuccessful argument. To-day, the concern with the 'quality of experience' has passed into the hands of men who seem to feel little need to defend rationally their own intuitions when grading the lives of their fellows.) Yet, curiously, the passionate anti-metaphysicians, the watchdogs of clarity and intellectual honesty, tend on the whole to leave the genuine cases of metaphysical infection alone. In the main, they gun only for past philosophers: living metaphysics bothers them far less.

Two (and more significant): just how important was the self-confessed 'metaphysics' which it was necessary to destroy with so much sounding of trumpets and against the resurgence of which such powerful ramparts had to be erected?

One may understand why our Martian historian, with nothing but a linguo-philosophic library recovered in the Outer Hebrides, should conclude that here was a society almost totally prey to metaphysics. But we who possess other information know that, whatever other defects this society may have, conceptual other-worldliness is really not so important among them. So why make such a fuss about it?

When people erect disproportionately elaborate barriers against X, though X is no real danger to them; when they are quite untroubled by X when it is thinly, indeed transparently, disguised; under such conditions we must suspect that, whatever they may say or think, they are not really worried by X at all, but by Y.[4] It is not *metaphysics* which really worries them. But something certainly does. Here we have a puzzle about contemporary philosophy. *What* is that something else?

The permanent revolution

Poor physics! It is difficult to suppress a feeling of superiority, of embarrassed compassion, when considering the subject of physics. In this century, physics has, I am told, undergone two revolutions. *Two!* And consider the large number of physicists, the resources at their disposal, the fact that physics is universal and that the scientific community in this discipline embraces members from a large number of countries. With all these enormous advantages, all that these numerous and well-financed scientists can achieve is two, a miserable *two*, revolutions, and in this century of science at that. One can only suspect that physicists are not merely lacking in external graces and polish—with those long hours in the lab, their nondescript backgrounds, their ill-balanced training, one can hardly expect anything better in that respect—but that they are also gormless, lacking in imagination, independence, and enterprise, content to carry on in hidebound routines. But it isn't really surprising. A scientific education simply does not develop those qualities of vision and originality and independence which are the hallmarks of a truly cultivated mind.

Consider, by contrast, a truly progressive subject, like philosophy. We have, in this century, undergone no fewer than *four* revolutions! And all this within the compass of one country, and very nearly within the compass of one or two universities. . . . And the number of philosophers is far smaller than that of physicists; the resources diverted to assist them, negligible; and the questions they deal with, by common agreement, are harder, indeed quite extraordinarily hard, perhaps beyond the limit—and certainly *at* the limit—of the capacity of human understanding. . . .

With these disadvantages and handicaps, facing these obstacles, philosophers have nevertheless produced *four* revolutions in one century! And what radical and fundamental ones, too! So fundamental that each set of revolutionaries consider their predecessors as exemplifications of the very paradigm of delusion and error. Such productivity, such fundamental and repeated originality, can be the fruit of no ordinary minds. It must, one feels, be the work of minds nurtured on that subtle but profound, elusive, but inescapably important *je-ne-sais-quoi* which goes with humanist culture. If only one could have more of it!

There is an interesting contrast between the progress of philosophy and that of science. In science, I am told, the supplanted theory lives on as a special case of the superior, more general theory, as an approximation to truth less close than its successor, but an approximation to truth nevertheless. In philosophy, the supplanted vision lives on, not as an approximation to truth, but as the very extreme of error. (For instance: the Idealist sense of total interdependence, and mind-dependence, was *the* error, for realists and atomists. The exclusive two-and-two-only-uses-of-language doctrine of Logical Positivism was *the* error, for linguistic philosophy.) This shows, of course, that the advances in philosophy are far greater (because far more radical) than those of science, and hence that the rate of progress is far greater even than would appear from the simple arithmetical consideration of number of revolutions per century.

There is another interesting difference. In science, one gathers, a new theory begins its career as a tentative hypothesis, and only acquires the standing of a generally accepted theory if indeed it has stood the test of time and scrutiny. (Of course, its initial propounder may, or may not, have had a passionate faith in it from the very start. But there is little he can do to impose this faith on others.) Not so in philosophy. Some of the most striking and influential theories of recent decades began their careers as unquestionable truths, and only became tentative theories *later*. They are liable to begin their careers on a pedestal not simply in the eyes of their authors: they are liable to arrive in a form such that they *cannot* be questioned, such that the very language in which they are presented, and the rules of discussion, preclude it. For instance, Ludwig Wittgenstein's influential *theory* that there was nothing philosophical or general to be said about the world and language, and that any attempt to do so was camouflaged nonsense and sprang from a misuse of language, was not presented as a *theory* at all. It was an assumption built into a procedural *rule*. Anyone who doubted it had to have his concepts examined, over and over, until he desisted. Thus the theory wasn't really stated; it was simply built into the procedure and into the criterion of its successful termination. It took quite a while to break through the rules and see that there was a theory there, and only *then* it became tentative.[5] In general, philosophical innovations tend nowadays to be like that: someone succeeds in changing the rules and starts playing the game differently, and for a time wins all games by his own rules.

One must add that the figure *four*—which already gives philosophy a professional rate of growth, so to speak, twice that of physics—is a conservative estimate. It restricts itself to what may be called the mainstream of the profession, by criteria such as numbers, occupation of prestigious Chairs, fame, and influence.[6]

There were, first of all, the Idealists. In modern philosophy, to be an 'Idealist' does not have the same meaning as it has in ordinary speech—where it means roughly to have a very high level of moral expectation. An 'idealist' in daily life is one who expects everyone to behave very well and for the best motives, or one who believes that men are at least capable of behaving in such a way, and above all one who endeavours to behave in such a way himself, and who, perhaps naïvely, expects himself to succeed and his efforts to be fruitful. Idealism in twentieth-century philosophy has another, though not quite unconnected, sense. It refers to a class of doctrines and themes, generally going back to the German thinker G. W. F. Hegel, and which include the following: the world is in some important sense a unity. Nothing in it exists on its own, or can be understood on its own. The proper understanding of anything involves seeing its place in the context of everything else, and hence involves everything else, indeed the grand totality. The totality is somehow spiritual in character. This doctrine and stress of the whole can also be applied to things within the totality, such as the society or the state. It is then open to the charge that it leads to the worship of the state or the collectivity. It is interesting to note that English thinkers were quite ingenious enough to combine, when they wished, a Hegelian outlook with a liberal theory of the state.[7]

The Idealists satisfied at least one kind of popular preconception of what a philosopher should be like: they claimed to tell their readers what the world was ultimately like; they argued from premisses which did not, at least knowingly, presuppose any one religious tradition or Revelation; and what they had to say was unquestionably edifying. They gave men a sense of the unity and interconnectedness and 'meaningfulness' of things. (They saw themselves as reacting against and overcoming what seemed to them the shallow empiricism of nineteenth-century thinkers such as J. S. Mill.)

They were, roughly speaking, followed by the Realists. Again, philosophical Realists are not the same thing as 'realists' in daily life, who are men who expect neither themselves nor others to be any better than they ought to be, and generally much worse. The realists believed that things were *really there*, and quite independent of the observer or knower. The Idealists, who always stressed the interdependence and unity of everything, tended in the end to fuse knower and object known into one indissoluble whole. In general, they tended to see everything as a cosy bundle—mind and object, citizen and state, etc. The realists by contrast insisted on breaking things apart, and this, in knowledge, led them to insist on things being *really* there, independently of the mind, and hence their name *realists*. Their tendency to break things apart tended to make them see both the world and thought or language as made up of parts. This tended sometimes to lead to, or presuppose, a theory about what happened when thought or language succeeded in being 'about' the world: the parts of one mirrored or reflected parts of the other.[8]

It was the next major school which made what was perhaps the biggest impact on the outside world: Logical Positivism. Logical Positivism rejected the Idealist view that the world, and virtually everything in it, was a cosy bundle, but it also claimed to reject the rival, realist view that the world was made up of its parts and that these were distinct (notably, that consciousness and its objects were distinct). It claimed not to have any doctrines about the world at all: for it castigated the conception of philosophy as a kind of 'super-science', i.e. theorizing about the world, distinguished from science proper by being more general, less experimental, supposedly more certain (and in practice more volatile) and more edifying. On the contrary: henceforth philosophy was to be about *meaning* and language. Its theory of meaning was splendidly simple: sentences were meaningful in virtue of recording facts, or in virtue of recording calculations.[9] The careful formulation of this claim runs somewhat longer, but this is the underlying idea. The classical English formulation of this position is of course found in Professor A. J. Ayer's *Language, Truth and Logic*. Sentences satisfying neither of the two criteria of genuine meaning are, strictly speaking, *meaningless*.

Logical Positivism seemed shocking, for its category of the meaningless embraces much that expresses, or accompanies, that which to many men 'makes sense' of their lives: moral and political principles, evaluation of all kinds, religious beliefs.

Logical Positivism was replaced by a movement best described as Linguistic Philosophy, whose central doctrines and practices spring from the later work of Ludwig Wittgenstein.[10]

Linguistic Philosophy, like Logical Positivism (with which the general public often confuses it), also disclaims any intention of legislating about or for the world: it too is about language, or perhaps not even that. (Wittgenstein denied that he was putting forward even a theory of language.) Yet inescapably it did suggest a picture of the world, and the picture suggested is in some ways closer to that of the Idealists than to that of the Realists and the Logical Positivists. It seems language is a very manifold activity, intimately and functionally fused with other human activities. The stress is on seeking the role of a linguistic expression in a larger whole. (This is a denial of the doctrine which sees meaning as the 'coverage' by a concept, so to speak, of a range of sensations, or indeed of the rival 'Platonic' theory which sees it as an attempt to penetrate the veil of appearance and reach out towards a higher reality.) It saw language as a manifold set of tools men use in the world: and past philosophy it saw as the noise made by misused tools. A language was said to be a form of life: in other words, these tools came not in isolation but as parts of linguistic traditions, which social scientists sometimes call 'cultures'. It saw itself as a technique for eliminating the awkward noises made by dislocated tools, or tools 'running idly'. No more positive task was there to be done—least of all any interference with 'forms of life'.

This school itself has tended to split into sub-movements. One influential segment has more or less abjured the general theory concerning the genesis of philosophic questions (the tool-and-rattle theory), but concentrated on the practices that were associated with it or commended in terms of it—above all, the investigation of linguistic habits, their most minute differences, and their social context. The rationale of this 'softly, softly' movement is unclear and tends to vacillate between the promise of a new science of language and the delivery of philosophic solutions (to problems that are not clearly specified) in about two or three decades.

One must add that since about the end of the 1950s some books have appeared by thinkers (notably Professor Hampshire and Mr Strawson) who had been closely associated with one branch or another of the linguistic movement, but which no longer fit neatly into the doctrinal or procedural pattern of that movement. These, however, really contained philosophers' philosophies, and were addressed primarily to professional colleagues. They do not appear to have stimulated emulation amongst them, despite the high praise they have received, and thus have not really, at least so far, affected the general pattern of thought-styles, in as far as the present decade can as yet be credited with a discernible pattern. (Again, one must stress that this fact does not imply anything, one way or the other, about the intrinsic merits of these books.)

If we adopt the figure *four* as the correct count of revolutions in philosophy in this century, this gives us fifteen years as the average life cycle of a philosophic revolution. This, however, is somewhat misleading, in as far as each of these revolutions begins its life while the preceding one is still in power, initially somewhat inconspicuous and hidden away in some recess of the intellectual landscape, and continues to live on after its days of glory, while its champions await the age of retirement.[11] It would be a mistake to compare the situation to the succession of dynasties in a well-centralized state, where one dynasty goes on ruling till the next one supplants it and seizes the unique centre of power. It is much more like those loose oriental states in which the new dynasty, long before it captures the state capital, already exists as an autonomous or independent ruler of some peripheral tribe, and where the outgoing dynasty, or members of it, continues some kind of existence as rulers of outlying redoubts before they are finally rooted out by their successors.[12]

The threatening abyss

Another relevant feature, obvious because overt and indeed much-advertised by the protagonists of these philosophies themselves, is a preoccupation with language, meaning and its obverse, nonsense. This preoccupation and its alleged beneficent consequences are after all claimed by these protagonists to be the distinguishing marks of the new era and of its merits. The advance is indeed breathtakingly radical; it replaces questions such as 'How many angels can sit on the point of a needle?', by questions such as 'In how many *senses* can an angel be said to sit on the point of a needle?'

The notion of what cannot be said, of the difficulty of saying things, of the traps which beset the attempts, is already conspicuously present with the Idealists. The realists are imbued with the need for utmost care in treading between the snares of speech. By the time we reach logical positivism and then the linguistic philosophers, this is no longer a preoccupation but an obsession. The identification of the stigmata of nonsense becomes the central theme of thought, and one which underlies and pervades all else. No puritan could have been closer to the thought of sin, no Victorian more intimately and pervasively embattled with the idea of sex, than were these thinkers with the idea of *nonsense*. It is not perhaps an unworthy preoccupation: but why is it so intense, why does it have them by the throat so much, why is it so persistent?[13] Why—and this is the crucial question—do they feel the danger of falling into nonsense to be so pervasive, so close, so haunting, and the goal of speaking sense to be so enormously desirable, so very difficult to achieve? Why do they not, like earlier generations, treat talking sense as the natural and secure birthright of sane men of good faith and sound training, and the talking of nonsense as a real but not very significant danger, like slipping on a banana skin?

If

> If you can keep your head when all about you
> Are losing theirs and blaming it on you; . . .
> If you can wait and not be tired of waiting,
> Or being lied about, don't deal in lies . . .
>
> R. Kipling

Such men are our latest philosophers.[14] The manifestos of the cautious-progress trend of linguistic philosophy tend always to sound like *If*. They often nudge us to remind us, lest we fail to notice, of their courage, their equanimity, their patience. Let *others* lose their nerve. Let others, having lost their footing, reach out for the spurious comfort of the general theory, or comfort their anxiety with the intoxication of loose and far-reaching claims. *They* themselves have their feet firmly on the ground, and their serene but observant gaze does not allow itself to be bewildered or misled. No anxiety for big and rapid returns can seduce them from a slow but steady progress. Calmly and modestly, they tackle and surmount each problem, one by one, like a good mountaineer whose relaxed and confident movements show that he has mastered his craft. They have the courage which 'can wait and not be tired of waiting'. The difficulties yet to come, or the recollection of difficulties surpassed, are not allowed to fluster them. They are never allowed to generate anxiety, panic, the clutching at the untested hold, the careless placing of weight on an unstable boulder, or that ultimate indignity, a frantic and indeed perilous grasping for safety. Such conduct they leave to others. What else were those grandiose and now half-forgotten theories, those portentous formulae and precarious inferences, but the behaviour of men lacking the calmness, the deliberation, and the resolution required for real and secure progress? What indeed.

All the same, one may suspect that this dignified, unflustered, one-by-one, generalization-free behaviour may after all have missed the point. If you do not feel a generalized intellectual anxiety, if you feel no need to find and make explicit and to evaluate the basic premisses of your activities, why the devil philosophize in the first place? There is no law against cheerfulness breaking through; but why try to turn it, in effect, into one further philosophic doctrine, and an extremely ill-considered one at that?

The unreality of time

Ironically, one of the themes which interest academic philosophers is the 'reality of time'. Even of late, they confess themselves intrigued by metaphysical would-be demonstrations of the unreality of time, and are anxious to champion its reality and to unmask the sophistries on the other side. Still, the battle they fight on this front does not seem perilous, even to them: whichever way the argument goes, they can always, when in difficulties, characteristically invoke irresistible reinforcements, a kind of philosophical nuclear striking force, the unanswerable consideration that common sense and language are on their side: the knock-down argument to the effect that even the opponent understands, and cannot but employ, *temporal concepts.* . . . Even the opponent, they triumphantly point out, whatever the apparent logical force of his arguments, understands full well what it is like to miss a train, he knows that the article in which he 'proved' the unreality of time was itself published on a certain *date*, etc., etc. This argument is itself part of the general philosophy which insists on seeing the role of concepts in a language, way of life, and validating them in terms of their possession of such a role.

Now I do not wish to challenge the full comprehension, indeed the mastery, of train-timetable concepts, of proof-correcting-deadline concepts, etc., on the part of these philosophers. Clearly, they *do* know how to operate temporal notions. But I do seriously doubt whether they have any idea whatever of what it is like to live in one century rather than another. Their philosophies make sense only on the assumption that they do *not*. Thus the denial of the reality of time has rather a deeper, and more realistic, validity than they suppose. Our problem is not why some people should perversely deny time, but rather why time should, for some people, have withered to nothing but train timetables.

Although this splendid timelessness has reached its full consummation only recently, it must be said that there has been a tendency towards it in academic philosophy for some time. Consider the contrast between Hegelianism proper and its modern local variant, the philosophy of F. H. Bradley: the difference, as Professor J. N. Findlay has recently pointed out, is precisely the splendid timeless immobility of the Bradleyan Absolute. In other words, most of what gives Hegelianism its interest—the metaphysical parable on human progress, one which seems to dispense with Agencies or norms external to the process itself—is lost. Bradley's Absolute is not merely, as Professor Ayer pointed out, lazy,[15] in as far as it does not itself deign to develop, though concerned with development: it is also irritatingly and tediously unspecific about just what development it is indeed concerned with.[16]

It is interesting to note that the relationship of modern logical positivism to the real positivism of Auguste Comte is exactly analogous to that of Bradley to Hegel. The values and norms of the two positivisms seem similar: the same commendation of positive science, the rejection of untestable waffle. But the interest of Comte depends in large measure on the fact that he saw, indeed that he was preoccupied with, *the social typology which is immediately implicit in the positivist theory of knowledge and science.* The crucial question for a positivist must be—the understanding of the difference between societies in which positive knowledge can and does flourish and those in which it cannot, and a concern with the transition from the one to the other. However much such a concern may be logically and rightly implicit in Logical Positivism, as it was recently fashionable, these implications were simply ignored—and worse than ignored: they were even denied, by appealing to the alleged moral and political neutrality of philosophy in general.

Proper Comtian positivism of course expressed or generated a characteristic *esprit* of the *Polytechnique*, and the effective promotion of hard-headed understanding and technical competence which it stands for. Fashionable local logical positivism in no way expressed or encouraged a spirit of any polytechnic, or even, to allow for differences in terminology, of the Imperial College of Science and Technology. On the contrary, it always somehow had rather an inexpugnable aroma of Christ Church, Oxford.

With the local variant of Logical Positivism, one feels that at heart its animus against Idealism was inspired less by the fact that the attacked Idealism was 'metaphysical' than by the fact that it was Victorian—starched, earnest, stuffy. The confrontation of Logical Positivism and Idealism was not that of two radically different cultures (as it should be if the formal arguments were taken seriously), but of two slight variants within one culture—one displaying the academic earnestness of the turn of the century, the other, the lighter airs of the 1920s and 1930s. Forms of untestable assertion and camouflaged valuation that are more *with it* than Idealism, more of our own time, do not rouse latterday positivism to fury, and may indeed pass unmolested or be treated with courtesy.

The difference between positive and other knowledge was credited to rather artificial entities (propositions, sentences, whatnot), and not, as is far more illuminating, to *cultures*, to traditions or ways of thinking (which can of course co-exist in one society). For a proper, though extremely moderate, formulation of the position, we had to wait for Sir Charles Snow's splendid pamphlet.[17]

Consider how very radical it would be really to take that doctrine seriously and insist that untestable assertions be—not, indeed, excluded, or even treated with contempt—but merely divested of spurious claims to substantiation, and forced to face the world undisguised. A society practising such an ethic would be transformed indeed. No wonder some nervous apprehension was provoked by logical positivism when it first appeared. But the nervousness proved wholly unjustified. This was a most reluctant Samson—and, as it turned out, a miraculously fortunate one. He removes the one truly central pillar of the intellectual and social edifice—the freedom to assert things without having any good grounds for doing so—merely in order to crush one pathetic little mouse, and lo and behold: nothing happens. The rest of the edifice seems unaffected, and both he and the other inhabitants live on happily and come to no harm.

But the most conspicuous display of timelessness in academic philosophy was due round about the mid-century. Bradley may be a timeless Hegel, and Logical Positivism a timeless variant of positivism proper: but the really striking example was the most influential philosophy of the post-war period. Wittgenstein's mature (linguistic) philosophy is, essentially, a timeless variant of the doctrine of the classical French sociologist, Émile Durkheim. (Neither Wittgenstein nor his followers seem ever to have noticed this.)

Durkheim put forward an extremely important theory of knowledge. (Perhaps our contemporary philosophers failed to notice this simply because the title of the book in which Durkheim expounds it does not mention knowledge at all, but implies that the book is about primitive religion.) This theory runs: both empiricism and apriorism are false. In other words, the knowledge we possess, the concepts we employ, can be explained neither as something merely extracted, from sense experience, nor again as a rapport with something super-sensuous, circumventing experience. Above all, the compulsive hold certain concepts have over our thought (e.g. causation, time—we seem unable to circumvent these even in imagination) simply cannot be explained along the lines of those two well-trodden philosophic paths. Instead, Durkheim suggests, it is society, culture, the totality of customs and practices of a social tradition, which inculcates and sustains our concepts, and makes it impossible for us to escape them.

Precisely this is also the core of Wittgenstein's mature philosophy. He too endeavours to avoid, indeed to destroy, both the empiricist and the apriorist models of knowledge. He speaks of *language*, but in so broad a sense as to mean, in effect, a *culture*—the totality of the contexts and functions within which speech takes place and which give utterances their use and hence their 'meaning'. He does indeed observe that language is a 'form of life'. Concepts are justified by possessing a role within a language, a 'form of life'. No other justification is possible.

Wittgenstein is, however, sadly inferior to Durkheim in his presentation and use of his theory. Perhaps it is true that our concepts owe their meaning, and their hold over our thought, to the manner in which they form parts of a way of life in which we have been brought up.[18] But Wittgenstein's philosophy is based on the assumption that this somehow constitutes a *solution*, that it provides an answer to questions concerning the validity of our ideas.[19] But plainly it does not constitute a solution at all. It may be true that we cannot stand outside all conceptual systems, all 'forms of life', in order to scrutinize some one or all of them: but equally, we cannot fall back into a cosy conceptual cocoon, the language/culture of our 'form of life', with the comfortable reflection that any attempt to transcend it is only based on some kind of error concerning the working of language. . . . We cannot do this, because there are no such conceptual wombs to crawl back into: the modern world is a Babel of 'forms of life', undergoing change with bewildering rapidity.

The real trouble with this kind of philosophy is that it wholly obscures both the tremendous *changes* which our society has undergone, and the *choices* which it faces. In its preoccupation with allegedly pathological deviations from sense it wrongly implies that there exists some viable *status quo ante* to which we could return. But there isn't. The Timeless Ones, who would insinuate that there is, really do more harm than the Luddites. Luddites, by romanticizing the past and rejecting the present (while generally enjoying its comforts, without at the same time contributing towards their greater diffusion), at least highlight the issue on which they adopt a self-indulgent, discriminatory, and wrong attitude. The Timeless Ones, while tacitly adopting the same attitude, also obscure the very existence of the issue itself.

The implausible Bluebird

This famous philosophy, which replaced logical positivism, was one of the Bluebird species. The general characteristic of this species is well known. Its argument runs: there is in man a Faustian or Promethean restlessness, a sacred flame, a noble craving for a pilgrimage and the Holy Grail, but beware!—the truth and the salvation are closer to hand than you think. The divine restlessness is misguided. One day, after we have wearied of the long pursuit, lost stomach for the distant desolations, the anguish and the toil of the search, behold!—the scales fall off our eyes, and we perceive that the treasure we had sought so far and perilously was ever close, homely and familiar and freely offered! If only we had known sooner! What tribulations and dangers we might have avoided! But no matter. The dear familiar homely treasure is now all the dearer, now that we know the futility and pain of seeking it in treacherous and sterile distant wastes.

Such is the story of philosophy. After two millennia or so some scales fell off some eyes, round about 1930, in Austria or Cambridge. Then, after 1945, there was almost a deafening noise as scales avalanched off eyes en masse, left, right, and centre, mainly in Oxford, but elsewhere too:[20] Truth stood revealed. The Bluebird was there, right there, at home, our own, ours only, in our own dear ordinary speech. It had no distant and alien, unsympathetic habitat: it was right there in the palm of our linguistic hand.

How was this marvellous discovery made? This is an interesting though by now familiar story. The view that philosophic truth has such a homely habitat is a corollary of a certain theory of language and of philosophy: Language is a set of tools we use in the world (which is correct). Philosophy is the noise made by dislocated verbal tools (which is almost wholly incorrect). Old philosophy—both its theories and its questions—are, to the proper running of language, as funny noises are to the running of a motor car: they indicate that some bit of the machinery is doing too much or too little. The job of the philosophic thinker or tinker is to remedy this, to restore the *status quo ante* by identifying and readjusting the misbehaving piece, and to eliminate the noise. (See pp. 16 and 22.)

This theory is not true. But why did it seem true to some? In the case of the inventor of this theory, Ludwig Wittgenstein, the answer is, in the main, that this theory is a sweeping and quite unwarranted extrapolation from a more or less correct diagnosis of his own development. It is true that the views of his own youth (formulated in the famous *Tractatus*) can be interpreted as the *very* funny noises made by the motor car of language when all pieces are made to do the same kind of thing (reflecting facts), instead of observing their more normal and complex division of labour. In his age he saw this and, with superb self-confidence, supposed that all other philosophy was the by-product of a similar error.

The corollary of this view is of course notorious, and constitutes the heart of the alleged 'Revolution in Philosophy': discover how each piece of language truly works, free yourself of misconceptions of how it should work, and impose no such external standard on it; and in consequence, philosophic 'puzzlement' will disappear.

Wittgenstein's mistake is essentially the mistake of a man who enters a discussion late, knows nothing of its history, and suddenly propounds a solution which seems a solution to *him*, but which, in fact, merely repeats the very problem which originally started the discussion, and certainly cannot terminate it. 'Forms of life' are a *problem*, not a solution. His behaviour is intelligible (on the assumption that he knew nothing of the real starting point of the discussion, which appears to be the case): what is more puzzling is that the others, who might be supposed to remember how it all began, allowed him to get away with it.

Wittgenstein's solution was: go back to how your language really works, free yourselves from the appeal of external and general norms of how it is supposed to work. This is, of course, the Bluebird solution.[21]

But philosophy started precisely because commonsensical notions became unworkable or inadequate. Men aren't really as disinterestedly Promethean as all that. If they reach out for independent, godlike norms, as they must, it is not so much hubris as necessity which motivates them. Generality, and the pursuit of independent criteria for the assessment of existing custom, cognitive or other, sprang, not from an error about language, but from a situation in which that custom was seen to be manifold, diversified from society to society (whilst yet those societies were flowing together into one civilization), unstable, unreliable, often inconsistent, and undergoing rapid change. One need only read Descartes, the starting point of modern philosophy, to see that he was *driven* to seek an independent starting point (which he found in doubt and in the self) by the chaos and contradiction of received ideas.

A secondary industry

We have now assembled some of the symptoms of this curious phenomeneon, contemporary philosophy: timelessness; the willingness to embrace a doctrine, or even a succession of doctrines, which only make sense if one is wholly oblivious of the social and intellectual transformations of the past four centuries or so; an affectation of imperturbability, a willingness to dispense with generality, which rather misses the point of philosophizing at all; this affectation somewhat belied by a hectic, amazingly rapid succession of total Revolutions (and Revelations); a sense of a lurking abyss of Nonsense at one's feet, of a feeling that one may be standing on the most precarious of snow-bridges over it, and that any careless movement will precipitate one into its dark recesses; a curious tendency to prepare elaborate defences along frontiers where virtually no enemy is in sight; a desire to return to the unco-ordinated 'common sense' of the possibly educated but unspecialized man, and the tacit assumption of the existence of an allegedly viable and well-tried form of life.

All this adds up to some kind of a clinical picture. The diagnosis which can be offered is of an interest far beyond the subject diagnosed.

Philosophy may not be the queen of the sciences (or indeed a science at all), but it *is* in a very real sense at the apex of the 'humanist' disciplines. I do not mean that it is necessarily superior to the others in its achievements, interest, quality of its practitioners, solidity of results, etc.; all this may be doubted. (In terms of interest, solidity of achievement, elegance, relevance, it can hardly claim superiority to history or sociology.)

But it is at their apex in a certain important logical sense. First of all: the nature of philosophic reasoning is fairly continuous with that of the other humanist disciplines, and indeed with the thought of daily life, in that it is not too difficult for an intelligent man to make the transition from the one to the other. (There is no enormous discontinuity, a yawning gap, bridgeable only by prolonged training, such as does exist between some of the advanced sciences and ordinary thought. An intelligent man can pick up philosophy simply by soaking in the ambience.)

Secondly, within this domain of mutually intelligible disciplines, it is the harder, more abstract, more general, perennially disturbing and the reappearing questions which are passed upwards to philosophy, even if, lately, there has been some tendency to disavow them. I do not mean that, in fact, an expert on literature puzzled by the nature of beauty as such, or a lawyer puzzled by justice, or a historian puzzled by causation or determinism, all reach out for the telephone and ring a philosopher of their acquaintance for the answer. They don't. (They might, in these days of Foundation-subsidized travel, arrange an 'interdisciplinary Conference', but that is another matter.) I do mean that the most general and fundamental questions, which do crop up in the course of historiography, jurisprudence, literary study, etc., *are* philosophy, and, when treated systematically, are classed as 'philosophy' rather than as parts of the specific discipline from which the question arose.[22]

This fact provides the principal clue to the diagnosis of the crisis or crises of philosophy. The feverish perturbations and weird comportment of philosophy are the symptoms of less visible, less dramatic, but no less important and more widespread difficulties in the wider conceptual economy of which philosophy is a part. We see here something like an Acceleration Principle, discovered in economics by Sir Roy Harrod.[23] Philosophy provides or services the basic conceptual equipment of humanist thought. If some anxiety is felt throughout the humanist culture, it is echoed with enormously magnified forces in the secondary industry, philosophy. The crisis of philosophy is the accentuated echo of the 'humanist' crisis.

As it is written

What is 'humanist culture'? Essentially, culture based on literacy. All human society and civilization presupposes language as such: but humanist or *literate* culture is not co-extensive with all human civilization. It is distinguishable from illiterate 'tribal' culture on the one hand, and from more-than-literate scientific culture on the other. The term 'humanist' is of course unfortunate, and survives from the days when a concern with mundane, 'human' literature was primarily distinguished, not from either illiteracy or science, but from theological, divine concerns. But for contemporary purposes, it is the literacy, and not its mundane or extra-mundane orientation, which matters. 'Humanist' concerns now embrace the divine. (Both speak the same language.)

Language is the tool of trade for the humanist intellectual, but it is far more than that. Language is, as Vico saw, more than a tool of culture, it *is* culture. Who would love had he not heard of love? asked La Rochefoucauld. And how many things would we do altogether if the concepts of those things were not built into the language of our culture?

The humanist intellectual is, essentially, an expert on the written word. One should not read this in a pejorative sense—as if to say, an expert on *nothing but* words. For words are a very great deal: the rules of their use are wound up with—though not in any simple and obvious way—the activities and the institutions of the societies in which they are employed. They embody the norms—or, indeed, the multiplicity of rival and incompatible norms—of those societies.

Humanist intellectuals, as experts on words, and above all on *written* words, are the natural intermediaries with the past and the future through records; with distant parts of the society; with the transcendent when the Word is held to contain the Message from it;

when the recorded word contains the rules of conduct, they are the natural judges; and so forth. A literate society possesses a firmer backbone through time than does an illiterate one. It is at least potentially capable of consistency. The literate intellectuals become the guardians and interpreters of that which is more than transient, and sometimes its authors.

This role was one which they once fulfilled with pride. The notion of the Priest or the Scholar, or even the Clerk, evokes an image which is not without dignity: for some men and some societies, it has more dignity than any other.

But this sense of pride is conditional on the fulfilment of the central task of this estate, which cannot but be one thing—the guardianship or the search for truth. If this is gone, only a shell remains. When the age of chivalry was over, Don Quixote was a joke. The military equipment of a knight could no longer be taken seriously. The question now is: how seriously does one now take the *cognitive* equipment of the *clerk*?

The answer is, alas: not very much. It varies a good deal, of course, with the subject matter, the milieu, the context.[24] But giving a general answer, it is correct to say that the clerk—i.e. the literate man whose literacy has led him to acquire good knowledge of the written word, an understanding of that which is written—has lost much of his standing now as a source of *knowledge* about the world. The educated public in developed countries turns to the scientific specialist when it wants information about some facet of the world. It does so even in spheres (e.g. psychiatry) where the record of the scientific specialist is not beyond all challenge. It suffices that the specialist is part of a discipline which itself is incorporated into the wider body of what is recognized as 'science'.

The deprivation of the humanist intellectual of his full cognitive status has happened fairly recently. Signs and portents, in philosophy and elsewhere, can be traced very far back: but as a general and widely half-recognized phenomenon, it is very new, and has occurred within this century, and almost within the last few decades. The magnitude and profundity of this social revolution can scarcely be exaggerated. There are still many members of the humanist culture who do not fully perceive what has happened. Some feel it, but angrily deny it: others feel and know it, and react with the kind of shame which needs must befall a caste when the basis of its identity and its pride has been destroyed.

It is for this reason that the rapidly succeeding, and increasingly weird, 'revolutions in philosophy' have a genuinely serious undertow. The underlying problem is the crisis of the caste of humanist intellectuals and the crisis in verbal knowledge, which is their defining expertise.

The rapid transformations of philosophy and the anxiety or obsession concerning meaning and nonsense reflect the underlying unclarity about the status of verbal thought altogether.[25] The use of language and of ordinary concepts has lost both its confidence and its innocence. It is this, ultimately, which really underlies the strikingly persistent and passionate preoccupation with meaning so characteristic of modern philosophy.[26] The heightened sense of language, the self-consciousness in the employment of it, the urgent desire to find theories as legitimizing or correcting it, the sense of an abyss of meaninglessness ever yawning, and viciously camouflaged, under our feet—all this springs from the fact that the humanist culture itself, the life of the word, the confidence in its capacity to relate to reality, is threatened.[27] The other traits and antics of recent philosophy are also related, in various more complicated ways, to the underlying crisis. For instance, the timelessness and the would-be neutralism are intimately connected. These philosophers either conduct their reasoning at a level so abstract that all social reality is out of sight, or concentrate on minutiae so microscopic that exactly the same effect is achieved. The normal vantage point of human perception, about $5\frac{1}{2}$ feet or so above the ground, is quite unknown to them. If they reflect on society and societies at all, they see it in a kind of Wittgensteinian night in which all cultures are the same shade of grey, in which it is, apparently, quite impossible to distinguish philosophically between them. If they had any sense of the total transformation in the course of the past four centuries, or of the one taking place now, they would perceive the impossibility (the strictly *logical* impossibility, the internal incoherence) of 'neutrality'. (Only the timelessness makes the illusion of neutrality possible.) When all rules are themselves *sub judice* and undergoing rapid change, no one *can* claim to be an impartial referee.

It should be noted that the basic insight, in the case of both Logical Positivism and Linguistic Philosophy, was, in each case, something extremely close to the two cultures problem. Positivism starts from the chasm between that which is science and that which is not. Linguistic Philosophy starts from the fact that language is an activity; an activity among others; not necessarily pre-eminent; an activity related to others not as (superior) theory to (mundane) practice, but as verbal activity to other and as dignified activities. This is something of which a humanist intellectual cannot but be aware, perhaps bitterly, irrespective of whether he learns it from Wittgenstein: for it is something of which his contemporary loss of status forcibly reminds him, and which contradicts that model of mind and language in terms of which his previous status and pre-eminence were once justified.

The crisis of a style of thought, and of a once proud caste which is defined by skill at it, is no trivial matter. One can think of a warrior caste in some tribe, prevented by a conquering colonial administration from continuing its calling and honouring its code, degenerating listlessly and withering away. But the end need not be so manifest and direct. The sons of proud chieftains may become pedlars of souvenirs to tourists, etc. Something of the kind may be happening to the humanist intelligentsia. A well-known Professor of Philosophy, close to the linguistic movement, making somewhere his contribution to the two cultures debate, observed that whereas scientists could invent nuclear weapons humanists could convey the issues hinging on them. Hmmm. This comes close to making an advertising agency the paradigm of the republic of the mind: the statisticians find out the facts, the humanists devise slogans for persuasion. But even assuming that every humanist is a potential Persuader—what an undignified end for those who were once the *Knowers*!

Societies sometimes endow the key activity of their members with an exclusive aura of dignity: among shepherd tribes, only herdsmen have dignity, and so on. In some cultures, knowledge and learning have claimed or even attained such a pre-eminence of respect. In the West, it has never had such a monopoly of prestige—though amongst some minorities it came close to it.[28] But even if not possessed of such a monopoly of dignity, it has a good deal of it, feudal and pseudo-feudal values notwithstanding, and quite particularly of course among those classes who specialized in this virtue. When such a dignity-conferring accomplishment is withdrawn, or suddenly comes to be seen to be illusory, the moral devastation is particularly great. When warrior nomads are forcibly turned into sedentary villagers, and ordered to be like those who were previously their despised protégés, the humiliation could hardly be greater. Now, in cognition as in production, roundabout, reproducible, changing methods are replacing the sensitive, locally rooted, but static and fairly low-productive ways of the artisans. The humanists are the artisanate of cognition.

The crisis is highlighted when the humanist has to teach or be taught. An important point about scientific knowledge is that it is fairly independent of the personal merits of its possessor. Of course, many species of it may simply not be accessible to a stupid man. At the other extreme, creative originality is only open to men of outstanding and personal talent. But in between, the average competent man really *knows* something (and is of use) when he has acquired a scientific qualification, even if it is a mediocre one. This is by no means obviously true in connexion with the middle-range, moderate-competent possessors of 'Arts' qualifications, and many teachers of such subjects are painfully aware of this. What has he to offer?

His literacy he shares with all other members of his society. His ability is a personal matter, which on the whole he does not owe to his advanced training. Just what has he to offer, *qua* graduate in the 'humanities'? On the 'humanist' side, an intelligent man without the qualification tends to be superior to a less able one with it, even for jobs *not* requiring great original creativity. This may mean that the skills or insights or sensitivities connected with 'humanism' are ultimately deeper, more intimately connected with our life and being, than the impersonally teachable techniques of science; and it may be, as Professor Madge has argued,[29] that whereas technical and instrumental rationality matters most *on the way* to fully industrial society, some kind of aesthetic perception will matter most when we finally get there; but it also makes one worried about the place of humanist subjects in a period of mass education, when literacy can be taken for granted (when, consequently, higher education must mean something more than intensified and extended literacy), when education must be at least compatible with self-respect on part of both teacher and student, and when it is not to our interest to encourage the invention, indeed the proliferation, of spurious claims. Some humanists, faced with the need to advertise their wares, have been all too ready to invent, or fall for, facile claims to alleged specialized skills. ('New Criticism' in literature, revolutions in philosophy, intimations and communings with tradition in political science—all these, whatever their intrinsic merits or demerits, appear to have the consequence of reassuring nervous teachers of the humanities.)

It is self-respect rather than material advantage which is involved. Snow observed that the Lucky Jimmery and Angry cult of the 1950s had something to do with the under-rewarded Arts graduate. Perhaps: but in this case, I take a nobler view of the motivation of my fellows. In a society in which there is a shift of stress from production to promotion, the Arts graduate is really quite well placed, materially. But prosperity without self-respect may corrode the souls of the best. Are we, who used to be those who *knew* and *discovered*, now really to be those who sell and persuade? This corrosive situation may be particularly acute in England, for accidental local reasons. Humanist education has its headquarters in educational centres which were once seminaries of a national religion. 'Humanist culture' then replaced faith as the concern of these centres, but it did not, on the whole, have very great prestige in the society. The reason was that those who had done well out of the Industrial Revolution did not care to stress the fact, and preferred to emulate the values of gentry, which did not include excessive self-cultivation. They preferred to see themselves as Romans, and their teachers as Graeculi. At a period when social ascension was a matter of making money and took several generations, it was schools, not universities, which were important.

But today, things have changed. Upward social mobility is a matter of climbing the educational ladder, and perhaps thereafter making money (rather than the other way round). In such circumstances, universities become supremely important. The semi-secularized seminaries were once only the peripheral outhouses of an Establishment which was not much concerned with them. Now, they suddenly become the principal Gateway on the way in. The humanist intellectuals find themselves in an extraordinarily powerful strategic position: they control the entry point, they must initiate the clamouring entrants, and supply the demand from the promotion side of an industrial society. (No wonder that a doctrine should arise which equates philosophy with the guardianship of conceptual table-manners.) They are indispensable to both sides. Under such circumstances, one is unlikely to need to worry unduly about remuneration: but one may well feel uneasy in other ways.

The general crisis has a number of sources, not one. One obvious factor is of course the towering superiority of science as a source of knowledge about the universe, with the sad consequence that the man sensitive to the meanings of words, to their connexions and inferential powers, their histories and recorded alignments in books, can no longer claim—whatever else he may still claim—that he is, primarily and above all and more than anyone else, a *knower*. Great material opportunities, combined with a deprivation of that which confers ultimate and inner dignity, may well lead to a deep and pervasive anxiety.

But another enormously important factor, curiously seldom noticed, is the *loss of monopoly of literacy*. The clerk is a nobody not merely because he is not a scientist, but also because in the developed societies *everyone* is now a clerk.

This is a powerful consequence of universal or near-universal literacy, of universal compulsory education, which was not foreseen and has still been scarcely noticed. To understand what it really is to be a clerk, a 'scholar', a literate, in his full glory and dignity, one must go to one of those many under-developed countries where literacy is still a minority accomplishment. The invention of dubious specialisms (e.g. 'linguistic analysis') is in part a consequence of this situation, of the loss of a genuine monopoly.

Most theories of knowledge are also, amongst other things, a charter of the social role and standing of the intellectual, cognitive class. (It is ironic that a clerkly culture whose very essence was verbal explicitness should sometimes turn, in time of crisis, to *ineffable* insights or skills in its pursuit of self-justification.) Whether these theories were good as such or not in one way did not make too much difference in the past: the institution they were intended to underwrite was not itself precarious. Now, it *is*.

The crisis of 'humanism' is a very real thing, and a kind of obverse of the problem of socially digesting science: how are the concepts in terms of which we see ourselves and live our lives to be related to those we take seriously as genuine knowledge of this world? It is unlikely that science will or could absorb all else: but it is even more unlikely that it can simply be ignored.[30] The issue of the 'two cultures' is utterly misconceived when it is seen, as it often is, as a problem of *communication* between two cultures. That problem exists, but it is relatively superficial and easy to solve: it requires only a new generation which has passed through less segregated educational channels. The real and deeper problem concerns just what, if anything, it is that the humanities have to communicate. The language of the humanities is incomparably closer to what we *are*, to the life we live, than is the language of science; but on the other hand it is not obvious that the humanities contain, in any serious sense, genuine *knowledge*. It is the chasm, perhaps intolerable, between real knowledge and identity which is the fundamental issue. The vernacular of life is now not even translatable into the Sacred Language of truth.

The problem is serious and must be faced, and it is sociological as well as philosophical: it concerns 'cultures' and their styles of thought and life, their cognitive potential so to speak, and the manner in which *knowing* and *being* are related within them. Recent philosophy has, unwittingly, received much of its impetus from this problem, but it has certainly not faced it squarely, or made much contribution towards its elucidation. On the contrary, it has proposed and encouraged facile solutions, which were part and parcel of that complacency so characteristic of the 1950s.[31]

The incompleteness of Snow's enormously salutary essay lies in the fact that whilst characterizing the two cultures he did not endeavour to go deeply into the differences of their cognitive potential, so to speak, and the way in which that is connected (or fails to be connected) with a general and moral orientation in and towards society. Modern positivism on the other hand was aware of the crucial cognitive chasm, but apart from handling it crudely it supposed that it had something to do with rather ghostly entities such as propositions or sentences, rather than cultures and societies. Hence in practice positivism tended to be either frivolous or scholastic or, curiously, both at once. Linguistic philosophy was quite correct in insisting, as against positivism, that it was human activities in manifold social contexts, and not isolated sentences carrying on some kind of cold liaison with 'facts', which were at issue: but it committed a disastrous mistake in supposing those social contexts to be stable, given, unproblematic—in supposing them to be a solution rather than a problem.

It is true that language is a form of life, and not just a series of verifications: but systematic verification happens to be a crucial part of certain forms of life, of industrial-scientific societies, and is conspicuously absent from certain others; and what matters is the understanding of the differences between these types, and of the various paths available from one to the other, and the assessment of those paths and of their social consequences. This requires an understanding both of knowledge and of social structure. There is a tremendous and almost—but not quite—incomprehensible difference between the past of humanity on the one hand, and its present and future on the other. The first task of thought is to comprehend this transformation, disentangle such alternatives as it may offer, and attempt some evaluation of them. In fact, the mainstream of recent formal and fashionable philosophy has done virtually nothing of this, or even tried. It consisted, in the main, of devices for ignoring change, and thus obscured rather than illuminated the choices we face.

The way forward does not lie in amateur and comically timeless linguistic sociology which takes 'forms of life' for granted (and this is what philosophy has been recently), but in the systematic study of forms of life which does not take them for granted at all. It hardly matters whether such an inquiry is called philosophy or sociology.

1964

Notes

1 'There were seldom any philosophical books to be seen. . . . Wittgenstein in those days often warned us against reading philosophical books. . . . This friend and disciple, J. O'C. Drury . . . when I complimented him on his collection of books . . . looked frankly shamefaced . . .', Karl Britton in 'Recollections of Wittgenstein', *Cambridge Journal*, **7**, 1953–4, 709–15; quotation from 710.
2 In detail, the situation is slightly more complex, owing to the fact that the terminology of philosophers is not internally consistent. Some of the ultra-modern ones now use the term 'metaphysics' in a non-pejorative sense, as describing something they themselves do (e.g. specification of general features of a 'kind of discourse', or whatnot). But basically the popular image of a would-be 'rejection of metaphysics' is correct, allowing for vagaries of terminology.

3 One may mean either neo-Marxist revivalism connected with the notion of 'alienation', abstruse enough to rival any theology; or theology proper *so* enlightened and sophisticated that it is impossible to see what deity or faith is being expounded or defended. (In the eighteenth and nineteenth centuries atheism was taught by rationalists, but now it seems mainly the province of theologians. Cf. A. MacIntyre, 'God and the Theologians', *Encounter*, **21**, September 1963, 3–10 and William Warren Bartley III, *The Retreat to Commitment*, New York, 1962.)
4 One hopes that such an inference is permissible, for we find it practised by linguistic philosophers themselves. For instance, Professor John Wisdom observes in *Philosophy and Psycho-analysis*, Oxford, 1953, 65: 'Now I contend that this is because it is not what he wants. When a man tells me he would love to ride a horse but, no

matter what animal I offer him, says "Not *that* one", then I think he does not really want to ride. Especially if, when offered a motor cycle, he takes to it with alacrity.' It is, of course, a general feature of this kind of philosophy that its practitioners believe that *others* are under a misapprehension concerning the true source of their perplexity. But though this suspicion is legitimate when applied to others, apparently it is not legitimate, alas, to apply it to them themselves.

5   'It is excellent that Wittgenstein's ideas should be treated, like other men's, as being capable of plain statement and reasoned objection. . . .' *The Times Educational Supplement*, 10 October 1958, 1474. Nearly a decade after the Master's death, the treatment of his ideas like other men's, and their desecration by actual formulation and even objection, has to be explicitly welcomed, as a positive innovation . . .!

6   I need hardly say that the inclusion or exclusion of something from this mainstream does not, on my part, involve any judgment concerning the objective merits of the philosophy or philosopher in question. It is not my view that the excluded items are necessarily or generally inferior to those included.

7   This was particularly true of the very influential Balliol thinker T. H. Green. Green was a kind of cautious version of Hegel, much as, later, J. L. Austin was a kind of cautious version of L. Wittgenstein. Cf. Melvin Richter, *The Politics of Conscience: T. H. Green and his Age*, London, 1964.

8   An admirable description of the Idealists and Realists is to be found in R. G. Collingwood, *An Autobiography*, London, 1939.

9   Logical Positivism disavowed philosophy as 'super-science', and hence in a way claimed to be no closer to the Realist than the Idealist images of the world. Nevertheless, its picture of languages was rather atomistic, and this picture was inescapably projected on to the world. An atomistic metaphysic was built into the doctrine, and not even particularly camouflaged. A natural way of reading Logical Positivism—i.e. one uninhibited by programme notes about how one should *read* it—is this; the world is made up of 'sense-data'. We note these; comment on them; sometimes also go in for calculations, which are never more than (at most complicated) repetitions, 'tautologies'; and we also, for some reason, sometimes make favourable or unfavourable noises, to express our feelings about sense-data or congeries of them.

10   Cf. his *Philosophical Investigations*, Oxford, 1953. A valuable exegesis is Mr David Pole's *The Later Philosophy*

of Wittgenstein, London, 1958.

11   I believe this last point is often true and has nothing to do specifically with philosophy. People of substance or of an age of discretion are very seldom converted, though of course they are, sooner or later, retired. This is a point which escaped Bernard Shaw in the reasoning which underlies *Back to Methuselah*. The coming of a race of Methuselahs might result not in accelerated progress but in scientific ossification.

12   The rapid succession of radically contrasted movements provides me with a premiss for an argument which is intended to highlight something specific to our period. But I must regretfully admit that the phenomenon described does not seem to be new: 'Lord Acton calculated that the average period of dominance of a philosophical school or movement was about twenty years', Professor W. B. Gallie, *Philosophy and the Historical Understanding*, London, 1964, 230. If Lord Acton and I are both right, the acceleration in this century has been merely one from twenty to fifteen years per movement.

13   Logical positivism and Wittgensteinian linguistic philosophy disagree radically in their theories concerning the stigmata of nonsense, but agree in placing this identification at the centre of things.

14   Cf. comments by Mr P. F. Strawson, 'The Philosophical Eye' (review of A. J. Ayer's *The Concept of a Person*), *Spectator*, **7060**, 18 October 1963, 500: 'At the other end [of the scale] is an area, cultivated assiduously and with some success of late, in which accuracy and discrimination of detail are primary concerns. . . .'
Or: 'I do not want to laud present [philosophical] fashions but there surely is a real advance in trying to go a little way certainly rather than a long way uncertainly.' Mr Jon Wheatley in a review of F. A. Hayek's *The Constitution of Liberty* in *Mind*, n.s. **71**, 1962, 435–6; quotation is from 436.
Or again: '[Professor Austin] . . . was willing to talk about one small point for a whole morning, or even, off and on, for a whole term or a year; at this rate . . . it will take twenty or thirty years before we can come out with an answer to our large problem. To this Austin would have said: why not?' Mr G. J. Warnock, 'J. L. Austin: A Remarkable Philosopher', *Listener*, 7 April 1960, 616.

15   A. J. Ayer, *Language, Truth and Logic*, London, 1936.

16   One way of underlining this is by reflecting that no one could have obtained Marxism by standing *Bradley*

on his head. By doing *that*, what does one obtain? The equally timeless *Tractatus* of the young Wittgenstein.

17   The anger aroused by the Two Culture theme amongst many is curious in view of Snow's moderation. It is true that he was a bit unfair to 'humanists' in seeming to take a certain kind of reactionary poet as their paradigm. But he never made a radical attack on the very foundation of their style of thought, such as was implicit in Logical Positivism. If *that* ruthless radicalism were combined with Snow's historically conscious and sociologically realistic formulation, we should have had something truly explosive.

The unjustified anger against Snow sprang, I suspect, from the following consideration: some 'humanists' tend to justify the position they hold in education, etc., by praising that which is 'all-round', 'many-sided', etc. They then make a curious tacit transition from praising many-sidedness as such to concluding that they themselves are somehow the clearest examples of it (presumably, in virtue of not being skilled at anything specific). If, however, science is explicitly counted as one of the crucial 'cultures', the equation of humanism with being the *compleat man* lapses. This, they feel, they cannot allow to happen. Their culture is their fortune, poor dears.

18   Cf. P. Winch, *The Idea of a Social Science*, London, 1958. This is an excellent formulation of Wittgenstein's sociologism, by an author who subscribes to it.

19   Cf. Professor S. Hampshire, 'Hume's Place in Philosophy', in D. F. Pears, ed., *David Hume: A Symposium*, London, 1963: 'Philosophy as a kind of anthropology of knowledge and belief is a conception revived in the later works of Wittgenstein. . . . The proper work of philosophy [according to this conception] is purely descriptive, to set out the linguistic facts that reveal our habits of thought. . . . We must try also to uncover the motives that prompt philosophical theories, treating these theories as fantasies of reason, which can be understood and, by being understood, undermined' (5). Earlier (4) he contrasts this view with the one which was rejected: 'the ancient ambition of philosophers: to find a criterion by which we can rectify our ordinary claims to knowledge, distinguishing the valid from the invalid claims. . . .' Hampshire quite mistakenly credits Hume with a similar acceptance of customary beliefs, and abstention from attempts at evaluation of custom, but he correctly singles out this attitude as central to linguistic philosophy. Theoretically, this attitude might be practicable *if* the world we live in contained one homogeneous and stable set of customs. If this is not the case, the recommendation corresponds to *no* conceivable line of conduct. What were the horizons of linguistic philosophers, to make them suppose otherwise?

20   Cf. 'The Post-Linguistic Thaw— Getting Logical Conclusions Out of the System', *The Times Literary Supplement*, 9 September 1960, 60. Traditional philosophy was due to be 'finished off', to 'be over'.

21   Consider a good summary of this position apropos of a lecture of Professor A. J. Ayer's, in a by no means unfriendly leader in *The Times*, 26 October 1963, replacing for some inexplicable reason the fourth leader: 'The source of all philosophical puzzles, paradoxes, and dilemmas is held to be [by contemporary philosophers] confusion in the employment of concepts, in particular the illegitimate transfer of a concept from one system to another.'

The really interesting assumption behind this by now familiar doctrine is that concepts have a rightful home and a rightful place and role in it, if only we could find it: then our trend towards a conceptual tower of Babel could be reversed, and all be well. Alas, it is irreversible. We might conceivably emerge at the other end, but we cannot retrace our steps.

Wittgenstein's best reason for adopting this subsequently much-diffused doctrine of linguistic custom as the true home of each concept (thereby committing himself to the idea of a determinate linguistic custom) is of course the denial of the possibility of some external norm of conceptual propriety—a denial which has some plausibility. It is interesting to note how this position can best be described as a kind of nominalistic Platonism— and that this is not a contradiction. Concepts are treated as norms—not because they are echoes of externally, divinely, given norms, but because there could be no external norms by which they could fail. The result is the same.

22   It might be argued that, in this sense, philosophy is also at the logical apex of the sciences. Logically, this might be so: but in fact, when physicists reconsider or revise basic concepts, say of simultaneity or of causation, to take the obvious examples, they do it by themselves. The systematic consideration of such issues in science does not give rise to another 'subject'.

23   The argument is: fluctuations in the economy as a whole are reproduced in very much exaggerated form, in those industries which supply the rest of the economy with its bulkier equipment, e.g. in ship-building. When demand is merely slack in the wider economy, it may decline drastically in the industries which re-equip the rest.

24   One obvious exception to the cognitive downgrading of the humanist intellectual is the field of history.

25   Cf. Mr George Steiner, 'The Retreat from the Word', *Kenyon Review*, **23**, Spring 1961, 186–216. Also E. Gellner, 'Is Belief Really Necessary?', *Hibbert Journal*, **56**, October 1957, 31–44; now ch. 5, below.

26   Certain reasons of a technical nature can be cited as the origins of the preoccupation with meaning and its limits, for instance the 'Theory of Types' in the philosophy of mathematics. I very much doubt whether these relatively specialized problems would have had the enormous impact they have had, were it not for the underlying cause now discussed.

27   'It is a human loss, a kind of lameness, to be unable to follow mathematical and inductive reasoning. Most philosophers are now lame.' Professor S. Hampshire, 'A Ruinous Conflict', *New Statesman*, **63**, 4 May 1962, 652–3; quotation is from 653.

28   I once listened to a Swiss professor explaining the meaning of Existentialism. He approached it as follows. There are certain things—God, death, for instance—in the face of which all men are equal. It matters not whether you are the meanest pauper, or—his finger rose to point upwards to heaven—a *professor*, it is still the same. . . .

29   Charles Madge, *Society in the Mind*, London, 1964, ch. X.

30   Consider the following observations by a contemporary philosopher, Professor J. M. Cameron, in a letter to the editor (headed 'Teilhard de Chardin'), *Listener*, **69**, 28 February 1963, 383: 'Making up such pictures (i.e. treating "the cautious and provisional hypotheses of the natural sciences at a given date as accounts from which we may extrapolate a grand picture of the entire cosmic process") *has nothing to do with serious work in the sciences or in philosophy and theology.*' (Italics mine.) One may

grant the point concerning theology. But in philosophy, can there be anything more serious than the results of science? Granting that these may be 'cautious and provisional', are any other putative sources of knowledge *justifiably* less so? (The point about a picture being 'grand' is simply part of conventional current philosophic denigration of any attempt at obtaining a *general* picture.)

In an earlier observation in the same debate (in a review of Charles E. Raven's *Teilhard de Chardin: Scientist and Seer*), *Listener*, **69**, 7 February 1963 256, Professor Cameron accurately describes the origins of this attitude: 'those of us who get our philosophic standards from . . . Wittgenstein . . .'. (Some other authors are also invoked, with perhaps less justification.)

31   Cf. Mr Bryan Magee, 'Political Philosophy Dies Again' (review of P. Laslett and W. G. Runciman, eds, *Philosophy, Politics and Society*, 2nd series), *New Society*, **1**, 10 January 1963, 27: 'The notion that political philosophy is dead was only ever acceptable to the politically complacent. . . . It seems no more than part of the all-pervading complacency and parochialism that characterized British life and thought in the 1950s.'

The notion that political philosophy was dead was of course a corollary of two recently fashionable philosophic doctrines, and was not infrequently asserted. Professor R. Wollheim observes in 'Facts and Morals' (review of Maurice Cowling's *The Nature and Limits of Political Science* and W. G. Runciman's *Social Science and Political Theory*), *New Statesman*, **66**, 9 August 1963, 170: 'The crisis from which [political philosophy] is suffering, which some diagnose as a mortal condition, arises from the application to it of two very general principles that *the majority of contemporary philosophers used to take as established*, at any rate until quite recently. . . .' (Italics mine.) The two principles indicated are the supposed moral impotence of (*a*) factual, (*b*) philosophical premisses.

Chapter 3 Reflections on philosophy, especially in America

A certain eclecticism is perhaps the most conspicuous feature of American philosophy. The deep structure which generates the whole range of views and positions in American philosophy is quite easy to locate. It is this: there are some fifty-odd States in the Union. These can be listed in one column. In a second column, one must list all available philosophic schools, something like this: positivists, pragmatists, Hegelians, Wittgensteinians, Existentialists, etc., etc.

There is now a very simple and absolutely reliable law, which runs as follows: to every possible pair of elements, drawn one each from the two columns, there corresponds *at least one* living, real concrete professor of philosophy. In other words, there is at least one Texas Hegelian, one Nebraska phenomenologist, one West Virginia Wittgensteinian, one Ohio Kantian, and so forth. Of course there may be more than one, but in all circumstances there must be *at least one.*

This extraordinary plurality deserves some comment. First of all be it noted that the diversity is but skin deep. The cars, houses, wives, divorces, and psychiatrists of a Utah personalist do not differ from those of a New Hampshire Heideggerian or a North Dakota neo-Kantian, or even a Louisiana Austinian. The ideological differentiation, in formal philosophy, seems to mean nothing in the souls or life-styles of the philosophers, or indeed in the society which harbours and sustains them. Some of my best friends are American philosophers, but I should find it hard to deny that this seems to be the main corollary of the strange and characterless diversity: academic philosophic thought plays little or no real part in the wider intellectual economy of America.

This is quite different from, say, the sociologists. With their virtues and their vices, they clearly both reflect the American intellectual climate and contribute to it. Not so the philosophers. It could be said that if the several thousands or more of professional philosophers in America were all assembled in one place, and a small nuclear device were detonated over it, American society would remain totally unaffected. The printers of university catalogues might feel the inconvenience of having to omit Philosophy 103, Metaphysics 261, Philosophy of Science 307, and so on, but there the inconvenience would end. No one else would notice any difference, and there would be no gap, no vacuum, in the intellectual economy, that would require plugging.

The difference from Britain is striking. British academic philosophers reflect very closely—indeed, they probably exaggerate—various notable traits of British culture and education. Their critics may feel that they reflect some of the more deplorable features of their period and milieu—the conflation of centres of serious higher education with finishing schools, the alienation from science, a weary insularity and complacency, and equation of stylistic pedantry with rigour, of spinsterish coyness with wit, of social thought with after-dinner rhetoric. But, for better or for worse, academic philosophy is continuous with the life which surrounds it, and plays a definite role within it. Its sudden elimination would certainly be felt, and could not possibly pass unnoticed. Not so with American philosophy.

There is here a curious contrast with the generation of William James. In a variety of ways, the Pragmatists really were a most remarkable and paradoxical success story. No one who reads James can have any doubts about the fact that he very self-consciously, deliberately set out to create a philosophy that was not merely valid, but also distinctively *American*. The Anglo-Hegelian metaphysics to which he was reacting may have been suitable enough for 'the more studious members of our protestant ministry', but it was unusable not merely for the 'Rocky Mountain toughs', but also for those who, like James, liked to think they combined the virtues both of Boston and of Cripple Creek. The Middle Way was also to be an American way. What is so remarkable is that James and the Pragmatists succeeded in providing a philosophy tailor-made for the specifications which they themselves believed that the American scene imposed. This is so impressive because, generally speaking, ideologies can not be successfully manufactured to order and to specification. Synthetic faiths generally just fail to take off. Ideological inspiration and social need must normally meet, if they meet at all, in an unplanned, unselfconscious, careless rapture. But James and his generation, despite their self-conscious awareness of what they were doing, did succeed, and to this very day, a visitor to America, when inquiring after the rationale of various institutions which surround him, notably in the field of education, will often find himself referred to the teaching of the Pragmatists.

Given this great and rapid success of what was virtually the Founding Father generation of American academic philosophy, the failure of the subsequent generations to play a significant role is all the more startling. There are of course thinkers who have deep local intellectual roots and who do make a profound impact: but it is striking that they are not formal philosophers, but men whose centre of gravity is elsewhere—in logic, in linguistics, in the history of science. Quine, Chomsky, Kuhn, have indeed made an enormous and justified impact, but the philosophic guild cannot really claim them. Their philosophic ideas are corollaries of substantive work done in another area

What is the explanation of this curious failure? There can hardly be much doubt about the fact of failure: generations succeed each other in the hope of achieving something of substance, and regularly fail. Collectively, the profession is autistic: there is a tremendous and somewhat comic professional output—one academic journal is actually a *fortnightly*!—but, despite this enormous quantity of reading matter with which the practitioners supply each other (and which no one else reads), it is doubtful whether they have injected even a single idea into the intellectual blood stream of the wider community which they are meant to serve. In fact, they have acted neither as a stimulus nor as a censor or guardian, they neither enrich nor prune. Whatever enters the blood stream from other sources has nothing to fear from their scrutiny. Their social nullity is complete. In as far as some philosophic ideas have entered, for instance, the ideology of the Protest movement—and elements of Existentialism, mystical Marxism, eastern faiths, phenomenology, can be discerned in it—these elements entered directly from abroad, or from sociology or other disciplines. They were never mediated by the philosophers who, apart from not being either innovators or censors, are not middlemen either.

A fully convincing explanation of this curious state of affairs is not available. But one must seek an explanation in two areas: one, the general terms of reference of philosophic thought in the modern world, and two, the specific institutional and ideological milieu of North America.

The terms of reference of modern philosophy are indeed difficult, not to say humiliating. Plato believed that there was a correlation between the importance and dignity of a subject on the one hand, and the rigour of kind of thought appropriate to it on the other. This was a plausible supposition, and in a decent, well-managed universe, one trusts that this is how things would indeed be arranged. Trivial, humanly unimportant matters could be dealt with in a logically sloppy and slipshod manner; whereas matters which are of great or ultimate concern to us would be honoured by the highest standards of logical rigour. Thus the decencies and human self-respect would receive their due.

The world which we in fact inhabit is, alas, not at all like this. In it the inverse relationship obtains. Rigorous techniques are available in many domains which, humanly speaking, are unimportant. Thanks to the rigour of those techniques, a consensus of experts is available in those domains which inspires the respect of onlookers. Many of these domains are rather like heavy-weight boxing: the criterion of excellence, and the manner of determining who satisfies it best, are so clear that there is relatively little room for intrigue, dispute, or disagreement.

The situation is alas quite other in the sphere of those questions that concern us most. Conflicting criteria abound, the manner of their application is obscure, movements proliferate, each of them claims to be in possession of procedures, principles, criteria, which generally re-endorse their own viewpoint and condemn that of their rivals, but which do not really have any evident authority when viewed from outside.

This situation may have multiple roots, but the ones that are specially worth highlighting are those connected not with the human condition in general, but with the *special* circumstances of western industrial man. Western civilization has two salient features, which have contributed to that unfortunate and humiliating inversion of the Platonic tie-up of rigour and importance. It is based on science and technology; and it is individualistic. The joint implications of these features are not always comfortable.

The individualism manifests itself in what might be called the protestant-Cartesian cognitive ethic: belief and opinion is to be judged before the bar of the individual conscience or consciousness. Assent to belief is ultimately a private and individual matter. The secrecy and loneliness of the ballot-booth only symbolizes the inherent privilege and predicament of private determination of assent or dissent. The cognitive condition of man parallels the constitutional right of the American citizen to possess arms. The reasoning also is parallel: as the firearm at the homestead was intended to be a check on tyranny, so the sovereignty of individual private judgment is meant to be a check on the dogmatism of institutions claiming to possess some kind of monopoly of truth.

Everyone knows that the reasoning in terms of small arms is anachronistic. Small firearms, such as can be owned by individuals may facilitate—notoriously, they do indeed facilitate—terrorism and assassination, but they constitute no serious threat whatever to a modern military machine. An American militia in the eighteenth century could defy the regiments of George III, but no modern totalitarian state could be defied by analogous means. Urban guerrillas do not disprove this. They can operate only sporadically, or against states morally unable or unwilling to use the force at their disposal, or against crypto-colonial pseudo-states, which are front organizations of foreign powers, and have no credibility for themselves or for others.

What is less seldom noticed is that the same anachronism which attaches to a weapon that can be made, handled, and maintained by a lone individual, also attaches to his *cognitive* equipment. As sophisticated and complex weapon systems have replaced individual small arms as the means of coercion, so a similar transformation has also occurred in our cognitive equipment. The protestant-Cartesian cognitive ethic—think for yourself, let all opinion pass before the tribunal of your private, individual consciousness—continues to receive a kind of residual lip-service, but has little inherent plausibility. The individual does not any longer have the illusion that he could possibly pass judgment on all the matters of belief which form the backcloth of his life. One is reminded of the advice given to an English poet by his father: no one can write a poem. Tradition writes it for the poet. All he can hope to do is occasionally to write a line. This, incidentally, is part of the significance of the remarkable recent vogue of Thomas Kuhn's *The Structure of Scientific Revolutions* (Chicago, 1962). The argument of that book spits in the face of the protestant-Cartesian illusion. Serious cognition is not an individual business at all, it says in effect: knowledge works only through 'paradigms', whose carriers are not individuals, but communities Revolutionary geniuses may perhaps contribute to the destruction of an old, or the erection of a new paradigm, but to enjoy one, to live in it, you need a community. The individual is not really a cognitive unit at all.

Thus there is a deep tension between our inherited individualism, which is still important and operative in many aspects of life, and the hard facts of our actual cognitive ecology. It is the tension between what Gaston Bachelard has called the world in which we live and the one in which we think. One might equally well express this in terms of the tension between two kinds of thought: thought which is continuous with daily life and its personal relationships, and in the terms of which consequently the individual sees himself—and, on the other hand thought which satisfies the highest contemporary criteria of effectiveness, and which is generally technical, specialized, and not at all continuous with daily life.

Part, but part only, of this tension may be due to a kind of historical time-lag. Our educational system has not moved fast enough, we have not digested the rapid and dramatic cognitive advances of modern times, and hence this gap between the ideas we use and those we respect. This no doubt is part of the story, though unfortunately it is probably only a part. Were it the whole of it, we could look forward to a definite solution of our problem

In as far as what is at issue is simply a time-lag, the solution would be simply the reform of the educational system, such that those who pass through it are adequately equipped to cope with the best available up-to-date kinds of knowledge. One could then look forward to the time when the notions which are deeply internalized and easily operated, and in terms of which we consequently *live*, are the same as those which govern the most high-powered, decisive, authoritative cognitive practices of our culture. It would then be possible to revert to the protestant-individualist ideal: judge for yourself! Each man, being in possession of a cognitive armoury almost as powerful, or at least not disastrously, profoundly less powerful than, the central armoury of the community, could decide whether or not he endorses authority or the communal consensus. And if he did not, he could without despair or absurdity defy it.

We all know, as soon as we articulate it, that this is mere fantasy. An individual is about as likely to forge, in the workshop in his back yard, firearms capable of challenging a modern weapons system, as he is of individually constructing and elaborating the criteria for the re-evaluation of a belief system. Descartes thought he could do it, and though this was an illusion even in his case, in the seventeenth century it had at least a certain plausibility. What Descartes could erect in his back yard was not markedly inferior, or inferior at all, to the co-operative effort of the scholastic belief machine, though one must also add that it was not nearly as independent of it as he thought and as his intentions required. But today, few men can have the Cartesian illusion; few can suppose that by dint of hard and totally independent, individual thought, they can re-assess the cultural heritage. Cognitively as in other ways, we are at the mercy of a complex division of labour which obliges us to put trust in others. A poet can hope to write a line here and there—but poems are only written by a tradition, not by a man.

But the specificity of our problem resides in the fact that there is such grave discontinuity between the idiom of the tradition which writes the poem, and the individual who writes the line. The cognitive tradition is very highly specialized, technical, and abstract. Daily life is lived in an idiom which is much less specialized, more concrete, and untechnical. Yet in the end, the protestant-individual values, *and* other factors, place the centre of gravity, the ultimate court of appeal, with the individual. Moreover, the major cognitive tradition generally does not contain moral, political recipes and injunctions. It is distant and in many ways neutral or indifferent. So the individual is the locus of the ultimate decisions on faith and morals not merely in virtue of the individualist doctrine which teaches that he *ought* to have this power, but also because no one else, at least in liberal societies, appears to have much desire to usurp it. And yet he cannot easily feel ready to assume such responsibility.

These then are the general terms of reference under which contemporary philosophy operates. Ultimate issues are still the prerogative of the individual and the idiom in which he lives—which means the individual *qua* individual, in his private capacity and not *qua* specialist (if he happens to be one at all). What is really important is that these decisions must indeed be made in the idiom in which he lives his life, not in the specialized idiom (if any) which he may happen to use in his professional hours. But this personal and lived idiom is untidy, messy, and known to be cognitively low-powered, in a society which is also familiar with high-powered, highly formalized, and rigorous cognitive techniques, which in a way set the norm. This lies at the heart of the tension. One might say: how can one continue to be a protestant-individualist in a society whose cognitive procedures are collective, technical, non-individual?

Faced with this problem, academic philosophies have reacted in a number of ways. At one extreme, there are those which claim to have discovered reasons for not discounting the private daily idiom after all—who believe that the ordinary world, the *Lebenswelt*, the concepts of ordinary language or whatnot, are really perfectly sound after all, *and* primary, and that there is no need to feel uneasy about them, and that the initial tension is based on a misunderstanding. All is well, really: we have not lost our cognitive citizenship, as we had supposed; our logical intuitions and assumptions in daily life *are* in order, and we *are* fit to be cognitive sovereigns. One is glad to hear this, but one only wishes that the reasons adduced in support of this position were a little more convincing.

At the other extreme, there are those who accept the superiority of technique, and endeavour to provide us with one good enough to propel us into that cognitive stratosphere in which we will at last be able to judge with confidence. And some doctrines combine the two approaches: it is amusing to note, in recent years, the emergence of specialized, patented *techniques* designed to give us access to our own subjectivity, or to the inner life of the concepts of our culture. Subjectivity, like original sin, used to be our prerogative, and we did not need to do anything to attain or enjoy it. But nowadays, a man needs a special technique and training even to commune with his own stream of consciousness, or to understand how he himself uses words. Well, so be it.

The correct attitude to this predicament is not something that is easy to find, and certainly not something to be settled in an article. But there remains the question why American professional philosophy has been so very uninspired, derivative, and unimpressive in coping with it. Part of the answer must lie in this: when the problem is, precisely, how to relate the thought of individual life, as *lived*, to specialized, professional techniques, then the prospect of insightful comments are small when they come, as they do, from a guild which is, by its general circumstances, so very heavily slanted in the direction of an humourless professionalism. The unspecialized nature of American undergraduate study (which is in itself an excellent thing), and the very heavily professional, career-oriented nature of graduate work, push the professional 'philosopher' towards movements which offer the appearance of technical specialization, of trade arcana. These can then consist of esoteric wills or abstruse reasons why the non-technical is sufficient. . . .

Moreover, it is still somehow difficult, for a high-powered American intellectual, to fall in love with the local culture. Henry as well as William James stand in the background. In America, love of the folk culture has been pre-empted by the folk itself. . . . The USA is unusual in having a *non-vicarious* populism. It is all very well for central and east European intellectuals to be populists, for they had a monopoly of such sentiments, and the peasants themselves whom they idealized knew nothing of it. (The English case is special. The earthy, idiosyncratic culture, on whose behalf a local variant of populism is articulated, as in the work of Michael Oakeshott, is an upper-class or upper-folk culture.) But it is hard to love a folk which already consciously loves itself, and has articulated its self-image and self-love against the intellectual slickers, who might otherwise be candidates for idealizing it. . . . So those who love the *Lebenswelt* choose an alien one, or alien approach to it.

These, as far as I can see, are the general terms of reference which determine the problem which is being solved so very disappointingly. A heavily professionalized, routinized profession is tackling an issue which, precisely, is about the relation of the technical-professional to the personal, individual, and ultimate; and in as far as it tries to satisfy some non-professional style of life, it tends to be alien models which alone have glamour for it. The result—an unconvincing, tedious, largely irrelevant technicality, and a sad dependency on foreign models, an absence of local roots.

1973

Chapter 4   On being wrong

The fact of corrigibility is simply that our convictions, valuations, and theories are liable to be mistaken. The question arises whether this sword of Damocles hangs over all our beliefs, or whether there are some privileged regions unmenaced by it; whether there are means of exorcizing it; whether we should even try to exorcize it, and if not, should instead resign ourselves to the possibility of error shadowing everything.

Perhaps the ideal of eluding corrigibility, of attaining infallible certainty, plays an essential role despite the fact that it can never be realized, and constitutes a kind of logical carrot which the donkey can never reach but which makes it progress. There may even be some kind of connection between the appeal of certainty and the fact that the precariousness of beliefs is also what makes them useful.

These problems have arisen in a number of different contexts, and I shall only bring out the connecting thread.

To begin with: Ordinary material object statements—statements about lamp-posts, handlebars, and window-panes, for instance—received attention from philosophers a few years back. Some pointed out that statements about such objects are infinitely corrigible, that evidence may always turn up making us realize that what we had believed about the object was not so. A certain kind of answer to this problem became fashionable. I say *kind* of answer, for it is an answer only in the way in which telling an awkward child to go away and play is answering its question.

The answer consists of saying that those who bewail the corrigibility of our knowledge are simply confusing various senses of 'knowledge', and applying criteria of evidence suitable in one domain to another. For instance: because in mathematics conclusive proofs are available, therefore knowledge in fields where such proofs are not available is felt to be unbearably precarious. All that the exponents of corrigibility appear to have done, it is said, is to have raised the fee entitling one to use the word 'knowledge' so high that only the most favoured convictions, or no convictions at all, can afford it. And the motive for this awkward and useless procedure is alleged to be the typically philosophic mistake of wishing to give a homogeneous and simple account of what important words such as 'knowledge' and 'certainty' mean; whereas the correct approach would have been to recognize from the very start that these words were bound to have different, though possibly related, meanings in different contexts. If this were the whole story the problem would indeed be spurious. But I shall try to show that preoccupation with corrigibility is much more pervasive, and far from being inspired merely by a limited, possibly technical or specialist, interest.

There is, for instance, in modern French literature, a widespread preoccupation with the infinite corrigibility of statements about personality. I do not know how many pages Proust devotes to Swann's preoccupation with the fidelity of Odette, or Marcel's with that of Albertine. With both, doubt is pushed to the point where it simply feeds on the truth that nothing entails the final exclusion of any interpretation of a person's behaviour. Yet it is rather unlikely that Proust was inspired by a philosophic programme requiring brief and homogeneous analyses of concepts such as 'knowledge of the character of others'. He was merely recording a widespread tendency of all who feel intensely about some object, to raise the standards of what is conclusive about it.

So impressed, indeed, are some writers with the inherent inconclusiveness of evidence concerning character that they sometimes suggest, mistakenly, that this weakness is peculiar to this kind of knowledge. The suggestion is even made that the certainty attainable about material objects is also attractive and desired in personal relations, where it cannot be had. This comes out, for instance, in the relation of the chief characters in Sartre's *La Putain Respectueuse*. Of course, with objects, certainty of a kind is obtainable by definition; we can ensure that a property is possessed by something by definition. But this device is not available to us with regard to people, who seem to possess an identity and existence independent of the conventions of definition. This I take to be the burden of the famous slogan that 'existence precedes essence'.

The preoccupation and indeed perverse enjoyment of the uncertainty of one's knowledge of others, similar to that found in *Remembrance of Things Past*, is also found for instance in an excellent recent novel by M. R. Margerit, *Le Dieu Nu*. The hero of this work vacillates between three women: his morally rather dubious sister; secondly, a married woman elusive and intriguing only because, as it turns out in the end, she is vacuous and indecisive; and, finally, a forthright, attractive, and intelligible young woman. Despite the obvious superiority of the last, at one stage the hero expresses his rejection of her by exclaiming that, unfortunately, he is no Cartesian: clarity and straightforwardness, however combined with attractive qualities, appeal to him far less than moral mists and ambiguities.

A more elaborate use of the awareness and, in this case, unwillingness to accept precariousness occurs in Anouilh's *Euridice*, produced in London as *Point of Departure*. The author's use of the Eurydice legend is this: the suggestion is that love actually entails desire for death, this being so because it involves convictions about the relationship which are too ambitious not to be falsified sooner or later, if by surviving one gives the future an opportunity of falsifying them. At the same time, for one in love, the thought of their falsification is hardly bearable. Indeed, even if one did not expect them to be falsified, they might seem tainted by the very possibility. Death is the only means of depriving the uncertain future of its power of tainting the present relationship. For Sartre, on the other hand, death in *Huis Clos* does not lead to certainty-at-last concerning personality. The ending of the accretion of evidence merely prevents further testing. Death thus ends inquiry without answering the question. This difference between Anouilh and Sartre is probably due to the fact that Sartre's characters tend to be concerned with qualities such as courage, rather than with fidelity.

There is more to be said about the logical peculiarity of 'death'. Death is indeed not an event in life, not even the last; to assert it of someone is to say that all the events of his life, including the last, have ended. It has recently been explained to us by philosophers that certain words, such as 'arrive', designate something infallible not because any human activities are infallible, but merely because just those words are applied only to successful performances. These are 'achievement words'. 'Death' is an achievement word.

There is a story by Gorki of a peasant who became a multiple murderer for no other reason than that one day he realized the fragility of human life, was shocked and repelled and at the same time attracted to transmute it into something which at least was firm and incorrigible—namely, death. Before his discovery, life must have seemed to him to possess a kind of security which afterwards he saw was spurious, and the shock of such a discovery may be similarly great for other people concerning other topics. One discovers something rather than merely alters the criteria of 'knowledge' when one sees that, say, the social arrangements within which one lives are what they are merely because they happen to have developed in that way, or that one's important convictions or values lack finality and conclusiveness. Later comes the discovery that such finality could not have been had.

Writers who are described as Existentialists earn this label at least partly in virtue of the fact that, while recognizing the urge to escape from corrigibility, precariousness, and uncertainty, they also maintain that it cannot or should not ever be satisfied. If I understand the notion of *mauvaise foi* at all, it is meant to characterize thinking which pretends to be or contains some guarantee of truth, some password to incorrigible certainty.

A similar theory is perceptible in something less literary and melodramatic: Professor Karl Popper's theory of science, contained in his *Logik der Forschung*, and his social philosophy, expounded in his *Open Society and Its Enemies*. The common underlying theme of both these works is the necessary and salutary nature of corrigibility, and the need for recognizing its inevitability.

I hope I shall be forgiven my levity if I give a simplified account of his theory of science with the help of the following parable: Imagine a matron dominating a social circle, within which her praise or blame can make or unmake anyone. She abstains from describing anyone as 'virtuous', restricting herself to 'virtuous as yet', and labelling as 'not virtuous' anyone who has lapsed even once. Thus the 'virtuous as yet' and the 'not virtuous' between them exhaust her circle. Although, of course, there is a one-way movement from the 'virtuous *as yet*' class to the 'not virtuous' class, she has given no hostages to the future. Now if you substitute 'scientific method' for the matron, and 'scientifically valid' for 'virtuous', you have, I think, a reasonably fair caricature of Popper's theory of science.

In one sense, of course, this device actually eliminates precariousness from the domain of science: if scientists operate only with 'falsified' and 'unfalsified as yet,' all inferences within science become formally logical. And indeed one of the aims of Popper's theory is to eliminate the myth of 'induction', the alleged 'principles of induction' having been a modest, empiricist way of practically insuring us against corrigibility.

But in another and more fundamental sense this model entails the frank recognition of the corrigibility of any scientific theory by allowing it to be only 'unfalsified as yet'. But this is a cross which should be borne joyfully, for certainty could be had only at the cost of vacuity.

It is difficult to see how one could tell whether this model is correct. Asking scientists would not be decisive, for Popper is not indulging in descriptive psychology; he is offering a logical reconstruction.

What motives could one have for working at such a science? I suggest without any proof that scientists are not imbued with an intellectual puritanism analogous to the moral puritanism of the matron in the story. They do not eliminate well-falsified theories merely from a disinterested pursuit of theories untainted by falsification; their attitude is, I should imagine, more utilitarian. Well-falsified theories are discarded because their falsification is taken to be an index to their future falsification. Were it not, one could hardly see a motive for doing science. Now possible motives seem to me relevant because unless perseverance in scientific work can be justified and a motive given in terms of the model, the model cannot altogether be right; unless, that is, it were conceded that scientific investigation is no more rational than blind guessing.

In the few emotively charged parts of the book, Popper extols the Sisyphus-like nature of scientific work. The very warmth of these passages shows an implicit belief in a strong, if regrettable, human urge towards finality, combined with the hope that this can be replaced by an alternative trait—namely, that of a frank acceptance of corrigibility. One can conveniently call these traits, such as a yearning for incorrigibility or an acceptance of precariousness, 'second-order' traits; for to say that someone wishes his convictions to have foolproof certainty is not to say *which* convictions he holds. Or to say of someone that he accepts the possibility of error in his beliefs is, again, not to say just which beliefs he has. Some 'first-order' filling in, so to speak, is required for these formal traits such as a desire for certainty. But while some filling is necessary, the mere possession of such a second-order trait does not predetermine *which*; a feeling of certainty, for instance, may characterize any beliefs.

The link between Popper's theory of science and his social philosophy is that in his view there is in social life, as in science, a powerful second-order yearning for incorrigibility and intellectual safety which is harmful, and which should be replaced by an acceptance or even cult of impermanence, corrigibility, 'openness'. In Popper's picture of political life the villain of the piece is neither the anti-social tendencies of individuals nor the corruption of governments, but the excessive social tendencies of individuals. His general diagnosis of certain harmful intellectual tendencies is that they are rooted in the yearning for social and moral certainty—for incorrigibility in effect. It is essential that we come to realize that freedom and the possibility of experiment entail that we shall never have security and certainty about the ordering and values of our society. The parallel with his theory of science is obvious.

The existence of strong second-order desires such as the yearning for certainty is of some interest in the psychology of morals. In societies in which some or all virtues have a logic similar to that of the matron, the devil has a permanent advantage. A man in whom the need for certainty is strong may sin owing not to some inherent appeal of the transgression itself, but through its logical charm. Virtue is infinitely corrigible, you can never be confident of retaining it; but 'being a sinner', on the other hand, has the merit of being reliably ascertainable in a finite number of steps, sometimes even after a single step. This purely logical consideration must be of inestimable help to the devil. Theological doctrines concerning the ever-present possibility of Grace are perhaps cunning attempts to deprive the devil of his advantage, by making sin infinitely corrigible also, and hence equally precarious.

A good deal of metaphysics, and certain kinds of ethics, may be seen as instances of the flight from precariousness. A typical form this ambition assumes is that of a pursuit of a Highest Good which includes among its merits that of not being liable to let you down. Spinoza is a good example of this: he informs us that he resolved to look for a Highest Good which, unlike lesser Goods, could not prove even partly an evil in disguise on attainment. The doubt that whatever he found might still let him down he silenced with the argument, reminiscent of the ontological proof, that it could not prove deceptive and precarious, being defined as just that which has no such snags.

The commonest advice for exorcizing precariousness is the ethics of recognizing necessity. Such ethics shamelessly turn upside down the normal meaning of 'freedom' which is 'ignorance of necessity', if it is to be defined in terms of necessity at all, and advise us to like whatever is bound to happen so to speak *ex officio*, because it is bound to happen. If we succeed in adjusting our desires and values in such a manner, the future can indeed hold no terrors for us. Such stoicism may be genuine in the sense of honestly restricting itself to recommending acceptance of whatever happens, without prejudging at all what it is that will happen. One can hardly imagine this really being practised, though one cannot but feel admiration for those who try. Yet it can also come to include predictions about the future more specific than the initial and modest 'what will happen, will happen' but claiming similar certainty. This is the case of those who elude precariousness by recognizing a necessity which is both specific and congenial to them (by some lucky coincidence). Both in the modest and genuine, and in the bogus and expanded, form, these theories are open to the criticism that games in which losing is impossible, winning is pointless. We cannot both take part in a genuine game and be certain of success, much as we would like to. It has been said that life is not a spectacle but a predicament; the truth really is that we need and like it that way, and even artificially turn spectacles into predicaments, with the help of bookmakers and others.

Ethical theories such as the one discussed may be combined with metaphysics to the effect that there are some general truths independently and reliably knowable, which yet at the same time account for all that is to be explained. If this were so, corrigibility would indeed be successfully eliminated, and intelligence or some kind of insight would suffice to free us from precariousness. The briefest damning criticism of this hope is Kierkegaard's remark that the system is always about to be finished next Tuesday. We can never be in possession of an all-embracing and self-guaranteeing truth with the safety-providing features required. Those absolute idealists who thought they almost had it as well succeeded in convincing themselves by leaving their system nebulous, vague, or tautologous. No wonder that those who took such systems at their face values were liable to feelings of nausea and inadequacy on contrasting it with the complexity of the real world. Such was the reaction of a student to metaphysical idealism reported by William James.

But if metaphysicians try to procure security for us by eliminating contingency, perhaps the motives of some empiricists are similar. For if we cannot totally eliminate contingency, the next best thing might perhaps be totally to eliminate necessary truth; and that is, notoriously, the empiricist's manner of spending his time, devoting himself to giving psychologistic or linguistic accounts of apparent instances of necessity. The model of the world suggested by extreme metaphysics, a model in which contingency is universally and symmetrically diffused, is not as consoling as the necessarily ordered world of the metaphysician; but at least it is better than the compromise in which necessity and contingency are mixed up higgledy-piggledy without even clear and orderly lines of demarcation. The very pure empiricist offers us the security of knowing that everything is equally insecure. As Thurber says, there is no safety in numbers or in anything else.

Metaphysical systems are really attempts at a kind of universal mnemonic device, an attempt to have and hold a set of easily retainable expressions which will recall and indicate the place of anything and everything, thus giving us safety in a chaotic world of transitory and confused things. Both lack of order and the precariousness of expectations are odious to an orderly mind, and both would be obviated by a successful metaphysic, were such a thing possible. No loose string would be left in a world which is all loose strings. Metaphysicians try to tie knots in the strings, empiricists point to their looseness, Existentialists make a virtue (of necessity or otherwise) of it.

1955

Chapter 5   Is belief really necessary?

The traditional picture of man is this: he is envisaged on a kind of cosmic market, hawking his soul (i.e. seeking a faith) as a poor peasant might his solitary cow. The sale is immensely important, for it is the only cow he has, the prices offered are very, very high.

The price of souls, contrary to the laws of mundane economics, does not fall with increasing supply. The buyers appear to possess literally infinite resources. . . . There is, however, a snag: most of them are unwilling to pay on delivery. They issue IOUs or dividend-bearing stock, and the assessment of risks against profits is a very difficult business. Pascal, one of the ablest salesmen amongst the belief-brokers, argued that the profits offered by his firm outweighed all possible risks, irrespective of how high we assessed those risks. His firm was promising infinite bliss, and its infinity was bound to outweigh any finitely (*there*'s the rub) assessed risk, however great. (But may not the risk be infinite too?) Another flaw in his argument is that it is cogent only if infinitely prolonged and accentuated bliss does not have a diminishing marginal utility. The numerous legends about men who sell their souls to the devil are a curious projection by a religion which is itself in this market.

Stating one's credo is a familiar, easily recognized response, like falling in love. But we may apply La Rochefoucauld's remark that few men would love had they not heard of it. Must one have an organized inventory of convictions and doubts? Such a *garderobe* of ideas and judgments is *de rigueur* in our culture, particularly for an intellectual. The possession of a nice set *defines* him. Many historical contexts with which we are familiar are marked by the emergence of comparatively pure belief-specialists, and an accompanying attitude to the role of belief in the life of any individual or society. The important features of that outlook are that *what one believes* is important, statable fairly briefly and uniquely, that it is optional, and that it transcends what is easily checked.

We can only speculate on the natural history of belief. For animals there is presumably no dissociation between belief and action—an animal can be said to believe those unavowed and unavowable assumptions on which it is seen to act. A straightforward dispositional account of belief suffices. But somewhere between that and ourselves fundamental modifications occur; the storing and communicating of belief by speech; the emergence of communal dispositions, whose implicit belief-implications could not be said to be the possession of the individual in isolation from his community—in other words of ritual; the emergence of ritual specialists; the separation through speech and record of belief from ritual, and hence finally the emergence of belief-specialists, in other words of prophets, priests, clerics, intellectuals. The above is merely a kind of possible, logical order.

Intellectuals are sometimes defined in terms of possession of certain skills, but that is an error. Some skills, notably literacy and sometimes a capacity to argue, are closely attached to being an expert on belief, especially in a culture where truth is verbal truth. (It usually is—ineffable truths are verbal truths *manqué*.) But the essential thing remains expertise in belief. Indeed the Sophists have earned their bad name through a reputation for having the skill without possessing, or caring for, Truth. The notion of *cleric* combines that of the scribe and of the authority on creed, and this conjunction can still be seen functioning in, for instance, the *fquih* of a North African village; but when it is dissolved, it is the latter component that is crucial. When everyone becomes literate, the descendant of the cleric is not the clerk but the intellectual. European history has accentuated this. Intellectual revolutions with social implications, or social ones with ideological accompaniments, have required a whole army of expositors and counsellors to explain what it is all about. In a more static society the cleric might have become primarily the bureaucrat (as perhaps happened in China), but that has been secondary with us.

Where freedom of thought prevails intellectuals are the brokers in this economy of beliefs. The habit of belief-allegiance, of investing in convictions, has spread beyond the transcendent—or back from the transcendent, one should say, perhaps—to any dubitable parts of science, politics, or art: anywhere, in fact, where the possibility of doubt and disagreement allows room for choice, manoeuvre, and the tension of uncertainty. The practice does not, at least in the short run, seem to have suffered from the diminution of transcendental beliefs. It has merely shifted its focus. Where freedom of thought is absent, intellectuals are bureaucrats of the nationalized belief rather than brokers.

The existence of a lively and sensitive belief-economy is one of the striking and perhaps decisive features of Western society. It is often asserted, with some justification, that freedom and tolerance, never wholly and permanently absent, are essential to it. What must be noted is that some intolerance and exclusiveness are also necessary. Scarcity is essential to economics—so a definition assures us—and in the realm of ideas, scarcity is generated by incompatibility. (At least, the fruitful scarcity of ideas is only produced this way. A mere poverty of ideas can be had without it.) Where all ideas are compossible, where anything goes and can be joined with anything else, no exchange, no replacement, no progress will arise: at best, an amorphous accretion, an unselective and uncritical syncretism. Perhaps this essential element of refusing to combine incompatibles came in through jealous and exclusive tribal deities—perhaps through the universalization of one of them.

An unwillingness to multiply explanations and a refusal to face the chaos of reality by a similarly disorderly set of beliefs were necessary. How unreasonable this insistence was *a priori*! With our hindsight we know it to have been fruitful, but this does not free some of the predecessors of science of the charge of silliness. Patently the world is not all water, or hot air, or green cheese. It was clearly a stupid notion that a single model must do for all cases that led Thales and his fellows into these absurdities.[1] It just so happens that, absurdly, they were right. In the social sciences, the question is still open.

A clue to the possible genesis of the fruitful intolerance may lie in the double meaning of the English word 'true'—'loyal' or 'correct-of-the-world', roughly. (German distinguishes between *wahr* and *treu*.) Communal loyalty has become the need for a unique truth *via* a stage where the former required the latter, perhaps. Some cultures make the worst of both worlds: a Tibetan lamasery combines a rigid traditionalism with sterile eclecticism.

Another half-error is contained in common assumptions about the role of belief in social control, alleged to be that of presenting a reasonably coherent picture of the universe in terms of which the individual can interpret his experience, and which allocates duties and rights, suggests expectations and so on. In fact, an important way in which belief facilitates control is through unintelligibility, through *blocking* the possibility of interpreting one's experience. This idea is of course explored in anti-clerical and polemical literature, but only with regard to specific beliefs, leaving incomplete a general theory of the social functioning and necessity of absurdity.

This necessity can be deduced from the maxim *comprendre, c'est égaler*. An intelligible belief-system, once mastered, leaves the disciple the equal of his master. He too can now draw further consequences, check the master's steps, and so on. No such danger arises if the system contains a decent dose of absurdity, which will paralyse the learner's power of independent movement within it.[2] (The arbitrariness of the rules of etiquette and in general of the *differentiae* of privileged classes has the same function: to make them rational would be to destroy their function.) Moreover, the unintelligibility leaves the disciple with a secret guilt of not understanding, or not avowing it, or both, which binds him to the master who is both responsible for it and seems untainted by it. The belief that the naked emperor is clothed is better social cement than that a naked one is naked—or even that a clothed one is clothed. It is not, as some philosophers thought, a common rationality, but community in specific irrationalities, which binds men. We enslave ourselves by seeing what is not there—or by not seeing what *is* there. Take a contemporary example: 'Linguistic philosophy' often works by pretending that what is intelligible is not.[3] A generation ago Frank Ramsay wittily defined scholasticism as pretending that what isn't clear is: a new species has arisen—pretending that what *is* clear isn't.

In brief, beliefs must be difficult to be satisfying. Thus it is a travesty to say that martyrs die for Truth. Real truths seldom require such dramatic testimony, nor is one either asked or tempted to give it. Martyrs have in general defended in the face of death beliefs which they would have found somewhat harder to defend in the face of logic.

A general purveyor of absurdity is religion—by its operational definition. An anthropologist, seeing someone adding two and two and making four, passes on. If however, *one* makes *three*, out comes the notebook and an entry is made under *beliefs*. Thus the vaunted universality of faith—which in any case only holds of societies, not of individuals—may boil down to no more than that all societies have beliefs or practices which to some others would seem absurd, and that all communities have collective rituals. (This last point is in turn a tautology, for a collection of people who never assemble for ritual are not a community.) Of course, not all theologians are ashamed of this. Kierkegaard elaborated the notion of 'offence' and maintained that it was inherent and essential and distinctive of Christianity. His attitude, insisting on the need for rational offensiveness, can be seen as a magnificent tactical *volte-face* in the struggle with rationalism, a positive exploitation of what others had only covered up as a weakness.

To acquire charisma through absurdity it is necessary to stake one's claim high. Salesmen of comparatively harmless spurious medicines may be prosecuted, but if they claim something so great that its falsity is no longer demonstrable, they not merely cease to be legally liable, but current canons of good taste, which protects sensitive souls, will proscribe criticism. Moreover, the very extravagance of the claim will attract the interest of the unhappy and needy of salvation or consolation. They can then be told that their very interest proves that in their hearts they know that the saving or consoling claim is true, and that their distrust only illustrates their as yet unregenerate nature—a point which has wisely been incorporated in the doctrine.

This use of absurdity is of course not restricted to religion. Notoriously, the absurdity of much military ritual is invaluable in breaking down potentially defiant recruits. The discipline of Communist parties depends not on the plausibilities, but the absurdities or contradictions of party line. It is less that these absurdities are enforced by party discipline, than that it is they which enforce discipline.

Another example is psycho-analysis, the opium of American intellectuals. (Whatever their nominal intellectual allegiances, from it they derive consolation and the notions and background-screen for seeing themselves and their lives.) The concept of 'resistance' is very close to Kierkegaard's 'offence'. He well knew how essential it is to 'transference'. Analysts themselves have commented on the oddity of the analytic situation, and there perhaps lies the clue to why resistance and hence transference generally occur. Those critics of psycho-analysis who adduce statistics showing that, for instance, the percentage of neurotics cured spontaneously and those cured by analysis is similar, may in fact be doing psycho-analysis a great service. If the effectiveness of psycho-analysis were cogently proven, if the patient in his need could really relax in a justified confidence that he will be helped, the tension which only hope and doubt can produce might be absent, and hence also resistance, and thus transference and the relationship essential to the therapy might not arise. *If* this is so, we should have an interesting example of a technique that can only work when its efficacy is objectively in doubt.[4] The initial appeal, the bait of psycho-analysis, lies in the fact that it has a unique strategic position: it to some extent shares (through medicine) in the prestige of natural science, without partaking of its tedium, technicality, indifference to the individual case, and human and moral irrelevance. Who would have dreamt that a technique could be both *scientific* and so delightfully, intimately personal?

It may be objected that the theory of the role of absurdity is only plausible with regard to more sophisticated cultures whose members *notice* absurdity. But just this may help to explain the ritual or mythopoeic extravagance of some primitives—as bringing absurdity home to those of crude logical perceptions. Puritan religions such as some forms of Protestantism and Islam operate on the aesthetic principle, applicable to the subtle and imaginative, that one good effect or symbol is better alone and unsupported by a baroque proliferation of minor ones, and that the imagined is more suggestive than the seen. Understood truths are sweet but unintelligible ones are sweeter.

Mores have grown up around the satisfaction of the belief function, the behaviour of the brokers and their customers. The sociology of belief has fluctuated between the doctrine that belief reinforces society by reflecting and symbolizing it, and that it consoles us for its evils by *not* reflecting it. Whilst sociologists have interested themselves in the social control aspect of the matter, philosophers, preoccupied with the epistemology of ethics, have on the whole neglected the ethics of *episteme*. Yet there is much to discuss here. There is a widely recognized obligation to believe, and a less widely accepted one to doubt—a difference only in part explicable in terms of the bulls and bears of this market. This conflict can also be seen as between committed belief (irrespective of what may be true) and truth (irrespective of what you may have committed yourself to previously). Some feel that switching one's belief investments is in itself immoral: 'True or false, my credo'. One does not let one's side down when it loses—indeed, especially then. Somewhat more rational seems the recommendation to experiment with stock in the hope of finishing with the best; and finally there is the romantic preference for the experimentation with various stocks quite independently of which is best.[5]

Another issue arises from the tradition maintaining that sincere belief excuses everything, that the sincerity and intensity of the conviction is more important that its truth or evidence, if indeed it is not a warranty of truth. 'Here I stand, I can no other.' The origin of this may well be the doctrine that sincere conviction was inspired by the deity, and that the individual was a better repository of truth than any institution. Latter-day liberals are sure less that individuals are inspired than that no institution is. Though still found, the high or exclusive valuation of sincerity is on the decline. It is recognized that sincere conviction too can be the last refuge of scoundrels. The reason for this decline is twofold, at least. First, prevalent psychological doctrines do not encourage us to take subjective sincerity at its face-value. Naturalistic theories, attributing often disreputable sources to our inner certainties and blockages, quite properly deprive them of much of their authority. Second, a series of philosophers from Hume to Bertrand Russell have spread the idea that the intellectual, the cognitively smart, is he who believes less rather than more,[6] and above all that it is irresponsible rather than noble to stake one's soul and, usually, the fates and interests of others on unsubstantiated convictions. This is a charge to which evangelists, Stalinists, and adherents of Causes and Faiths are open. Faith seems something dubious not intellectually, but *morally*. There was a time when an atheist's word was unacceptable in court. Would it not be more reasonable to refuse the testimony or promises of a believer? A man who, for the solace of his soul, is prepared to prejudge or prejudice the nature of the universe and the fate of mankind, *on inadequate grounds*, is not likely to shrink before a little deceit or dishonesty. *A priori*, I am inclined to distrust those who sell their souls to God or party (or to a psycho-analyst).

It must however be admitted that this *a priori* argument for the immorality of believers is not confirmed by their actual conduct, or at least by that of the intellectual ones amongst them. This fact may however have the following explanation. First, minorities that have stones cast at them by a smug majority little qualified for the task often exhibit an average level of morality above the general. There is nothing like being a member of a minority with uncertain status for putting one on one's better behaviour; and amongst intellectuals, the status of believers *is* uncertain. Secondly, believers caught up in the present revival are still living on the inherited capital of a humanist, sceptical, tolerant and universalist ethic which is associated with Rationalism. But it behoves us to be careful: how long can such values survive without the doctrines that were their basis?

The two considerations undermining high valuation of sincerity alone—the argument from Freud and the argument from Russell, so to speak—cut across each other on the issue of toleration. Scepticism may make for tolerance, but the seeing of convictions in the context of the whole personality does not. Given that beliefs are indices of one's nature, they can hardly claim inviolable status: a society that fights disease cannot proclaim a sacred right for all and any symptoms. Illiberal regimes often have no objection to truly free thought, they only do not tolerate criminals—and it so happens that certain beliefs are infallible stigmata of a criminal nature. The outlook of modern psychology is not conducive to a belief in the sacredness of the individual conscience and conviction, and indeed members of psycho-analytic schools are not given to crediting rivals with *bona fides*. Still, liberalism, like democracy, can be (and has been) deduced not only from the goodness, but also from the wickedness of man, and this second premiss remains available.

Once men are caught by the salvation-through-verbal-formula outlook, the situation they find themselves in is this. Imagine a highly disagreeable prison. A new inmate arrives, and after a time informs his fellow-prisoners that he has a foolproof plan for a revolt that will liberate the prisoners. The prisoners, who have been had before and know something of the Governor's methods, suspect him of being an *agent provocateur*. . . . But in the nature of the case, there is no way of checking up. He wins over some of them with threats; when his rebellion succeeds, he will punish all those who did not believe in him. But not until the day of rebellion is attempted will the prisoners know the truth, and the decision must be taken *now*. The belief-systems facing mankind are like the new prisoner's claims—only the crucial day of confirmation is in general postponed *sine die*. A painful situation this. The need to believe may be a neurosis—but it is also a 'good source of it. The captaincy of our souls is a bother.

The comic pathos of this situation is most visible in those prayers to God asking for faith. If that *cri de coeur* has any meaning, it is already satisfied; if, on the other hand, the doubt is genuine, those who utter it must know that they cannot solve an open question, an issue *sub judice*, by prejudging it. . . . This total lack of logic has not prevented that cry from often being heard. The classical form of inner struggle, that intellectual exercise which has given Western inner man his muscles, consists of trying to prejudge the issue and yet not quite allowing oneself to do so.

From the viewpoint of knowableness, the universe is an excellent torturer. The essence of efficient torture is not to lay on pain thicker and thicker—which only sooner or later leads to the numbing of sensitivity and resignation—but almost to deprive of hope whilst not allowing a peaceful and assured despair, and to enlist the sufferer's own efforts in the production of pain. Those who wish to square themselves intellectually with their universe by capturing it in a final and all-embracing formula are lost; not even a sceptical retreat into cognitive abdication will be allowed them. The contemporary version of such modest tactics is to say that heterogeneity is essential and unifying formulae are not to be found—but *that* too is a unifying formula, and pretty unsatisfactory. The continental version of faith-abstemiousness, the Existentialist disclaimer of moral guarantees outside the individual's choice, is itself an ethic and a guide, a would-be source of security. But the universe has many ways of ensuring that there is no proven faith and no guide—not even the one that there is no true faith and no guide.

The metaphysics of liberty in relation to belief has its oddities. In one sense, nothing is more under my own control than what I think: to lift a feather off my desk is not much bother, but to substitute one phrase in my mind for another is less. If anything is under our control, ordinarily our thoughts are. But in another sense, what we believe is less under our control than anything else; in fact, not under control at all. If we do not like the roundness of the earth, we may one day flatten it into a pancake: but never, never shall we alter the truth of the least and most trivial of propositions. The Law of Excluded Middle, as well as the supposed manifestation of the voice of God, has made us feel we *can no other*.

It is just possible that the importance of verbal belief and of salvation through formula is drawing to a close, that a *credo* will become as archaic as a totem. Let us look at some factors possibly making for this.

One is the decline in importance of verbal communication in general. It may be that the educated man is ceasing to be he who is highly literate and can express himself well, and is becoming he who can operate the calculus. The prestigious forms of knowledge today are the rigorous, technical, mathematical kind; rightly so perhaps, for they more than verbal culture give increased control. It may be that the attribution of importance to belief depends on the assumption that the truth about the universe is verbal, and that some set of words, and some *type* of concept or symbolism, is 'truer' than others or even absolutely 'true', independently of the context, purpose, operations in which they are used. This is a questionable assumption, and not only does modern philosophy question it, but modern life also brings this doubt home to us in daily life.

Perhaps the basic error of past thought was to take verbal questions uncritically at their face-value, trying to find answers to questions without suspecting how odd they were.[7] Perhaps it is possible to replace this attitude either by constructing rigorous calculi in which questions allow of precise answers, or by a dissolution of those questions by examining the terms used in their operational context in daily life. These two possibilities are being explored, each by one active philosophical movement. If either succeeds, the intellectual custom of coquetry with beliefs and doubts, *inner life*, is doomed. Then nothing will remain to be discussed except technical matters and undecidable matters of private taste.

Note that such cosmologies as our age produces are constructed precisely as gadgets are: the method of cosmologists is avowedly pragmatic, seeking models that will incorporate tenuous data. No permanence, or 'truth' in any stronger sense, is sought.

A civilization that is pragmatic rather than absolutist, technical rather than adaptive, mathematical rather than verbal, *Americanized* as we perhaps unfairly say, may have little room for verbal pre-occupation, for the pursuit of that precise explicitness which has been with us from Socrates to G. E. Moore. (When it attributes power to words, as it does in psycho-analysis, it is not in virtue of their truth, cogency or precision.) Perhaps not much should be made of this, but where Damon Runyon (and many others who articulate the inarticulate) comes from, only mugs ask questions, or indeed answer them. A gadget civilization, when it does not use the precise slide-rule, requires the tacit *cottoning-on*, the operation *know-how*, not the unsatisfiable fumbling after the ultimate, metaphysical *mot juste*.

Many themes in modern philosophy ironically provide this trend with a verbal rationale. Let us look at one in particular—contemporary philosophy of mind. The traditional model of mind in a very general sense was such as to imply or suggest that general beliefs mattered, and everyone had to have them, at least implicitly. The model saw mind as a receptacle, picture, or mirror of the world: a picture that perhaps distorted, selected, added—but still, fundamentally a canvas of kinds. This suggests that it *must* have boundaries, and perhaps a general pattern arrivable at by leaving out the details: we *must* have a *Weltanschauung* as well as a multiplicity of little *Anschauungen*. (Ever auto-suggestive, being told that we must, we tried to develop one.) A picture *must* have a frame or a boundary where a frame could be fitted. I suspect this model still underlies the thinking of those anthropologists who attempt comparative studies of *outlooks*.

Fundamentally, the contemporary philosophy of mind consists of the puncturing of this model. Mind is what intelligent people do, and the way they do it. Analysis of mental words shows this, and understanding of the veritable functioning of scientific inquiry confirms it, machines isomorphous with specific mental function possibly prove it. Those of us who do not clearly know what they believe may relax: we are not deficient or lacking in self-knowledge. The supposed obligation to get clear about it all rested on a mistake. . . .

In modern times, Faith has lived in a kind of Strindbergian *ménage* with *Reason*. The final possible cause of a decline of belief may be that this partner is in eclipse too. Not merely no longer a faculty, and deprived of normative authority by Hume, it has also lost much of its status as a kind of Censor of cognition. There seems to be very little that a stern Reason enjoins or forbids: only 'uninterpreted systems' are the home of a really severe logic. Outside them, everything seems much looser and more fluid than had been thought. An iron Reason is not merely not immanent in history or in positive knowledge, it is even absent from its last refuge, mathematics: formalized mathematics are based on set theory, and systems of set theory are optional. . . . A Reason so emaciated is no longer a worthy opponent of Faith. ('Believing in Reason', once a paradoxical expression, seems appropriate now.) Indeed looking at the contemporary religious revival, one has the impression that it is a decline of faith in reason, indifference or disrespect for truth, rather than a revival of faith: people who are part of it seem nebulously *in favour of religion* (rather than believers in specific doctrines) and hardly pay it the compliment of realizing that it claims to be *true* and has to be assessed as such.

1957

Notes

1 Or so a contemporary philosopher of the currently fashionable school might argue. The alleged discovery of the latest philosophical school is that the mistake was not in the particular unities found, but in that unity was sought at all. Wittgenstein was the Heraclitus of language and thought. Heterogeneity is the clue: in Mr Berlin's metaphor, the fox must replace the hedgehog. My general point is that had we been ever foxes, science would never have emerged. But more specific points can be argued against the foxy philosophy which claims to deal with each problem on its merits, unhampered by the mania for unity: namely, that this foxiness is spurious. What really happens is that the unifying ideas, the notions of what is a problem and of what counts as a solution and where solutions are to be found, are left implicit in the technique and not openly avowed. This has the incidental convenience that they cannot be criticized, and can be disavowed by those who use them. For, let's face it: no one of us has more than a limited number of party tricks. The man who claims that he has none or is prepared to use any number, that he has come unprepared, is kidding us and himself: especially if his performance is good. It is interesting however to note than an ideographic science has developed not where it was predicted—in the social sciences in general or in history—but in philosophy! A possible rival for this status is psycho-analysis: but there again, one may be sceptical about claims to ungeneralizable understanding of things unique, implicit in incommunicable therapeutic skills.

2 Let it not be supposed that such charisma through unintelligibility can be had only through long words borrowed from dead languages, and pretensions to transcendental insights. A great discovery of contemporary philosophy is that brief Anglo-Saxon words and an immanentism which scorns to transcend one's own familiar speech habits (let alone this world) will do just as well. It is the oddity of the rules of the game that counts, and they are not only odd but hidden by being unavowed, by virtue of the Principle of the Spurious Fox (see previous footnote).

3 I have in mind those who assure themselves that they do not understand perfectly clear, if disputable, doctrines such as a phenomenalism, determinism, etc., failures which, with their strange reasons, impose as great a strain on the mind as the older abilities to understand statements about the Absolute, etc. Arguments, or rather techniques, which silence without convincing are being used now on behalf of a putative common sense, or rather the outlook of an unimaginative, unsceptical, dullish, and rather extroverted man, instead of being used to buttress a more melodramatic outlook: *there* is the only novelty, and not in any increased honesty or clarity.

4 Psycho-analysis, like linguistic philosophy, is a special and interesting case. For instance, it meets the yearning soul's desires at a very cheap price in terms of general verbal beliefs, which differentiates it sharply from most belief-brokers. It is equally cheap on the ethical plane. It is expensive (apart from the literal sense) in subjecting the patient to a situation and in insisting that misery is self-caused—a heavy guilt indeed.

Like linguistic philosophy, it implicitly subscribes to a type of what may be called the feminine theory of cognition: that truth is not a matter of exploring or penetrating an external reality, but of gestation and parturition. For linguistic philosophy, truth is incapsulated in our actual speech-habits, and only needs a special midwifery to bring it out. Or more precisely: philosophy brings no truths but only extirpates error, and error springs from misinterpreting our own speech-habits, and a careful examination of them corrects this. The midwifery of psycho-analysis has the attraction, in addition to its ethical tolerance, of being more than logically *tolerant*—placing a positive premium on the relaxation of our logical super-ego.

The earliest form of the feminine theory of cognition is of course the Socratic method. Any don who has, usually from laziness, tried to bring off the slave-boy trick with students, knows how phoney it is, how difficult it is to elicit the truth by questions without *suggesting* it.

A question for the psycho-analytic reconstruction of history: if human reproduction were like that of fish, would metaphysical theories of knowledge, the idea of *Durchdrengungskraft des Denkens* in Einstein's phrase, ever have occurred? But one must add that there are (at least) two types of metaphysics: those based on the model of penetration and those based on (concepts of terms) *fitting* (reality) *like a glove*.

5 Cf. Goethe, *Faust*, and Lessing's choice between the contents of God's right and left hand: one contained truth, the other its endless pursuit.

6   The final parody of this trend is the contemporary philosophy which openly asserts that no conclusions other than platitudinous are acceptable. The *mot* is attributed to its leader that in philosophy you know that you are getting somewhere when you are getting bored. (How, one wonders, is the boredom of achievement distinguished from the boredom of attrition?) In what tones do they cry *eureka*? Philosophy once prided itself on inducing wonderment where bovine acceptance had been before. This present philosophy prides itself on restoring the *status quo*. For it, wonderment is, necessarily, a sign of an error or muddle, never of illumination or discovery. The social ideal of imperturbability has been turned into a cosmological heuristic principle.

7   Let it be said that if the mistake of past thought was the failure to reflect on the oddity of philosophic questions and to realize that language may in them be used oddly, it may also be the mistake of the present philosophy to rule out, implicitly, that the world may be odd too. Past philosophy took language for granted and puzzled about the world. 'Linguistic philosophy' takes the world for granted and puzzles about language. (The assumption is that truth is to be found at home— by clearing up our concepts: that philosophic enterprises are defeated not by external difficulties but by self-created ones, like armies that break down under the task of supplying themselves, without the enemy having to do anything about it.) My own guess would be that *both* language and the world are odd. That would leave us in the indeterminate situation of one equation with two unknowns. That doesn't surprise me, for life is hard.

Part two   On ethics

Chapter 6   Maxims

It may be true that the traditional philosophy of mind went wrong in treating states of mind as occurrences and in treating the relation between them and actions as causal. It would however be a mistake to assume that therefore there is no use for notions such as 'rule of action', or Kant's 'maxims', or that such rules and their relation to action cannot be defined in a manner not involving the above two interpretations. A rough account of something Kant said would be that events happen in accordance with laws, and actions in accordance with conceptions of laws. He was then saying something important about the logic of 'action', and part of my aim is to interpret his and similar statements in a manner which will be compatible with the results of contemporary preoccupations with the way certain psychological usages mislead us, and yet enable rules or maxims to do some of the work for which they were invented.

There is perhaps a not too unnatural sense in which all actions can be said to be applications of rules, and, from the motives just indicated, I am trying to discover or invent such a sense.

Consider a schoolmaster watching a pupil perform some action, and commenting to a colleague, 'He knows a lot about history, quadratic equations, and . . .'. A celestial observer with unlimited time and sources of information might completely enumerate everything the observed pupil knows, believes, likes. Completeness could perhaps only be had at the cost of some reduplication because convictions and preferences can be described at different levels of abstractness; this doesn't matter for the present argument, and will be seen to be relevant later. One further point: expressions like 'Tommy knows that . . .' and 'Tommy believes that . . .' must for the purposes which will emerge shortly be lumped together, because although they imply wholly opposed things about the reporter's agreement with Tommy, yet their implications *about Tommy* are largely similar.

Having made a complete inventory of what Tommy accepts, (as true, preferable, etc.) the items of which we can describe as 'the ideas he has', whilst Tommy is innocently performing some action, the celestial observer might then split up the items into two groups. One group will consist of the ideas relevant to the action which Tommy is just performing, of those which, if Tommy did not accept them or if he accepted some alternative, would lead to a modification, or abstention from, the action. The other group would consist of those which make no such difference. Both lists would include items such as 'He knows London is south of Edinburgh', and such as 'He considers travel an agreeable experience'. Such heterogeneous items do indeed mix happily in biographical works.

The rule on which the action is based or of which it is the application, is the list of *relevant* biographical features or facts describable as 'ideas' in the sense suggested above. This definition of 'rule of action' helps to do what some writers wanted rules to do, i.e. provide criteria for distinguishing actions from mere events. Biographical facts about a person's ideas are not relevant to mere events in the way in which they are relevant to actions. To omit the pejorative 'mere' and ennoble an event into the category of actions entails that it has an intimate connexion with the biographical facts of the believing/thinking/preferring type. This continues to be of interest even if we give a dispositional account of some or all of these biographical facts.

Consider some consequences of this. The rule on which the person is acting being open, i.e. applicable to other situations—which it will not always be in effect if the list of ideas contains demonstratives or very specific descriptions or any other *localizing* expressions, so to speak—the person must at the time of action be committed to acting similarly in analogous situations. If an analogous situation turns up and he does not act similarly, this shows that his character has changed, that he has changed his convictions, attitudes or preferences. All this may look like aprioristic psychology; I am in fact only making explicit what is implied in the above definition of 'rule' and offering a suggestion towards the definition of 'change of character'.

All that is claimed so far is that there is an intimate relation between any action and a subset of a person's mental characteristics such as convictions and preferences and that there is some point in calling this subset 'the rule' of which the action was an application. Some but not all of these features will be cognitive. The force of this qualifying epithet is that a biographer reporting one of the cognitive ideas can always describe it as true or false. It is worth noting that the biographer may do this explicitly by using the words 'true' or 'false', or on the other hand implicitly by choosing the appropriate verb introducing the idea. By saying that Tommy knows, instead of *believes*, he is implying that the conviction to be described is a true one. The division of ideas into those which are characterizable as true or false and those which are not is important for my argument.

Let us return to the question concerning how the subset of relevant ideas which make up a rule are selected from a person's total set. Suppose the person in question has a dossier in which his ideas are listed, one per sentence. Those ideas which are described by sentences which could cease to be true of him without this leading to an appreciable modification by him of the action as a physical event do not enter into its rule; the others do. This dependence of action on belief is indeed logical and not causal, for a part, though not the whole, of the evidence for what a person believes is whether, as we say, he acts on it. But there is a causal element present, or rather there is an indication of where to look for a causal connexion, viz. between the events constituting the agent's acquaintance with the evidence for the truth of the cognitive ideas on the one hand, action as a physical event on the other. Not all ideas need be such as to allow of evidence, and indeed any set constituting a rule must, as I shall attempt to show, contain some which are not; some or most, however, will be. There is another slight complication: 'evidence' tends to mean 'good evidence', whereas the facts leading to conversion to a belief and hence to an action may be inadequate. I propose, however, to mean by 'evidence' in this context whatever causes conversion and can significantly be quoted by the person concerned as justification of it, irrespective of whether, by some standard, it is a good justification. Noticing evidence for a change of belief causes or helps to cause actions; the point of time, which can frequently be ascertained, at which as it were the evidence becomes effective, i.e. the time at which the evidence has sunk in and after which the agent would act otherwise than he would have acted previously—that point of time dates 'conversion'. Conversion is often veridically recorded by verbal behaviour, though of course to be converted and to say that one is are not the same thing. One does not feel inclined to say that the verbal behaviour expressing conversion ('since yesterday I have believed that . . .') is an intermediate causal link between noticing the evidence and the action but rather that it, like the action, is a consequence of noticing the evidence. I am not quite clear whether this disinclination is logically or empirically founded; it may be that we use language so as never to allow this kind of causal efficacy *merely* to the uttering or hearing of words, and shift the responsibility on to the 'really meaning' or 'really understanding' of them, which puzzlingly turns out on reflection to be just the uttering or hearing plus actually acting in accordance, i.e. something not eligible for the status of cause. On the other hand it may be also just an empirical prejudice; philosophers have warned us against the belief in the magical power of words, but there also exists at least as strong a tendency to believe in their magical impotence. One of the reasons why psychoanalytic theories surprise one is that they look as if they entail that merely *saying* something, in certain circumstances, has far-reaching effects.

The above analysis throws some light, I think, on why psychologizing *a priori* and, for that matter, apriorism with regard to history, has an appeal that survives more tenaciously than similar temptations do in the theory of the natural sciences. A Humean theory of causation to the effect that it is useless to investigate either of the related terms alone for purposes of finding evidence for a causal connexion tends somehow to be more acceptable with regard to nature than with regard to humanity. There is a suspicion or hope that human behaviour 'makes sense', a notion perhaps similar to whatever some philosophers meant when they said that the universe was 'intelligible'. One feels inclined to say that it is somehow an accident if nature makes sense—falls into a coherent pattern, but that it is surprising if a human being does not: as if there were an *a priori* expectation of order with regard to the latter but not with regard to the former. In a sense, I think, this belief in the presence of the *a priori* in our psychological statements is correct, though not the diagnosis with regard to how, and where it arises. It arises at two points: in the connexion between evidence and convictions or ideas, *and* between the latter and action. Supposing convictions, ideas, preferences *were* events and *did* function as effects and causes, it would indeed go against the grain to say that they were such *à la* Hume, i.e. for no intrinsic reason. The truth is probably that although indeed their relations to evidence and action are not contingent, they are not causal either.

This, I think, partly accounts for the ghost in the machine, himself rather machine-like, being composed of elements with rather surprising logical properties, i.e. elements which though apparently discrete yet manage to have necessary relations with each other. The attack on the ghost in the machine may dispose of these elements, but on the other hand leaves one, rightly I think, with a sense of something important omitted, of an excessive assimilation of statements about intelligent human performances to successful performances in general, irrespective of whether the agent or agency is conscious or not. It seems to omit something which Kant's statement about action being in accordance with conceptions of laws and events simply in accordance with laws brings out. My discussion of the relation between evidence, belief, rule, and action is an attempt towards a further clarification of this.

As already stated, the temptation to believe in *a priori* discoverable psychological connexions comes in at two points: with regard to the relation between a state of mind and an action (e.g. 'it was because he was angry with him that he hit him') and between evidence and the state of mind (e.g. 'because he saw a card up his sleeve he was angry'). Neither connexion looks contingent but somehow rational or appropriate; at the same time with regard to both counter-examples are to be expected and occur, so that if someone wishes to interpret these connexions as causal and yet somehow *a priori* knowable, he is forced to put them into a new category of either *a priori tendency* statements, or *a priori* correct as opposed to actual connexions, a kind of correct standard route from which actual tracks can deviate.

Ideas face as it were two ways; on the one hand they are dispositions to act in a certain way, yet on the other *many* of them are cognitive, i.e. are about something and it makes sense to talk of them being true or false and being valid or not in virtue of some evidence. A person's belief can be rational or otherwise, in whatever sense a theory is or is not rational given some evidence. A part of what we mean by calling an action rational is that the rule on which it is based is composed of beliefs which are rational in the above straightforward sense; or rather, that those of the components of the rule to which evidence is at all relevant are rational in that sense. This should bring out how very misleading it is to say that 'he hit him because he was angry' is like 'the glass broke because it was brittle'. You can alter a person's anger by conveying information to him; but *talking to glass notoriously makes no difference*, unless you believe in animistic theories, which consist precisely of treating events as actions, or believing them to be based on ideas and mental states which in turn are susceptible of being changed by the presentation of evidence. Though it may be true that ideas and states of mind are not occurrences, it is extremely important to note those of their features which differentiate them from things such as that of brittleness. These features are: the fact that some of them are true or false and dependent on evidence, and that all of them can be verbally quoted by the agent as justifications of his action, and that events, i.e. actions, can be influenced by the presentation of evidence or arguments relevant to the ideas involved in the rule. Admittedly one discovers about one's own dispositions in a manner similar, in a very general way, to the discovery of the brittleness of glass; but glass does not tell us of its own brittleness in self-justification, and much of importance follows from that. The causal connexion between the noticing of evidence and action is part of what we mean by such psychological terms as 'conversion' and 'conviction'. These causal connexions tend to make sense in a certain way, in that the evidence, with an intelligent person, modifies the behaviour so as to make it more effective in achieving some aim, this more effective behaviour being something dependent on that piece of evidence. One part of the anatomy of the ghost then arises thus: by (*a*) adding superfluous links in the causal chain between seeing-of-evidence and action, and (*b*) then inventing a kind of plasma in which these extra causal processes take place. This tendency probably springs in part also from a dislike of allowing inter-temporal, discontinuous psychological causation.

Rationalistically inclined moralists, noticing that states of mind and ideas are quoted in justification of actions and also that some at any rate of the factors involved in such explanations as it were embody propositions, i.e. are true or false, were tempted to believe that what was meant by 'wrongness' or at any rate what defined the same class of actions was the kind of irrationality an action can have in virtue of the beliefs on which it is based being either false or even incompatible with each other. This would have had the merit of answering the 'Why be moral?' query, for no one sets out to be illogical. But before such a theory could be plausible it would have to be shown that such a criterion does in fact define a class at least vaguely similar to the intuitively selected class of wrong actions. What however happens is that if the criterion of rightness is formulated as requiring that all the mental states or ideas *susceptible* of being rational in the way in which theories are, should be so, the criterion becomes too liberal and defines not right actions but all actions performed by intelligent and well informed agents. If on the other hand it is formulated as requiring that *all* the factors on which it is based should be rational in that sense, it becomes too strict and *no* action *can* satisfy it, as Hume has shown. It is interesting to see why Hume was able to show this. The reason is that explanations or justifications of actions in terms of motives, desires, intentions, beliefs . . . , or rather in terms of the complete set of the relevant ideas and states of mind (= the rule, similar to Kant's 'maxim'), have much in common with explanations in terms of sufficient causal condition—except, of course, that they are not causal. A correct account of a person's maxims or rules of behaviour is one from which we can infer to the action being attempted in certain circumstances, —that is just a part of what we happen to mean by a correct account in such a context, and that is why we can say that a man is committed to acting similarly unless his relevant ideas change. But it follows from the fact that we want explanations of actions in terms of motives, rules of action, maxims, to be sufficient explanations that any list of ideas relevant to a certain action cannot consist *only* of the cognitive ones, i.e. of those characterizable as true or false alone. The reason for this is that we have evidence for what a person believes other than the evidence implicit in that one action: his verbal behaviour, other actions, or the kind of data on which his beliefs are based plus knowledge of how he habitually makes up his mind. Given that, it follows that it is possible, what in fact often happens, that the identical set of beliefs, judged by evidence prior to the action, does nevertheless not lead to the same action. (If, as a matter of fact, identical convictions always *did* lead to similar action, neither Hume nor anyone else might perhaps ever have noticed that 'reason is inert'; it would still be true.) In order then to retain ideas or motives accounts as *sufficient* explanations, we must supplement the story about the convictions by an addition about decisions, preferences, or feelings. Whatever other functions these expressions have, one they have in common is that of always being usable for supplementing the story about beliefs, thus making the explanation by motives a sufficient one, one from which in the given circumstances that action and no other would follow. They are of course peculiarly suited for this job because, *not being cognitive*, i.e. not being tied to anything, they can never be shown to be impossible, false or as perhaps even unplausible in any situation and thus can always without contradiction be invoked to complete the explanation. A man may, in full knowledge of the facts, prefer a course of action leading to the destruction of the world in order to save his little finger; the 'preference' here is not necessarily the name of some ghostly event, but is a quite legitimate addition to his inventory of ideas, legitimate and necessary if we are to explain his action in terms of motives in the way in which we habitually do so. Explanations by motives, ideas, mental factors generally are sufficient explanations and beliefs are some of the relevant factors; but identical *beliefs* may and do lead to differing actions, and hence it follows if indeed these explanations are to be sufficient, that other, non-cognitive, factors such as decisions, preferences, feelings must be present to account for the action. In a sense these states of mind *can* be invented rather like equation-balancing particles. All this is only a restatement of Hume's main proof of reason being a slave of the passions. But this restatement is useful in showing where the Emotivist and the Existentialist go wrong; for neither of them really wants to say that moral actions, judgments, policies or attitudes necessarily have anything to do with a process or activity called emotion or decision respectively. What both *have* noticed is that those ideas which are classifiable as true or false and for the truth or falsity of which accepted criteria exist cannot by themselves constitute sufficient explanations; and they rightly wish to classify the necessary additional factors in terms of the method of validating their truth or appropriateness. But the point about these ideas is that, although any particular one (preference, choice, feeling) is always selected from a number, often a large number, of possible and incompatible alternatives (in which they resemble the cognitive factors) yet there is no method of singling out or justifying the choice of that one from the others, (in which they differ from the cognitive factors). And it is just this which is being brought out when this lack of method of validation is called validation by feeling or 'decision'; for the force of saying that something is a matter of feeling or decision is really that something has been chosen from a number of alternatives but that *no* justification can be offered for the choice. Nothing singles it out in the way an *experimentum crucis* singles out the tenable theory or in the way a sign post singles out the right road.

By a rule of action I mean then the list of the ideas, in this sense, some cognitive, (e.g. beliefs that . . .), some not so (e.g. preferences for . . . over against . . .) which justify an action and from which one can infer to an action being attempted in a certain kind of situation, the kind of situation perhaps being itself specified in the rule. The examples of maxims Kant gives include a specification of the conditions under which the maxim becomes operative.

I may, incidentally, seem to be over-stressing the possibility of inference from a rule to attempted action; in practice, we use rules to justify and explain more often perhaps than to infer and predict. But the possibility of explaining an action by the rule presupposes that the former can be inferred from the latter, that, as suggested above, the rule is a sufficient condition of the action or at least the attempt, given certain circumstances. Inference matters less in practice because we seldom have much evidence other than his actual action for somebody having a maxim.

Still, we can predict fairly well in the case of persons of strong character, that description being used for people whose rules of action are fairly rigid and effective and can consequently be reliably identified in advance of action. It might be objected that the behaviour of people of weak character is also predictable; indeed it is, but there is an important difference. We can construct the rule in accordance with which the person surrendering to a temptation is acting. Still, if he is really 'surrendering to temptation', or 'not in full control of himself', it will be useless to present evidence or arguments undermining some part of that rule, for despite intellectual agreement behaviour will not be modified—this being entailed by the meaning of 'surrendering to temptation'. In these cases, the constructed rule is analogous to descriptive scientific laws governing *events* whereas *actions* are performed in accordance with the *conceptions* of laws, i.e. in accordance with rules proper. My point is that the force of 'conception' in the preceding sentence need not be some act of contemplation but must be, at least, the kind of sensitivity to evidence and argument described above. The reason why psychoanalytic theories present an irrationalistic and deterministic picture of man is partly at any rate that they suggest that the latter of the above two ways of behaving obtains more frequently than we thought, that many of our behaviour-patterns which we thought based on good reasons were in fact independent of them. A detailed consideration of the kind of evidence considered sufficient to unmask a reason as a rationalization would I think bear out my statements about the logical relation of rules and actions.

There is here an apparent circularity: we allow a dispositional analysis of ideas and states of mind and yet wish to treat it as something independent of the action for which they account. But this circularity is merely apparent; for although the evidence for ideas and states of mind may be behaviour, including verbal behaviour, yet the presence of an idea is not necessarily or even frequently validated by any single action. For instance: we may know what somebody believes from what he told us, from the fact that we know that he has a great respect for evidence and that conclusive evidence for the belief in question was at his disposal; if subsequently he acts *as if* he did *not* believe it, we don't necessarily say 'he did not believe . . .' but may say 'he did believe that . . . , but he was swayed by an impulse' or something of the kind. No general rules can of course be given for just when verbal behaviour is weightier evidence than action; in actual situations we usually know.

The need to give an acceptable account of rules of action, 'maxims', 'states of mind behind actions', springs from the importance of the purposes which require these notions, which moreover do not disappear with the realization that action involves not so much 'knowing that' as 'knowing how'. Ethical classifications of actions notoriously have to consider actions not merely as events but in terms of the rules behind them if they are not to be paradoxical, which moral theories stated only in terms referring to the physical aspect of actions, e.g. pure consequence-ethics, tend to be.

My aim is, so to speak, to show the compatibility of the psychological scaffolding of the *Grundlegung zur Metaphysik der Sitten* with *The Concept of Mind*. I suggest that Kant did not interpret in any objectionable way the psychological works built up to expound his ethics. I base this assertion on evidence such as his insistence on the presence of self-deception, i.e. lack of necessary correspondence between the actual rule of action and the one asserted autobiographically, and on the irrelevance of whether the agent is clever enough to *formulate* the rule at all. Admittedly such a case would also depend on showing that his preoccupation with determinism did not arise from mythical interpretations of mind.

But it is not only for moralists, classifications that we need something like the rule terminology; ordinary classifications require it as much. Many action words stand for groups of possible ways of behaving such that some members of the group will have little *physical* similarity with each other. Their inclusion in a common group is due mainly to the similarity of their rule or the 'thought behind the act'.

Apart from the uses it already has, such a terminology may well turn out to be indispensable for the analysis of notions such as that of unconscious motivation, which might amount to the presence of the rule plus a disinclination to formulate it to oneself or others, and a disregard of its presence as evidence for the falsity of some beliefs about oneself. But this disinclination and tendency to disregard themselves constitute a second order rule, and the logic of 'unconscious' requires that this rule of expression be equally unconscious. This, of course, sets us off on an endless regress, but there is nothing vicious in this. The regress is analogous to the one occurring in certain old definitions of 'consciousness' as entailing that the conscious person not only knows, but also knows that he knows, knows that he knows that. . . . Either regress only becomes vicious if interpreted as requiring an extra entity or process for each recurrence of the verb 'know', or the phrase 'disinclined to avow and consider as evidence', respectively. What is roughly entailed is that, in one case, the agent should be capable of giving the correct answer however often the recurrent question is repeated, and that in the other case he should not be capable of giving it. An action inspired by an unconscious motive might be described in this terminology as an action based on a rule wholly impervious to information and persuasion presented in the ordinary manner, and to that extent similar to a causal mechanism as opposed to an intelligent response, but sensitive to information presented in a certain way, i.e. with the help of psychoanalysis.

Finally it is important to point out that any event occurring in a person's biography which one wishes to classify as an action can usually be explained by a number of different rules, or sets of relevant considerations, differing in degree of abstractness, though mutually compatible. Thus the same process can be described as the action of tightening a bolt, assembling a vehicle, earning a living, or helping the export drive, though, to repeat the premiss, there are *not* five or more processes. The point of having different 'actions' is that different sets of considerations are relevant on deciding that the various features, of differing abstractness, should be what they are. Normally, when asking what a person does, and why, we tend to be interested only in some one feature and not in the whole number. There could perhaps be a clumsy sense of 'rule' covering them all; a more useful sense is the limited one which groups only the considerations relevant with regard to some one feature. To speak of an action is to speak of a physical process, some aspect of which is being sensibly interpreted in terms of the considerations leading up to it, the criteria of suitableness for such an interpretation being, as

suggested, the possibility of avowal and influence through information. It follows that any event interpreted as an action with regard
to any one feature will be liable to other interpretations with regard
to other features. But: for reasons connected with the logic of explanations by motives, only one interpretation can be correct with
regard to any one feature. It is likely moreover that most if not all
events occurring in biographies will be interpretable as actions with
regard to some features and not so interpretable at all with regard to
others.

1951

Chapter 7   Ethics and logic

There are ethical theories which surprisingly tie up moral validity with classifications of logical form such as universality or particularity. Kantian ethics make use of the first of the logical terms mentioned, and Existentialist ethics of the second. I shall not in this paper be concerned with either Kantian exegesis or with describing any of the actual forms of Existentialism, though I shall use a possibly simplified form of either theory to discuss why there appears to be a connexion between logical form and ethics, and with what reason. If my simplified types turn out to be caricatures, I only hope they are illuminating ones.

My general argument could perhaps be summarized in the following way: when people act they are also prepared to give reasons for their actions. The reasons they will offer will have a logical form, which will tend to be one of two kinds. Either the reasons employed will be of an impersonal, general, abstracted kind, or they will include a so to speak biased reference to some privileged person, thing or event, privileged in the sense that quite similar but not numerically identical persons, things or events would not by the agent be counted as equally good grounds for the relevant action. Naturally, such a privileged particular would have to be *named* and not just described in the justification of the action, for a description would apply equally to the similar particulars which, *ex hypothesi*, would not count as grounds and thus should not be covered by a genuine justification which really told us the reasons the agent has for acting in the way he does.

Thus we have two kinds of justifications of action, those which employ only descriptions and thus constitute open rules, and those which contain logically proper names and thus are not open. Ethical theories have been built round this distinction, to the effect that we should act in such a way that our possible justifications should be of one or the other kind. My aim is both to describe how these theories arise out of our habitual modes of justifying our conduct, and to discuss what philosophical reasons can be offered in defence of either theory.

For purposes of this discussion I assume it to be analytically true that all actions are based on a rule or a maxim.[1] This assumption, which in the appropriate sense seems to me justified, is obviously necessary if the suggestion that there is a connexion between logical form and ethics is to make sense. For actions in the sense of events cannot have a 'logical form', though the maxims on which they are based can and must. The required thesis can perhaps be put in the following way: with regard to any action, a command can be constructed such that it enjoins that particular action and no other. If one then appends reasons specifying why each of the various features of the action is required to be what it is, we have a rule or maxim in the desired sense.

I shall begin by discussing the apparently irrelevant question whether there is such a thing as 'love at first sight' or not. This question is, if my reading in dentists' waiting rooms is at all representative, frequently and with interest discussed in the pages of women's journals. The tone of the articles on this subject, the way examples are brought up and so on suggests that the authors are under the impression that they are discussing an empirical question; that, in fact, they know by what tests l.a.f.s. could be recognized, the issue thus being merely whether anything satisfying those tests actually occurs. But a more careful reading would I think show that this is a superficial analysis, and that the question is in part or wholly logical, about whether anything *could* count as l.a.f.s.

Consider the following possible *a priori* grounds for denying the existence of l.a.f.s.: for X to fall in love at first sight with Y, X must after his first encounter with Y develop an attitude or feeling towards Y which, *ex hypothesi*, he has towards no one else. But assume, as is plausible, that X could only have noticed a finite set S of Y's characteristics[2] during that first encounter. If now X encounters a person other than Y who however like Y is characterized by S, two possibilities arise: either X manifests towards the new possessor of S the same attitude or emotion as he manifested towards Y, or he does not. Either of these two (exhaustive) alternatives can be taken to be conclusive evidence of the absence of love, and thus jointly to constitute an *a priori* case against its possibility.

In the former case, the fact that X does not really love Y is shown by the very recurrence towards someone who is not Y, for 'love' (or perhaps 'romantic love') is defined in such a way that it can only have one object. It might pertinently be objected at this point that uniqueness, or primacy for that matter, are not, as existence is not, logical predicates, in other words that they cannot legitimately be included in definitions. This may be so, but, for better or for worse (for worse as I shall argue), some concepts with which we operate *are* defined in terms of uniqueness, in conjunction with other characteristics. For instance: Y is considered X's 'beloved', but when it is found that X has a relationship towards Z similiar to the one he has to Y, some people at any rate will withdraw the description of 'X's beloved' from Y, without indeed granting it to Z either, thus showing that for them *uniqueness* is a part of the definition of 'beloved'.

The alternative is that X does *not* have the same attitude or feelings towards the new possessor of S as he had towards Y. But this equally constitutes conclusive evidence for X not really loving Y. For S is all he knows of Y; if, consequently, on re-encountering S the original emotion or attitude is not re-evoked, this shows that it had not really been connected with its apparent stimulus and object, that it had been accidental, arbitrary, and without any of the significance which one normally attributes to emotions or attitudes of that kind.

With regard to either alternative, then, decisive considerations show the impossibility of correctly predicating 'love'. In practice, of course, we avoid the paradox with the help of the notion of primacy, or some similar expedient. S in conjunction with primacy does give us uniqueness. But primacy of encounter is not a characteristic of Y. It only tells us something about the history of X himself. Much will be made to hinge in this argument on the fact that certain classes of action and attitudes must include in their maxims such autobiographical, agent-mentioning clauses.

I have chosen l.a.f.s. only because the point emerges with particular clarity, owing to the fact that here the limitation of the information available about the object of the emotion, and the possibility of that information also holding of some other object, emerge very noticeably. There is a number of attitudes, dispositions to act, for instance loyalty, patriotism, devotion to some specific tradition or leader, which are all logically similar. They all involve the agent in having some specific attitude towards some one object and that not merely or at all in virtue of the properties of the object in question: if, for instance, a country is discovered possessing all the characteristics of the patriot's country which he was ever aware of, this will probably not induce him to extend his loyalty and share it equally between the two countries, as would in a way be logical in view of his inability to distinguish in any important way between them. But such is the logic of patriotism. Similar problems have hitherto only been noticed in connexion with identity and the use of logically proper names: how can we use a proper name seeing that no characteristics of the nominee are parts of the definiens of the name, so that they can all cease to be true of him or become true of someone else, without this warranting either a restriction or an extension of the use of that name? My point is that there are dispositions or attitudes which select their objects in a similarly puzzling manner. I shall call these E-type preferences or valuations. Behaviour manifesting an E-type valuation cannot be universalized, i.e., its maxim cannot be deduced (in the sense in which an exemplification is deduced from the rule it exemplifies) from an open rule formulated with the help of only property words and variables, but, of course, no proper names. All this has already been shown: an agent acting in accordance with an E-type preference cannot be said to be acting in accordance with some rule from which his preference follows as an instance, for he would not act in accordance with that rule with regard to another instance if one turned up; *that* has been made the defining property of E-type preferences.

The point is that an object of, for instance, love, must by definition be unique (and the same goes for object of loyalty, etc.); whilst there is at the same time no guarantee that these objects are objectively unique, that they possess distinguishing characteristics not shared by such objects as have not been singled out for that attitude. There are of course, as already mentioned, certain relational characteristics which can always be found to help single out the object uniquely; primacy of encounter, *accident* of birth, and so on. Amongst civilized and liberal-minded people a certain shame tends to attach to being influenced by such subjective or accidental factors, to selecting the objects of one's important attitudes (such as loyalty, worship, or devotion) in a non-universalizable way, without a rule which one would be prepared to see applied in all analogous situations.

It might be contended that with the help of the kind of relational characteristics mentioned above the important attitudes under discussion *could* be universalized; but this would, I think, be mistaken. The genuine patriot does not wish to see others equally devoted to their country of birth or ancestry to the possible detriment of other countries, possibly his own. Such an attitude characterizes only the games-player, to whom, logically, the continuation and quality of the game must be a more genuine consideration than victory; but I take it that genuine patriots do not see international conflicts in which their countries are involved as games.[3] Similarly, the genuine lover cannot admit that his love would have had a different object had the order of his encounters been different. Similarly the believer with the 'Credo quia absurdum' attitude is not condoning the belief in *other* scandalously absurd religions. If, as often happens, the awareness of the asymmetrical, arbitrary nature of one's position is accompanied by a tolerant willingness for others (or oneself had things gone differently) to have their rival accident-biased attitude, that is equivalent within my system of definitions to a cynicism incompatible with *genuinely* loving, believing, etc. And this surely corresponds to our notion of the real romantic lover or the convinced believer, neither of whom can abandon the conviction of the unique appropriateness of the object of his particular attitude.

It is sometimes suggested that we have access to 'Being' through the fact of our own existence, inwardly experienced, and that this, rather than the subject–predicate form of language, is responsible for the psychological resistance to phenomenalism or the 'applicability of a predicate' analysis of 'existence': for the feeling that 'to exist' somehow must amount to more than that. This metaphysical feeling seems to me to spring from this: my 'being myself' seems to me independent of the predicates which apply to me and to be something that would survive the replacement of all of them by others. Hence the 'exist' in 'I exist' cannot be accounted for by the predicate-applicability analysis with even such plausibility as attaches to it elsewhere. (It would also follow that Identity of Indiscernibles does not apply to self-conscious beings.) This feeling may be totally unjustified, and I bring it in not to defend it but as prima facie evidence that 'awareness of oneself' as we normally think of it is an E-type attitude.

Given that I have clarified what I mean by E-type valuations, I should also show that they occur, that actual instances of purposeful behaviour are based on them. But I can only plead that this be accepted as a highly reasonable and plausible hypothesis, for the experiments that would be required to *prove* it are in practice almost or totally impossible to arrange. We cannot build a country resembling closely that of our hypothetical patriot, or re-arrange the temporal order of the lover's experiences, to test whether indeed their conduct is inspired by an E-type preference. I am confident that this is so, but for anyone not sharing this conviction the subsequent argument can be of little interest.

There is an alternative kind of valuation which I shall call type U. For instance: a judge ideally applies a rule wholly devoid of any personal reference, a rule containing merely predicates (descriptions) and logical terms. This, I suppose, is at least a part of what is meant by the ideals of the 'rule of law' and 'equality before the law', which suggest the desirability in some sphere of completely impersonal decisions, i.e., decisions formally deduced from abstract premises and consequently not varying in application from person to person, except, of course, in the manner prescribed by those abstract premises. But judicial impartiality is not the only instance of U-type valuation. Type U valuation is equivalent with one possible and important sense of 'rational', corresponding roughly to the common notion of 'acting on principle'. It is this sense of 'rational' which is relevant to the Kantian connexion between rationality and morality, and to the fact that E-type valuations and cults such as that of loyalty, the Fuehrerprinzip, 'credo quia absurdum' and so on are patently incompatible with Kantianism, and with the vaguer class of attitudes describable as liberalism or rationalism in general.

Having established my dichotomy between E-type and U-type

valuations two problems concerning the classification of valuations as one or the other arise:

(i) Whether an action or tendency, or, more precisely, the valuation 'on which it is based', falls into category U or not depends on whether it is derivable from an open rule or not. The identification of this rule is indeed a matter of speculation concerning what the agent would do in other circumstances, and not of recording on an intra-cranially located dictaphone such verbal accompaniments as the action may have. Now just as a phenomenon may be subsumable under a number of mutually compatible theories of differing generality and may be subsumable under some theory of smaller generality and not under any theory of more than a certain degree of abstractness, similarly a valuation may be derivable from a less general open rule but not from a more general one. This being so, we do not know whether to consign it to type E or U, for with regard to different levels of abstractness it satisfies the criteria of entry of either. This point is crucial and will be discussed later.

(ii) Is the use of the first person singular in the maxim to count as the kind of asymmetry which consigns the relevant act to type E? It might be argued that a person biased in his own favour is not irrational in the same sense, if indeed irrational at all, in which the person drawing a distinction in his conduct where there is none in the facts, so to speak, *is* irrational. In other words, is intelligent egoism irrational? This is a merely terminological matter. Intelligent egoism is not universalizable in the same way as I have shown that genuine patriotism or romantic love are not; it is *not* rational in the sense of 'being influenced only by considerations which one is prepared to see operative generally and not by merely local factors', and consequently must be consigned to type E, despite the fact that there is a perfectly good sense of 'rational' equivalent to 'intelligently selfish'.

Roughly speaking, my distinction is between actions based on rules and those which are not. I shall go on to suggest that Kant's mysterious universalization recommendation can be stated as requiring that our actions be based on rules or plans of action that can be formulated with the help of a symbolism employing only predicates, individual *variables*, operators and logical connectives; and that this second order rule or general plan itself employs in addition to the items mentioned above only predicate *variables* instead of actual predicates.[4] Given that, I am trying to show how Kant's recommendation is an exaggeration and development of the actually effective U-type valuations, why and whether he thought that the formal recommendation actually had concrete entailments with regard to conduct, and what general reasons, with what merit, could be put forward for the validity and bindingness of that recommendation.

The recommendation of the alternative logical form to our pro-grammes of action, namely of particularity, also elaborates or rather makes explicit the logic of a class of actually effective valuations, those earlier described as of type E. This doctrine also has certain difficulties of application such as those mentioned with regard to Kantianism, and general reasons can be offered in justification of its validity.

Historically, E-type valuations occur twice: once as all the old, non-universalistic, loyalty type of ethics, and the second time in the reaction to the rationalistic, universalistic ethics, in those cults of the *acte gratuit*, of the unbacked decision, of blind self-assertion which are often lumped together as modern irrationalism. Philosophically, as politically, extreme traditionalism and a cult of unreason based on some acquaintance with and rejection of open ethics may combine. Hitler and Pétain were not accidental allies. There is no corres-ponding cleavage within rationalistic, U-type values.

A further historical point seems to me to be worth making: it may seem odd to pit a simplified Kant, of the *Grundlegung*, against a simplified Kierkegaard, of *Fear and Trembling* (for this is what in effect I have been doing), in view of the fact that Kierkegaard was reacting not against Kant but against Hegel. (In fact Kierkegaard might equally well have made Goethe the object of his invective and ridicule. Goethe's omnivorous determination to make the best of all alternative worlds reminds one of the dialectic of opposites and mediation making sure that nothing was left out. Such proceedings do indeed satisfy something in us. We feel a regret every time some choice makes us abandon irrevocably one alternative, and feel wist-fully that in an ideal world we should be able to enjoy *all* possibilities in a perfect synthesis, or, in English, have our cake and eat it. Goethe tried to do this by being his own Cunning of Reason.) But to return to the justification of opposing Kierkegaard to Kant rather than Hegel. Hegel located by means of an ingenious and ultimately tautologous system, the rationality which Kant had in a sense exiled to the noumenal, in historical development and the national whole.[5] But this historicist and immanentist side of Hegel, important though it may be for other purposes, seems irrelevant to the central Universalist–Existentialist quarrel, and is therefore ignored in this discussion. The Universalist (or Rationalist, or Essentialist) case is therefore being represented by streamlined or if you like, stylized Kant, rather than by a Kant rewritten for an immanentist, holistic and historicist mind, which from one aspect is what Hegelianism amounts to.[5]

Having shown both theories to be ideal and exaggerated types elicited by philosophers from kinds of valuations actually operative, let us examine the fundamental reasons for advocating the *validity* of these types. In both cases these reasons are connected with a theory of freedom (this being clearer with regard to Kant) and with 'being really oneself' (this being clearer with regard to Existentialism and indeed being connected with its name).

The possibly camouflaged universality has of course often been noticed in ethical judgments; what recent perceptions have lacked—apart from seeing that some moral judgments are a type E—has been any kind of justification of moral judgments having this form, any attempt to tie up this form of theirs, as Kant did, with their obligatoriness. Recent discussions in particular seem to make the 'analysis of moral judgments' a purely *de facto* matter, with the answer having a purely contingent status. The analysis of the German word 'schimmel' is 'horse, and white', but there is no necessity for a language to contain such a word—indeed English doesn't. Similarly, some 'analyses of ethics' make the answer sound similarly accidental. But this simply won't do, for the question concerning the correct analysis of ethical statements is itself ethical; by which I mean that when we ask it, we wish to know not how the inhabitants of Huddersfield or of Bongo Bongo use them, but how they should. (This criticism does not apply to the 'Emotive Theory', whose analysis does tie up with obligatoriness—by denying it—and which is not a mere *de facto* theory, for it really concludes that ethical judgments must be emotive because there is no other logical pigeon hole for them to fit. The fact that it is thus deduced from a general position rather than based on a direct examination of ethical judgments is sometimes used as a basis for attacking it—but it seems to me to be, on the contrary, a merit. To show that ethical judgments cannot but be of a certain kind is a way of showing that they must and ought to be of that kind—perhaps the only way.)

According to Kant, a man making an U-type valuation and attempting to act in accordance with it *because* it is of that type is *therefore* free, and only such a man is free.[6] This appears to him to be so because the only alternative to being influenced[7] by the form of one's maxim, by the fact that it is deducible from an open rule which in turn could be schematized with the help of individual and predicate variables alone, is to be influenced by the content of the maxim, by the empirical, 'it so happens' preferences specified in it. But the content of the maxims refers only to the preferences which, as a matter of empirical psychology, we happen to have. But to be influenced by these empirical contents of one's maxims, or, more accurately, by the empirical inclinations corresponding to the concrete ends specified in those maxims, is to be determined by something which in view of the arguments of the Second Analogy of the C.P.R. is part of the mechanism of nature; it is, consequently, to be unfree. But that being moved by the form of the rule, by the fact that it is of type U, is to be exempt from the causal system of nature, follows for Kant from the fact that our faculty of generalizing, of conceiving or operating with open rules whether in the indicative ('theoretical') or in the imperative ('practical') mood, is not a part of nature. It is for him not continuous with and a refinement of ('passive') sensibility, but radically distinct from it and somehow 'spontaneous'. I do not propose to discuss here his doctrine of 'spontaneity', the doctrine that valid rules of thought can be effective in our thinking because of their validity and independently of whether the psychological laws which happen to be operative luckily coalesce with them or not. But it is worth remarking that the arguments in favour of this doctrine, based on the conditions under which we can sensibly attribute validity to our thinking, are equally effective with regard to Theoretical Reason and Practical Reason, or, if you prefer, with regard to inferences in the indicative and imperative moods. In a period such as ours when genuinely felt scepticism is far more widespread with regard to ethics than with regard to science, the argument can of course be far more persuasively formulated with regard to Theoretical rather than Practical Reason.

A number of things is presupposed if the Kantian model is to work. To begin with, we have the puzzling claim that logical form, or validity, can be causally, psychologically effective, a claim which Kant partly tried to make plausible with the help of the doctrine of the 'self-wrought' feeling of respect for law, and which in the end he declares to be an intrinsically irresoluble mystery. This claim I do not propose to discuss.

Another gap in the Kantian argument is this: suppose we accept that criterion and justification of validity of moral commands lies in their 'form' rather than content, this by itself does not single out which form; and if 'universal' and 'particular' are kinds of forms, then both are so equally. In other words, why single out universality as the ethically important logical form? I do not think Kant could offer a very good answer, for it follows from his general position that a merely sentient being, without the rational faculties, would be as little capable of making singular or particular judgments as of making universal ones. Still, psychologically one can see what led him to this assumption: somehow, universal judgments seem further removed from mere 'Anschauungen' than the others.

But furthermore, the argument presupposes that the privileged logical form of moral commands by itself determines a specific class of commands. This presupposition can usefully be split into two: that it uniquely determines one command in any given situation, in other words that it is a sufficient criterion of duty,[8] and, less ambitiously, that this form is at least compatible with some commands, though possibly mutually incompatible ones, so that additional premisses, presumably intuitive 'moral laws' of the commandment type, are required before duty can be determined.[8]

To begin with, the formal recipe prescribing that our maxims be of type U fails to determine uniquely a line of conduct. With regard to any course of action whatever, it will be possible to devise a maxim which will be universalizable, i.e., one which will be of type U and which will be, in that form, approved by the agent. After all, all that is required from a maxim for it to receive grading U is for it to be expressed solely with the help of predicates, etc., eschewing any proper names or personal pronouns. But we can, with the help of these quite impersonal predicates, include so much detail in the maxim that in effect, though not as a matter of logical necessity, it will only have a unique object, i.e., the immediate situation in which the agent wishes to apply it. In effect, its application will be as limited as if the agent had as his maxim the patently E-type plan 'I, now, wish to do such and such though I do not approve of anyone else, or myself at other times, doing so; I am quite happily making an exception in my own favour, or in favour of the present moment.' But having used a U-type rule, he will in fact have no need of making 'an exception in his own favour': for he will be able happily to sub-scribe to the open U-type rule, knowing that thanks to the plethora of detail included, a sufficiently similar situation will not arise. If I put in enough details about myself, though formulated in an impersonal way so that those details could characterize someone else, then in practice that someone else would have to *be* I before the situation would become adequately similar and the maxim be re-applicable. This is really the force of 'Tout comprendre c'est tout pardonner', which becomes analytic, for 'Tout comprendre' becomes equivalent to '*being* the other chap'.

Similarly, if too few details are included in the maxims, it will be difficult to find *any* that will be universalizable at all (as opposed to the situation where, with too much detail included, *any* maxim ever acted upon *was* universalizable). If we progressively eliminate more and more from the details specified in the initial conditions of the rule of action, the number of occasions on which the act specified in the apodosis of the maxim becomes ordained correspondingly increases (at any rate, it cannot *de*crease, and the circumstances under which it would fail to *in*crease would sound as if the speci-fication of the relevant details was merely a practical difficulty, which some favourably placed person, possibly the agent, can hope to some degree at any rate to solve). But it seems to me that the above argu-ment makes clear that the indeterminacy of boundaries of relevance are objectively there, and no amount of intimate acquaintance with the circumstances of the action such as may be granted, sometimes, to the agent, can avail against it.

An alternative way sometimes adopted as a means of coping with this difficulty of Kantian theory is to say that the formal principle of morality was not meant to be a sufficient criterion of morality, that Kant meant it to be supplemented by 'moral laws' of the ordinary, commandment type. This interpretation, which is perhaps tenable as far as mere textual evidence goes, can be nevertheless rejected on a number of grounds: first, that if an interpretation of a great philosopher is possible which makes his doctrine both commonplace and silly, it should not be adopted unless we wish to use that interpretation as grounds for discontinuing the study of that philosopher. Had Kant been merely another dogmatic intuitionist, surely there would be no justification for studying that doctrine in his difficult writings, seeing we can find the unexciting falsehoods of which it consists in more accessible places. What people who adopt this interpretation forget is that Kant called his philosophy Critical, not Uncritical. Had he considered a supplementation of the formal principle by a set of moral laws of the commandment type necessary, he would presumably in accordance with his method have asked how they were 'possible', in the special sense he gives to this query, and have perhaps written a Critique of them. Furthermore, these supplementary moral laws would make the formal principle redundant.

I wish now to return to an earlier theme, namely that the Kantian recommendation is an exaggeration of features found in certain types of valuation, notably in the imperatives of an impartial, egalitarian legal code. If, as is claimed in the preceding paragraph, the formal Kantian recommendation has no entailments such as he thought it had, can it also be maintained that a specific type of valuation approaches it more closely than alternative kinds?

The answer is that although, as maintained above, all courses of action are universalizable, some are more so than others: though all are universalizable (i.e., a U-type maxim can be found for them) if we try hard enough by means of piling on the conditions specified in the apodosis of the maxim, with some we need to try less hard than with others (the amount of detail to be added being less), and what we do add may come more naturally.[9] The man who cheats in an exam may universalize his procedure by including so many impersonally stated autobiographical data into the apodosis of his maxim that the maxim would never in fact apply in any other case. He would in fact be indulging in sophistry, though this could never be strictly demonstrated, for whether he honestly adopts the queer overburdened maxim or not could only be tested in the situation where it became re-applicable without this time serving his interests, and, thanks to precisely this overburdening, such a case is most unlikely to arise (which indeed was the object of the sophistry). But a genuinely moral (by Kantian standards) course of conduct, inspired by considerations in which the fact that the agent *is* the agent, so to speak, does not figure, the agent having in a way abstracted himself and not allowed his bias in his own favour to influence him, is much more obviously and genuinely universalizable.

But whilst the considerations expressed in the general precepts of an egalitarian, universalistic ethic *are* highly impersonal, in the sense of not being loaded in favour of any group or individual, they are not *totally* formal. All proper names and most descriptive predicates have been eliminated from the maxims of a man acting in accordance with such an ethic: but only most, and not all, the predicates. And this in-eliminable empirical content of the maxim, however abstract and general, makes the Kantian model of moral action ultimately unworkable. For either it must be eliminated—but then from the *mere* form of the moral law no concrete directives can be deduced, for, as shown above, many directives, given a little ingenuity, will fit into it equally; or it remains as an independent element present not in virtue of being the sole contents compatible with the form, but *chosen* for some independent, and, necessarily, empirical reasons.[10] And to say that the maxim contains empirical elements, especially specifications of aims, *not* entailed by the mere form of the moral law for the sake of which alone the moral man can act, is to say in more ordinary language, that he is acting at least partly (namely, with regard to his choice of just those empirical elements as against possible alternatives) not from duty but from inclination.[11]

This is the appropriate point at which to shift our attention to the logic of Existentialist ethics, for the decisive starting point for Existentialism is precisely that irreducible element which resists Kantian Essentialism, so to speak, and which can neither be dispensed with nor deduced from the purely formal principle.

Frequently, one hears accounts of Existentialism in roughly the following terms: Existentialism rejects abstract descriptions of the world and life, and concentrates on the concrete stuff of human experience of life. This kind of account reduces Existentialism to a preference for journalistic sketches as against statistics and analysis, or for impressionistic painting as against diagrams. But that is not Existentialism.

Existentialism is the doctrine that choice (whether of faith or behaviour) ought to be or is bound to be (vacillation between these two positions is inherent in the doctrine) based on an ungrounded 'leap' and cannot or should not be deduced from a formal, and consequently blessedly non-arbitrary rule such as the one Kant hoped for (though, as already stated, owing to what essentially is no more than an historical accident the founder of Existentialism was reacting not against Kantian Essentialism, but against Hegel's historicized version of it). The negative clause in my above definition is much more important than the positive one, and consequently it does not matter that the positive one is metaphorical. The ultimate weakness of Kantian Essentialism was that *no* actual valuation, or attitude (= set of valuations) *could* fit the rigour of pure formality (be completely of type U), that no actual specific valuation was entailed in the formal moral principle. The weakness of Existentialism is that no valuation can possibly escape being of the kind enjoined by the doctrine, at least to the extent of containing the irreducibly arbitrary (in the sense of not deducible from formal considerations) element. This fact is responsible for the incontestably true aspect of Existentialism, its indicative formulation to the effect that to some extent at least all our valuations are of type E. It is equally responsible for the failure of the doctrine in its imperative formulation: for to the extent of possessing *an* arbitrary element all valuations are of type E, and consequently *that* cannot be made into a principle of selection; and as for the recommendation to make our valuation as much of type E as possible (the cult of the *acte gratuit* aspect of Existentialism), *that* second order recommendation can neither be justified nor is it itself, with its great generality and abstractness, particularly of type E. On the contrary, it paradoxically provides a general open premiss for E-type maxims, thus in a way undermining their E status. If one embarks on a policy of inconsequentiality one *has* acquired a kind of general policy. In any case, I do not think it makes much sense to attach numerical indices to the arbitrariness-saturation of valuation, a miss in this context being as good as a mile; and this is another reason why Existentialism fails to become a recommendation by being necessarily and universally followed anyway.

It remains to discuss what the appeal of the E-type of valuation and its generalization and erection into a principle, corresponding to the 'Escape from heteronomy and arbitrariness' appeal of Essentialist ethics. Ultimately, in both a logical and a factual sense, choices and decisions are made by concrete, here-now people and not by principles. The logical sense has been elucidated earlier: it amounts to saying that formal principles are not, contrary to certain metaphysical doctrines, strong enough to entail valuations. The factual sense amounts to this: that even if the formal principles were strong enough to entail valuations, these would nevertheless only in fact be *made* thanks to and *in* the concrete *existenz* of individual men, choosing or preferring to adopt them.

If the universal principles are somehow built into the world-process as forces in the 'historicist' way, the performance of an arbitrary, E-type action becomes the only way of asserting or attaining one's freedom—like making a face at an otherwise all-powerful headmaster. (Cf. Dostoevski's 'Notes from Underground' for this appeal of the unreasonable act.)

There is something paradoxical about the recent revival of interest in Kierkegaard, in view of the fact that he considered himself to be primarily combating Hegel. The reputation and attention devoted to Hegel having at the present time reached an all time low, the enthusiastic exhumation of Kierkegaard would seem superfluous. This paradox supplies a clue to a radical difference between Kierkegaard's and latter-day Existentialism. The contemporary version is really a *faute de mieux* Existentialism, a more or less regretful recognition of the fact that there is no, and could not be, immanent, or transcendent, Reason, this entity being envisaged as a combination of the hypostatized criteria of validity and an actually operative force ensuring that thoughts or even things will satisfy those criteria. Kierkegaard's attitude was totally different: he did not regret its absence, on the contrary he feared the possibility of its not being absent, wishing as he did a universe in which the burden of selecting what is valid in belief and action remained on the shoulders of the individual.[12] For that reason he seemed positively to relish the absurdities of religion: the more scandalous the absurdity, the lesser the danger that it might be incorporated in a rational system guaranteeing its validity.

I have tried to show that the recommendations of both Kantian and Existentialist ethics fail in their respective ways to be satisfactory, the one through being impossible to comply with, the other inescapably operative anyway. I have also tried to show that these two theories are not accidental fallacies or confusions, but naturally arise out of the fact that human beings not merely act but have statable reasons for their actions. The two theories under discussion arise through the exaggeration of certain features of the logic of giving reasons for a course of conduct. They arise 'naturally' rather in the way in which Kant tried to show in the Transcendental Dialectic of the C.P.R. that certain metaphysical doctrines were natural by-products of human thinking. Given a tendency, inspired by considerations concerning the possibility of attributing validity to our thinking, towards transcendentalism with regard to our thinking faculties, *that* in conjunction with the fact that some of our valuations are of a certain kind, namely type U, will naturally lead to a Kantian ethical theory; given, as a philosophical reaction, an emotively charged insistence on immanence and concreteness (consider the 'Existence precedes essence' slogan), *that* in conjunction with the fact that some of our valuations are of a different type, namely type E, will naturally lead to Existentialist theories of conduct.

One might ask, in the end, whether, although the two extreme recommendations fail to be serviceable signposts, we could not after all extract an ethic from the logical form of maxims by adopting as a general recommendation that we should universalize as much as possible, that, even if complete derivation of the content of the maxim from its law-like form is impossible, that we should strive to retain as few underived, arbitrary elements in our maxims as possible. (*Perhaps* this is all Kant intended to say, and my criticisms of Kantianism have missed the mark.) Similarly, a modified (though hardly moderated!) Existentialism might maintain that although we all indulge in the *leap* anyway, we should do so as much as possible, that we should minimize the extent to which we justify our behaviour by more general grounds.

I think that both these attitudes are, as a matter of historical fact, operative, and influential at least partly in consequence of the philosophical reasons adduced in their favour; but I do not see by what standard external to both one could choose between them. This very fact would seem to give the victory to the Existentialist side; but this should not obscure the fact that we can also choose to be Kantians.

1955

Notes

1 I have tried to show this in 'Maxims', ch. 6 above.
2 Of some one appropriate logical type, if you are pedantic about counting such things as 'characteristics'. Professor Popper has pointed out to me that the argument does not depend on this finitude, anyway.
3 In actual fact the attitude of what I describe as genuine patriotism, and that of the abstracted, so to speak aesthetic enjoyment of the games-connoisseur frequently co-exist, with the help of some double-think. I am talking of simplified types, and in saying what they can and cannot do am discussing what is and is not compatible with their definitions, and not of psychological possibility.
4 All these rules would of course be only formulable in a symbolism designed to accommodate imperatives as well as indicative statements. I am just assuming that such a symbolism is possible and that it would be fairly similar in its logic to the familiar symbolism. I have not attempted to work it out.
5 For an interpretation of Hegel supporting these contentions see J. Hyppolite, *Introduction à la philosophie de l'histoire de Hegel*, Paris, 1948.
6 This is notoriously a tricky piece of Kantian interpretation. I am for the sake of simplicity assuming the validity of the interpretation of Kant which makes him say that we are only free when doing our duty; an interpretation which is in accordance with *one* at any rate of Kant's uses of 'free'.

7 This means something like 'varying one's behaviour in accordance with . . .' and *not* 'pushes, in billiard ball fashion'. It is sometimes argued that Kantian ethics presuppose a philosophy of mind construing motives as efficient causes, and that this invalidates his ethical theory. Neither the premiss nor the inference of this argument is valid.
8 *Which* of these represents what Kant intended to say is, again, a matter of controversial Kantian interpretation. The weaker and second interpretation gives rise to fewer difficulties and can be defended with reference to the text, but I nevertheless prefer the first as being more interesting, illuminating and characteristically Kantian, in that it follows obviously from typical Kantian premisses and shows us where they lead. If Kant were merely another intuitionist, he would hardly deserve the attention he receives. Cf. p. 88
9 Not much should be made of this naturalness, for it will be relative to the language employed, i.e. to the kind of action-concepts occurring in it. When definitions of action-concepts are constructed, the definiens will be a concatenation of characteristics which, suitably phrased, can become parts of a maxim. But, as shown, the possibility of universalization depends on which elements are included in the maxim. When we wish to include a particular set of these in a maxim, we can of course do this very simply if that set happens to correspond to the definiens of some natural action-word, by just including the name of that action.

Otherwise we must either invent a name and construct its definition, or include all the features which would have figured in that definition in the maxim itself.

10 Necessarily, for in the Kantian scheme there are only two alternatives for the groundings of a part or whole of the contents of a maxim; either to be entailed by the very form of the moral law, or to be empirically founded.

11 It is of course not made unambiguously clear in Kant's ethics whether he meant the formal principle to determine all the important details, or not. It really amounts to whether he meant to expound an ethic of obligation or one of permissibility, whether he thought that morality was like Italy, where everything not forbidden is allowed, or like Germany, where everything not allowed was forbidden. I feel inclined to say that he tried at least to be on the German side mainly because that makes for an interpretation which is simultaneously more difficult to defend philosophically and (a frequent conjunction, this, in issues of Kantian exegesis) more interesting, in that it more clearly follows from the general theses inspiring Kantian ethics, such as that of the 'heteronomy' of all empirically motivated conduct.

12 In a way, Kierkegaard was to metaphysical optimism what *Brave New World* is to scientific optimism.

Chapter 8   Knowing how and validity

The *knowing how–knowing that* dichotomy is used by Professor Ryle to obviate the fallacy that all intelligent performances entail that the agent contemplates, considers or in any other episodic sense knows some proposition. There is however an alternative mistake, which is suggested and not guarded against by Ryle's treatment. This is a mistake of treating *knowing how* as a type of validation, as a legitimate answer to 'How do we know?' questions. I do not know whether in fact Ryle himself commits this mistake. The Presidential Address to the Aristotelian Society, 1945, gives the impression that he does; the relevant chapter in *The Concept of Mind* does not. What I shall say is consequently only fair with regard to the earlier work. My reason for saying it nevertheless is that *The Concept of Mind*, whilst not repeating the mistake does not give any explicit warning against it either, and the mistake made by Ryle in the first, 1945, formulation is likely to be repeated by some at any rate of those who accept his main point. There seems to be already at least one instance of this happening in print, this being Mr Toulmin's article in 'Defence of "Synthetic Necessary Truth" '.[1]

The case which I shall elaborate is roughly that there is a tendency, requiring to be checked, to make *knowing how* do what 'intuitions' used to do. The temptation is seductive because the job done by intuitions, that of unquestionably answering with an air of finality the question about the way of validating some standard, always has a certain appeal. It is no doubt tempting to do this with the help of *knowing how* rather than of intuition in view of the fact that there clearly is such a thing as *knowing how*, whereas there is no such thing as intuition. Before showing that to make the notion of *knowing how* perform the function of intuitions is a misuse of it, I shall first of all try to show the non-existence of intuitions.

The confident assertion that there are no intuitions, that no-one has ever had an intuitive apprehension of rightness, an implication, deity or of anything else looks like a piece of unjustifiable dogmatism. It is sometimes said that if anybody appeals to intuitive evidence, we cannot refute him directly but can only hope to do so indirectly by drawing out some unpalatable implication of what he intuits.[2] But as people seldom intuit what is unpalatable to them, and as after all it is no great trouble to eliminate any undesirable indirect implication of their special insight by means of an additional *hilfs*-intuition liquidating the embarrassing logical relation, we should not get very far that way. But there is another way, for the denial of intuitions is not, despite appearances, an ordinary negative existential proposition. If it were, it could indeed never be reliably established. But there is no need to set off on an endless collection of evidence that Smith, Jones, Robinson . . . do not have intuitions, for the philosophically important concept of intuition can be shown to be self-contradictory. There are indeed senses of 'intuition' in which it is not self-contradictory, but only in the self-contradictory sense can intuitions perform the illegitimate task assigned to them. Such plausibility as theories of intuition do have derives, I think, from a concealed fluctuation between the permissible but innocuous, and the self-contradictory but powerful senses of the word respectively.

Intuition is required to be a something which is simultaneously *both* the evidence, in the sense of initial conditions of an inference *and* the guarantee of the legitimacy of the inference from the evidence. There tends to be actually a triple impossible identification—of evidence, the rule of inference from that evidence, and the guarantee of the truth of that rule. This identification is the essence of 'intuition' and is shared by otherwise quite diverse myths. Consider, for instance, a non-Humean theory of causation, which will have to claim that the causal property is intuited in the cause or the effect in isolation. The logician will rightly point out to anyone holding such a theory that a causal inference cannot be made from the cause (the initial conditions of the inference) alone but only from it in conjunction with a generalization. If the logician goes a step further and interprets the requisite awareness of the generalization as necessarily episodic, he will be committing the mistake which Ryle is concerned to eradicate. But this obviously does not mean that the intuitional theory of causation was right, or that the logician was wrong provided he restricted himself to pointing out that causal inferences are not valid in virtue of the initial conditions only.

What holds of causation holds of ethical, aesthetic, theological, logical, and any other candidates for intuition equally. The intuitionist in morals, for instance, does not, I think, wish to say that being intuited as obligatory *is* what makes an obligation valid, if only because that would free anyone unburdened with such intuitions from obligation. Similarly, the mystic does not wish to blaspheme by saying that his special experience *is* God. What both would rather like to say is that there is a special experience, with an inference from that experience to *something more* than it; and that somehow the experience is a guarantee of the validity of that inference. But this only requires to be stated clearly to be seen to be impossible. The defender of intuitions may attempt to evade the argument by saying that it would hold if we were concerned with ordinary, natural experiences; but that here we have to deal with special non-natural ones. But the argument does not depend on the inclusion of intuitions in the category of natural events, however that category may be defined. It depends only on intuitions being something which happen to specific people at specific times.

What then makes theories of intuition plausible, and what are the legitimate senses of the word? To begin with, ordinary people, scientists, mathematicians, writers all obviously do have hunches; they do make inferences, state theorems, predict effects without thinking of the underlying rule, possibly without knowing it, and even more often without having proved it, in whatever sense if at all it is susceptible of proof. It is incidentally the fact that Ryle's central thesis is right and that rules are not frequently present as occurrences, which leads to the misinterpretation of the above phenomena as intuitions. If you wish to call them intuitions there is perhaps no great harm in it, provided it is clear that all you are doing in describing them as such is telling how a certain inference, guess or trick was or could have been carried out or arrived at—i.e. without extraction of the rule of procedure underlying it, without explicit formulation and proof of it. You are *not* giving a logician's account of why the inference or guess was valid or true respectively. The intuition in the harmless sense is valid in virtue of something or other, but *not*, like the mythical intuition, simply in virtue of having occurred.

There are also more specific kinds of phenomena making for the theory of intuition. There are all the irregular unique or unprecedented hunches, some accompanied by an irresistible feeling of conviction, which *turn out* to be correct. There are also those philosophically interesting topics where no-one has succeeded in eliciting the rules—we do not know the sufficient and necessary conditions of something being right or beautiful—and where there is reason to believe that these rules never will be discovered. In the general cases of the preceding paragraph the validating rule *was not* present in an episodic sense; in all these cases for one reason or another it looks as if it *could not* be. But again, intuition in these cases is not valid because it occurs but in virtue of something else. A qualification is necessary here: if certain kinds of subjectivist theories are true, if the aesthetic or ethical hunch is not a clue to something else but simply *is* the aesthetic or ethical property, then it does become self-authenticating, by saying nothing. It again fails to be a *hunch* in a strong sense.

There is another special class of things which some people may hanker to grade as intuitions—gestalt-perceptions. When I see a pattern in a cloud or on a Rorschach card I do not see only what I saw there before I saw the pattern, but nor have I made an inference from what I saw there before; what happens is that I . . . well, words fail me; what happens is just that I see a gestalt. The reason why words fail me is not, I think, any deficiency of language or merely my insufficient command of it, but the survival of the prejudice that when we see something we must either see what we could have seen in the same object at any time or we must be inferring from it. This makes us attempt to give an account of gestalten in terms of one of these two, whilst the whole point of the discovery of gestalten is that the above dichotomy is not exhaustive. Gestalten are obviously important for ethics and aesthetics. Take the case of ethics; it is plausible to assume that judging a person, unlike perhaps making decisions about returning books by post, involves a kind of bio-graphically synoptic perceiving of a certain pattern. Maybe some people or classes judge in a completely atomic manner, by adding up observances and breaches of isolated obligations. Some others perhaps judge in a fully teleologically unified manner, in terms of conduciveness to some solitary overriding aim. In fact I do not think either of these extremes often obtains. One usually judges in a manner which is a mixture of these types, supplemented by attention to a kind of emergent pattern sometimes called way or style of life. The perception of this element can be described as intuitive, but again, it is *not* such in the sense of being the validating factor. The fact that a certain pattern is noticed or perceptible is not what makes that pattern the desirable one. Misdemeanours and disapproved behaviour-patterns also have gestalten, e.g. *la vie bohème*.

My motive for flogging the dying horse of intuitionism is not sadism alone. It is also that the tough-minded terminology of *knowing how* is liable to be used for the same purpose in place of the comparatively unfashionable terminology of intuitions. What has happened is, I think, this: the misinterpretation of *knowing how* as *knowing that* was perpetrated initially by logicians and moralists who were primarily interested in questions of validity and only incidentally interested in the philosophy of mind. Still, their mistake in the latter field was liable to lead them into metaphysics which in turn were liable to affect their conclusions with regard to their main question. Ryle, on the other hand, interested primarily in the philosophy of mind, firmly eliminated the myth of the co-extensiveness of *knowing that* with intelligence, but in turn misinterpreted, at any rate in 1945, *knowing how* as a logician's category (a type of validation), or as a reason for why logicians' categories were inapplicable, which really amounts to the same, as I shall attempt to show. In reality the *knowing how–knowing that* dichotomy, all-important for the philosophy of mind, is not coordinate with, but on the contrary cuts across, logical classifications such as analytic, synthetic, synthetic a priori, pragmatically justified or unverifiable. Ryle in 1945 seemed to conclude that because something was shown to be a matter of *knowing how*, the question concerning which of the logician's pigeon-holes it was to go into was silly. But this is not so; consider, for instance, the case of inference. Ryle rightly points out that the notion of *knowing how* is required for explaining the source of Lewis Carroll's paradox in the story of Achilles' conversation with the tortoise. But the fact that a skill is required for the application of a rule of inference does not mean that the rule need also be a valid rule: the fact that it is applied, the fact that someone knows how to use it, does not by any means make it valid. Rules are not relevant to the novice's performances only. False or self-contradictory rules of deductive inference may be constructed and people may acquire the skill of operating them and manufacturing fallacies and contradictions. Any philosopher, for instance, who has spent some time discussing the logical antinomies has acquired such a skill.

Let us turn to the motives one might have for treating, in general or over a limited field, *knowing how* as a logical category, as a type of validation. I can think of three of these reasons, two of them incidental and possibly not operative, and the third the main and effective cause of the mistake. I shall discuss the two minor ones first.

Firstly, there is the bogey of scepticism. It is notoriously plausible to say with regard to quite a number of important skills, such as those of making inductive generalizations or behaving correctly, that if we succeed in eliciting the appropriate rule, and translate the *knowing how* into explicit *knowing that*, we may find ourselves in a position of having to consign it, for purposes of logical classification, to the class of unproved or unprovable items of *knowing that*. Philosophers who dislike sceptical conclusions do so for at least two reasons: firstly, the traditional one that they sometimes feel that their function is the justifying of beliefs, and secondly for reasons connected with some aspects of contemporary philosophical method. The effect of Professor G. E. Moore's habit of asking '*what* are x?' instead of '*are* there x?', reinforced by the theory that philosophy is concerned with language as used, has been the tendency to rule out sceptical conclusions a priori. It is of course possible to philosophize in such a manner that one cannot arrive at sceptical conclusions, just as it is possible to produce the illusion of increased income by printing money. But when sceptical conclusions are ruled out beforehand by the very method employed in discussing the problem, the validation of the cherished beliefs becomes of a rather dubious kind, like an increased income produced by a doubling of salary accompanied by a doubling of prices. Some people, as is known, are nevertheless happy in such situations. But the use of *knowing how* to answer scepticism does not constitute a merit. Scepticism in various fields seems to me a theory and not necessarily the apodosis of a *reductio ad absurdum* argument. It may well be an important feature of some human activities that the rules underlying them cannot be justified.

It is worth mentioning at this point that one of the functions of language as the most important, or possibly the necessary, conditions of *knowing that* is its job of facilitating criticism, comparison, discussion, and improvement of skills. Unverbalized skills are by their very nature unobservable, except when actually employed, and then exercise of them is liable to inhibit observation; they can be developed and improved only by the laborious method of trial and error. Those, however, which by means of verbalization can be pinned up in a glass case can often be compared, modified or rejected far more speedily and efficiently. I am not, incidentally, denying that some untranslated *knowing how* must always be present, even in the verbal discussions, this being true for all the reasons connected with Lewis Carroll's paradox.

The second reason is that with regard to certain topics, such as art or sport, the extraction of the rule, the translation of *knowing how* into *knowing that*, may be very difficult, or impossible, and whether it is successful or not, the attempt itself may be unhelpful or even harmful to the performance. When dancing or playing table-tennis, it is fatal to think about what one is doing. We need only remember that unfortunate case of the centipede. Another but similar trouble may arise in ethics. I gather that certain social groups subscribe to ethical codes which incorporate as one of their rules the prohibition or discouragement of ethical introspection and critical speculation; to ruminate about whether what *isn't done* really is not to be done may itself be a thing that isn't done. All these cases, where *knowing how* occurs, but *knowing that* is difficult, undesirable or undesired, are liable to tempt one into misconstruing *knowing how* as a category of validation, or into making its presence a reason why no validation is necessary, which, as I have suggested, amounts to much the same. For some genuine logical category of validation, of *reason for selection*, in effect, must always apply *wherever there is a choice from amongst alternatives*[3] if only that residual category signified by the pejorative term 'arbitrary'. There *are* alternatives in painting a picture or dealing with a situation, and therefore . . . Q.E.D.

The final and main reason for misusing *knowing how* as a category of validation is the ambiguity of 'knowing how' and similar expressions. To say that somebody knows how to do something is to say two things: that he can *do* it, and that he can do it correctly. This can best be seen from considering a denial, e.g. 'he does *not* know how to argue'. This may mean either that like the tortoise in Lewis

Carroll's story, he simply isn't capable of making the step and inferring from the premises at his disposal; but it may equally well mean that he does make the step, but the wrong one and comes to a conclusion which does not follow. When we assert that he *does* know how to argue we are simultaneously denying both these possibilities. One may fail to notice that two things are being said because 'knowing how' is never predicated unless both hold, and the second can't hold unless the first does.

To say that two things are meant by 'knowing how' is not the same as to say that two processes are referred to by it, this being the fallacy which Ryle rightly attacks. Only *one* process is indicated, but what is *also* being said is that the process satisfies some criteria; this is mentioned by Ryle in *The Concept of Mind* but ignored, and I think implicitly contradicted, in the 1945 paper. To say that someone knows how to argue is, apart from mentioning his disposition to behave in a certain way, also a statement that what he does when the disposition actualized is an instance not merely of argument, but of *valid* argument. It is to say that he will observe the appropriate rules; 'observe' not indeed in the sense of 'look at' but in the sense of 'act in accordance with'. The denial of the 'two processes' theory should not blind us to the duality of meaning of expressions such as 'knows how to . . .'.

This point can also be made by saying that *knowing how*, like, for that matter, 'knowing' *tout court*, is an expression for achievements. 'Knowing how' is, to be precise, a triply laden expression: for when I say 'Tommy knows how to skate' I (i) refer to a disposition of Tommy's to do what is describable as skating (ii) imply that he succeeds, which (iii) prejudges to some extent the question of what the criteria of good skating are, by entailing that they are such as are satisfied by Tommy's performance. Only (i) refers to a process, indeed; but important as it is to notice this, it is also important not to ignore (ii) and (iii). The sense in which 'knowing how' is presupposed in all knowledge, which Ryle insists that it is in the 1945 paper, is sense (i) only. There are at least two reasons why there is a tendency to confuse the various senses: firstly it appears that we tend to be interested only in successful performances and have no terms corresponding to 'knows how to . . .' but possessing only its minimal force. The nearest (axiologically) neutral term seems to be just the humble word 'doing'. The second reason is that *some* words for actions, but some only, analytically entail what the criterion of successful performance is. 'Playing football', for instance, does, though 'skating', 'composing' or 'behaving oneself' do not; the activity of playing football *is defined* partly in terms of trying to score goals or tries, i.e. in terms of the criteria of success. In the case of such activities the distinctions that I have drawn are not relevant. I shall, whenever the distinction becomes important, refer to the neutral sense of 'knowing how' which begs no questions of validity as sense (i), and to the strong sense as (ii).

Toulmin, in the article mentioned above, does seem to think that *knowing how* has a special relation to synthetic necessary truths. The suggestion would seem to be that the latter are either valid in virtue of being kinds of *knowing how*, or that for this reason the question of validity does not arise. If this were true it could undermine my case that Ryle's dichotomy is irrelevant to classifications of logical form. To begin with, Toulmin classifies as synthetic a priori all those propositions which are necessary but with regard to which the guaranteeing definitions are not easily available but would have to be specially constructed. Well, Toulmin can if he wishes use 'synthetic necessary' in this way; indeed he explicitly abstains from claiming that the kind of proposition he is interested in corresponds exactly to the type normally discussed under that title, by christening them 'Type-Q propositions'; but it is worth noting that in *that* sense language will be overcrowded with synthetic necessary truths,[4] the vast majority of which will not be of the kind which is normally discussed in connection with the problem of synthetic a priori propositions. To say that language is overcrowded with Toulmin's type of synthetic necessity is to say that language is full of entailments which no-one has bothered to formalize and which it would be unnatural to formalize. Really plausible candidates for synthetic necessity are not those entailments with regard to which the definitions have not been in fact constructed, but those where the construction of the definitions comes up against certain problems. If a term A figures in an entailment 'A entails B' and we *can* construct a definition of A which includes 'entails B' and a definition of A′ which resembles the definition of A in all respects *except in so far as it does not include 'entails B'*; and if it is clear that A′ *does not entail B*, no problem arises and most of us, though not Toulmin, are satisfied that the entailment is analytic. This procedure, however, does not always work, at any rate easily, and it is when it doesn't that there is a point in talking of a genuine candidate for synthetic necessity. For instance, I can define 'red' as 'like the Soviet flag, and not green' (definition A), or alternatively as just 'like the Soviet flag' (definition A′). Unfortunately the entailment 'not green' still holds even for A′, and therefore cannot be attributed to its inclusion in the definition A. This kind of difficulty has, for instance, been very clearly exhibited by Mr D. F. Pears[5] with regard to certain temporal features.

Toulmin says that his synthetic necessaries have something to do with *knowing how*. Yes, indeed, for he has defined his class of them in terms of lack of formalization; and to say that something is a matter of 'knowing how' *is* to say that it is an intellectual but unformalized, unverbalized operation or that the verbalization is irrelevant. *Knowing how* has come in not because of synthetic necessity but because of the lack of formalization. But the weak *knowing how* (i) is present equally in unformalized statements of any kind, synthetic, analytic, and the rest. For they all involve doing, if only operating with undefined symbols or recognizing applicability or suitability without explicit criteria. More important still, this *knowing how* (i) is also present in false statements. *Knowing how* (ii) is *not* necessarily involved, unless Toulmin restricts himself to *successful* or *correct* exercises of the kind of *know-how* which he considers to be of 'Type-Q', and then of course it will be present by definition, for *knowing how* (ii) = *knowing how* (i) plus success, by some criteria. It is the smuggling in of these criteria in not unpacked *knowing how* (ii) that is the danger. Hence in neither sense is there a special connection between *knowing how* and synthetic necessity such as Toulmin suggests.

Toulmin seems to believe that the opposition to the doctrine of the synthetic a priori is based primarily on dislike of the 'inner eye', special insight, etc. This belief of his partly accounts, I think, for his keenness to introduce *knowing how*, for he seems to think that if *knowing how* replaces special intuition the basic objection will vanish. But even if special intuition were always relevant, which it is *not* in Kant, who after all matters most in the context of synthetic a priori propositions, *knowing how* would not be an eligible heir. To say that a proposition is synthetic or analytic or of any other kind is to say what kind of proof would be seen to be relevant to it *if* the appropriate definitions *were* constructed; 'intuited' was a spurious addition to this list, sometimes coupled with synthetic a priori. It is *not* to say anything whatever about whether the 'rule' of the operation *has* been made explicit.[6]

In his final paragraph Toulmin points out, talking of mathematicians' and logicians' shortcuts, that intuition is a good thing but no substitute for proof. True enough; but one should stress the same about *knowing how*, which also is not the *kind* of thing that can deputize for a proof. I am not claiming that all skills made explicit *are* susceptible of proof; and admittedly those which are so may be so in different senses. Nor am I denying that what have been claimed to be synthetic a priori principles, e.g. causation, may perhaps be illuminatingly described as performance rules rather than as propositions. What I want to guard against is the possibility of *knowing how* being in any way used to silence or 'solve' discussions of validity or to suggest that these are based on a misapprehension. *Knowing how* is an excellent thing, but it is no substitute for proof, evidence or grounds, nor, alternatively, for admission of arbitrariness.

1951

Notes

1 Stephen Toulmin, 'A Defence of "Synthetic Necessary Truth" ', *Mind*, n.s. **58**, 1949, 164–77; cf. esp. the penultimate paragraph.

2 Cf. for instance P. Nowell-Smith, 'Freewill and Moral Responsibility', *Mind*, n.s. **57**, 1948, 45–61; see esp. 53.

3 This is analytic—for a 'type of validation' is just the kind of way we choose the true or valid proposition from amongst possible alternatives.

4 Toulmin must, however, obviously also imply that there is some kind of correspondence between 'Type-Q' and synthetic a priori by discussing it in connection with the forms, the general polemic concerning the latter.

5 D. F. Pears, 'Time, Truth and Inference', *Proceedings of the Aristotelian Society*, n.s. **51**, 1950–1, 1–25.

6 Cf. for instance, G. Frege, *Foundations of Arithmetic* (trans. J. L. Austin), Oxford, 1950, 3.

Chapter 9   Morality and 'je ne sais quoi' concepts

In an interesting recent paper[1] Mr R. M. Hare examines the notion of universalizability. One interesting issue that emerges is the connection between *universalizability* and *morality*. By means of an imaginary dialogue (pages 304 and 305) and his comments on it, Hare conveys that he considers the connection between these two notions to be analytic. Roughly: if 'moral' does not *mean*, at least, 'universalizable', what else could it mean? If it were not allowed to mean or entail that, we should not be able to assign *any* meaning to it, Hare suggests. If recommending some act with the help of the word 'ought' does not entail or imply that we are recommending the same for analogous situations, what could it mean?

Claims that some connection is analytic can be attacked by a certain standardized move, namely by producing the fork: either you accept the Conventionalist view of analyticity in which case your initial claim is *ipso facto* trivial, or kindly produce an alternative interpretation of what your alleged inherent overlap of meanings amounts to. Now this *is* a standardized and questionable move and hence there would be little point in making its force felt against Hare's argument in particular, unless a special relevance obtained. This however may well obtain.

How would Hare actually verify the alleged overlap of meaning? The imaginary conversation conveys that if 'ought not' does not mean 'a person *like* me in circumstances of *this* kind oughtn't to do *that* kind of thing' (italics mine), if in other words the command or recommendation is not tacitly 'universalized', then no meaning is or can be attached to calling it moral or using the ethical word 'ought'. Now if Hare actually tried out this conversational experiment one of two things would, I suspect, happen. Either his interlocutor would lack philosophical sophistication and Hare would fail to get his point across, and thus that experiment would not count, or he *would* be so sophisticated and then his response would merely reflect his philosophical position—and we know that some philosophers are not in this sense Kantians—and again the experiment would not count.

Or suppose that, less trivially, we wished to know whether universalizability was 'built into' the codes of alien groups as it appears built into the moral consciousness of Hare's. Unfortunately, we shall have to have made up our philosophical minds about the issue under discussion *before* we begin our translation and anthropological interpretation, and not, alas, after it. For before we decide just which of the terms in the alien language we translate by 'moral' words in English, we shall have to decide by what criteria—necessarily philosophical ones—we shall isolate what we call their moral terminology from the rest of their vocabulary of exhortation, command, appraisal, etc. It is sometimes said nowadays that cultural relativism is not as well founded empirically as had been believed, that moral *notions* do not vary a great deal though their application may. In terms of Moore's deceptively clear-seeming distinction, it may be said that 'what is *meant* by *good*' varies little or not at all, but 'what *is* (held to be) good' does. Now this to me seems to show something about the general conditions of translatability, but nothing about anything else. For example: I simply have no choice but to translate the Berber word 'iehla' as 'good', and therefore I *could* say that 'the concepts are identical though Berbers do not appear to find goodness in the same things as Englishmen do'. I could say it, but it seems to me to follow closely from the limits of what can be done when translating, and from nothing else, and to throw no light on Berbers and Englishmen or the alleged similarity or difference of their moral concepts, and a great deal on the limitations of translations. I conclude from this, in the first instance, that we must distrust such demonstrations of alleged moral similarity-under-the-skin, and that we must distrust Moore's distinction, and that the difficulty of showing analyticity through synonymy with regard to moral terms is even greater than that difficulty in general.

In particular, I conclude from all this that the evidence for the analytic connection alleged by Hare cannot be *de facto* synonymy or partial overlap of meaning, for we seem to be able to find this only by blatantly circular proceedings. If then we do not take Hare's imaginary conversation as a model of the evidence but merely a device of exposition, we shall have to look for the actual evidence or proof elsewhere.

Now one explanation that seems to me plausible is to say, looking at it from the outside, that a certain kind of egalitarianism and a related sense of justice is so deeply tied up with morality in Hare's mind and the tradition of which he and most of us are a part, that neither he nor the rest of us can really separate them. I suspect that historically speaking this is so, and what follows is that the tie-up of morality and universalizability is in a sense trivially analytic, in other words that we can, if we wish, use universalizability to circumscribe 'the moral' by a linguistic *fiat*, but that in consequence certain phenomena which by the other criteria would be called moral will be excluded from that class. For instance, a moralist such as Professor Ginsberg who is interested in the historical development of morals prefers to use something like universalizability as a criterion of the *level* of ethical development, rather than as a *qualification of entry* into the field of morality in the first place. In so far as the difference here between Hare's and Ginsberg's position is merely terminological, I conclude that this way towards validating Hare's tie-up of morality and universalizability is trivial, though of course the valuation of universalizability which Hare and Ginsberg share is far from trivial.

This second approach towards validating the connection alleged by Hare having also proved unsatisfactory, I turn towards the kind of validation attempted by Kant, which seems to me so good that I find it hard to explain why I do not wholly accept it. This argument is that *qua* rational we have reasons for what we do, and that reasons must be open and universalized (this being analytically so, though not in Hare's usage). The question then arises why we should be rational in this sense, and the Kantian ultimate answer is that only thus are we free from irrelevant, contingent efficient causes, and that we pre-suppose such freedom anyway in as far as we ascribe validity to any of our reasoning or conclusions. This last argument seems to me true notwithstanding periodic would-be refutations of it in terms of the discovery of the difference between historical and logical reasons.[2] Kant can be interpreted as saying that only if we 'universalize' are there any 'logical reasons' to counteract historical ones. Now this Kantian approach produces a feeling of conviction and non-triviality in me which the conversation imagined by Hare does not. The argument runs: In as far as I act, as opposed to just being a thing acted upon, I must have reasons, and in as far as I have reasons they must be open. For reasons which do not apply to other cases are no more reasons than an explanation which can only explain one thing is an explanation. Kant held all this to be analytic, but a synthetic element entered when this whole complex was tied up with obligatoriness or morality. Now it seems to me that something like the Categorical Imperative can indeed in a weak sense of proof be proven, in that if we wish the justifications we give for our actions to observe the same canons as our explanations of nature in a society whose science is not circular but genuine, we must universalize our maxims.

This seems to me better than the imaginary conversation in Hare's paper which would leave the anti-Kantian quite cold, whereas this argument would at least force him to say that he does not wish to be rational in valuation in a sense analogous to that in which scientific explanations are rational.

Some light is thrown on all this by observing what happens when

actual conduct fails to live up to what that universalizability requirement would demand. The frank egoist 'makes an exception in his own
favour' as Kant says and he is not philosophically very interesting.
The cunning and hypocritical egoist indulges in the construction of
an *ad hoc* maxim so devised as to allow him to make such an exception without this being formally demonstrable.

It has however struck me recently that this device is not as generally
used as I had believed and as Hare suggests in his second broadcast[3]
on this topic. Admittedly, your petty little egoist is much addicted to
it, but he is not nearly so interesting philosophically as the so to speak
ideological irrationalist, the Fascist, mystic, etc. *He* does not
elaborate a clumsy overburdened and loaded maxim which serves to
show that he may act as he wishes but those of opposed persuasion or
commitment may not; he is simultaneously simpler and more elusive
than that. He uses one of what I shall call the *je ne sais quoi*[4] concepts.
He admits that he discriminates between rival objects of loyalty, or
worship, or just human respect, or love, between which no significant
empirical difference that would justify the discrimination can be
found, and he does not stoop to pretend that he has found a basis for
discrimination amongst the irrelevant empirical *differentiae* of the
rival objects. No, he firmly asserts that there is an important difference but one that is only perceptible to the select, who may in turn be
identified by a similar procedure, or that it is something incommunicable in words or at all, or something that cannot be even
conceptually isolated from the complex of which it is a part, etc., etc.
Sociologically speaking, this device may be an extreme case of the
fact that many patterns of social conventions or beliefs *have no*
underlying reason and this with good effect, for thus learning them or
refuting them becomes impossible for outsiders. *Comprendre c'est
égaler*, but where there is nothing to understand you cannot equal, at
least not by rational procedures.

There seem to me to be many *je ne sais quoi* concepts; for instance,
'personality' in the sense promised by certain advertisements, intuition, 'it', 'oomph', and perhaps even 'beauty'. What they have in
common is the suggestion or implication that there is a difference but
it cannot be located or stated. When in a certain context we say that
someone 'has personality' we do not simply mean that he has a
certain effect on us, we also mean that we cannot isolate what it is
about him that is responsible for it. Of course he has certain characteristics, but those characteristics in someone else would not have
that effect or even have the opposite effect. That this is so and that we
cannot explain it is what is already contained in or implied in the
concept 'personality'. The concept 'personality' has a curious logic;
it specifies an effect and implies that it is unexplained. *Personality* in
a certain sense can *never* be explained, not because there are things in

this world of which we can say a priori that they will never be explained, but because 'personality' is, from the *observer*'s viewpoint, a
non-achievement word. Or put it this way: There is no such *thing* as
personality, but we can combine in one notion certain effects and the
idea of inexplicability.

The ideological irrationalist adopts precisely this device *vis-à-vis*
his preferred object. The device is in certain well-established cases
even protected by social custom, in so far as it is considered bad taste
to discuss certain valuations or attitudes, and hence their ineffable
status does not even need to be explicitly asserted. For instance, to
discuss faith critically with a believer is nowadays considered not
quite the thing, partly perhaps in consequence of the tolerant temper
of the times, partly perhaps in consequence of the Existentialist
manner of looking at religion as a very private event and *not* as an
arguable conviction.

Rather pale versions of *je ne sais quoi* concepts are professionally—
and inexcusably—manufactured by philosophers. 'Intuitions' in the
sense in which these alleged occurrences are claimed to validate or
justify some propositions or procedures—in ethics or other fields—
are of this kind. What happens is that an unaccountable discrimination occurs—say between valid and invalid moral rules—and such a
je ne sais quoi concept is brought in as an all-too-convenient *deus ex
machina* to explain it. Of course the term may be used innocuously,
when its '*je ne sais quoi*' status is clearly, honestly and frankly conveyed, as when we say something like 'I only know this to be true
intuitively' meaning that I accept something not knowing why 'on a
hunch' and hope that a justification will follow. This frankness always
characterizes Existentialists—by definition—and makes them more
likeable and tolerable in a sceptical world than intuitionists.

A real parody of the vicious kind of use of these concepts occurs
when they are first introduced in order to justify some distinction—
say between ethical truth and error—and then their 'presence to the
mind' is conceived on the analogy of a physical sense. It then seems
necessary to admit that this channel of alleged information must be
capable, like all others, of conveying error as well as truth. *Then* a
kind of second-order *je ne sais quoi* concept, to sort out truth and
error within the hypostatized version of the first, is required. . . .

Of course, academic intuitionists and apprehenders of ineffable
concepts and distinctions are seldom if ever also ideological ir-
rationalists in the real world outside philosophical discussions, so
they don't really do much harm. They do, however, provide a kind of
comic genteel model for the logic of moral attitudes of men such as
Hitler. I have elsewhere argued [5] that no one has ever had an intuition
or mystical experience, etc., and that this *is arguable*, not being an
empirical matter, as it seems, but a logical issue. Of course this does

not preclude the fact that people do have odd experiences when they consume mescalin or listen to Billy Graham. What it does preclude is the classification of these experiences as somehow cognitive.

We may now return from our longish but necessary and worthwhile excursus into the nature of *je ne sais quoi* concepts. What is their relevance to the issue whether morality and universalizability are analytically connected, or indeed connected at all? I think their existence and role can be interpreted in a number of ways. Most of what can be listed as non-universalizable valuations or preferences,[6] e.g. blind loyalty, worship, romantic love, would in practice receive buttressing-up from *je ne sais quoi* concepts. The arbitrarily chosen object would be said to be selected not for no reason, but for unsayable ones. But it is quite natural to class many such non-universalizable valuations—especially with this support of theirs—as 'moral', though this goes against Hare's claim that universalizability and morality are analytically connected. Hence they are not merely not connected analytically, but not connected at all in the minds of those who class some of those non-universalizable valuations as moral; and that in some cases this occurs is a reasonable interpretation.

The facts can however equally be used to support Hare's claim, and fairly. The important thing then is *that* these valuations do not come up alone but that they *are* supported by *je ne sais quoi* concepts. These pseudo-notions are the compliments particularistic vice pays to Kantian virtue. With rare exceptions, the champions and upholders of non-universalizable values do not frankly say they are such (amongst the rare exceptions to this being some characters of novels of Dostoevski, André Gide, and Sartre). Nor do they take the petty and cumbersome way of camouflaging their particularity under a mass of detail. They prefer to camouflage it with the help of ineffable reasons. The ineffable entities specified or hinted at by these reasons may have an ethereal habitat, or more recently, as in the case of D. H. Lawrence, be housed in the intestines, or with the Fascists, amongst the blood corpuscles. All this varies with fashion and is, logically considered, irrelevant detail. What does matter is that the use of a *je ne sais quoi* concept implicitly admits the principle that universalizability is called for, even if it then circumvents it through the ineffable uniqueness of something.

The truth—and if true, kind of truth—of the connection between morality and universalizability is not yet clear. *Je ne sais quoi* concepts are more important than 'over-loading of maxims' as a device of camouflaging non-universalizability, and that throws some light on the former issue.

1956

Notes

1   R. M. Hare, 'Universalisability', *Proceedings of the Aristotelian Society*, n.s. **55**, 1954–5, 295–312.
2   For instance, by A. Flew in 'The Third Maxim' in *The Rationalist Annual*, London, 1955, 63–6.
3   Compare R. M. Hare, 'Have I a Duty to My Country as Such?', *Listener*, **54**, 20 October 1955, 651–20.
4   Cf. Hume '. . . that certain *je-ne-scai*[*sic*]-*quoi*, of which 'tis impossible to give any definition or description, . . .' *A Treatise of Human Nature*, Book I, Part III, Section VIII.
5   Ernest Gellner, 'Knowing How and Validity', *Analysis*, **12**, 1951, 25–35; above, ch. 8.
6   Compare my paper on 'Ethics and Logic', *Proceedings of the Aristotelian Society*, n.s. **55**, 1954–5, 157–78; in this volume, above, ch. 7.

Part three   Some ancestors

Chapter 10 French eighteenth-century materialism

An important facet of the European philosophical tradition is represented most clearly and characteristically by a group of French philosophers of the eighteenth century. The group contains some of the most famous names in French literature and includes, among others, La Mettrie, Voltaire, Diderot, d'Alembert, and d'Holbach. These writers cannot be said to form a philosophical school, nor were they all philosophers in the modern sense of the word. Some, like Voltaire and Diderot, were literary men; some, like d'Alembert, scientists and mathematicians. But each in his own way gave expression to a certain characteristic point of view that may be called the syndrome of progressive thought. We shall first take a general survey of this syndrome and then consider in more detail one particular manifestation of it—the work of d'Holbach.

Major themes of the Enlightenment

The characteristics of the syndrome of progressive thought are anticlericalism and hostility to religion; rejection of supernatural or 'spiritual' explanations of phenomena; an insistence or preference for explanations of phenomena in terms of the structure and activity of matter; a positive expectation that everything in nature and man can be explained in natural intramundane terms; determinism; empiricism in epistemology; hedonism and/or egoism in psychology; belief in reason as the guide and arbiter of life; rejection of the authority of tradition; utilitarianism in ethics, and utilitarianism and/or democracy in politics; pragmatism with regard to the theory of truth; relativism; and belief in the power of education and of government and in the possibility of deliberate improvement of human life.

Manifestations of this syndrome tend to be more sharply articulated in Roman Catholic countries than elsewhere, and not surprisingly; for its elements were first assembled in opposition to Roman

Catholicism. Perhaps the manner in which they were assembled owes something to the Church's *example*, as the selection of the constituents plainly owes almost everything to its *opposition*.

It would be wrong and, so to speak, parochial to erect a general typology of thought along the lines of adherence or opposition to the elements listed.[1] The alignment of views for and against the progressive syndrome, as I have called it, is rooted in a historical situation rather than in some universal and basic dualism.

The expression 'materialist', as used in common speech, owes much of its meaning to the syndrome described. To say that someone is materialistic or is a materialist in his views, policies, or practices is not normally a way of saying that he proposes theories about matter being the only constituent of the universe. Rather, it is a way of implying that his thinking has some of the characteristics on our list. A man may come to be called a materialist because he allows only for hedonic or egoistic motivation in men, or because he allows no considerations other than the specification of tangible advantages to influence policy, or because he refuses to allow the possibility of inexplicable or unpredictable factors influencing events.

'Materialism' in a narrower and more technical sense can be defined as the doctrine that only matter exists, and hence that all other phenomena and features of the world are explicable as manifestations of the organization and movement of matter.

Materialism in the narrower sense is indeed *one* of the constituents of the set of beliefs and attitudes which make up materialism in the broader and looser sense.

The reason for the use of the same term to describe both the wider and the narrower 'materialism'—as often happens when we get an ambiguous term designating a doctrine or attitude—is that materialism in the narrower sense is held to be the crucial and most important among the materialist doctrines in the wider sense. Both adherents and opponents have supposed that materialism in the narrower sense is the premiss from which the wider set of ideas can be deduced. In fact, it is not even clear whether all the doctrines of the wider set can easily be made consistent with materialism in the narrower sense (or, in some cases, with each other), let alone whether they are deducible from it.

The set of ideas that I have described as the progressive syndrome are the fruit of the French eighteenth-century Enlightenment. The individual ideas are not on the whole original; they generally have far older roots and a longer history. But their joint crystallization in a connected system of ideas constituting a characteristic and easily distinguishable outlook is the work of thinkers who, if not always French by nationality or residence, wrote in French and made their first and strongest impact on the climate of opinion in France. Their influence in preparing the ground for the French Revolution is a commonplace of history books.

It would, of course, be a very misleading simplification to suggest that there was a general consensus, or even a clearly discernible majority opinion, among the many active writers of the period. Nevertheless, certain themes stand out—either by being upheld more often or more effectively, or by standing out more conspicuously in opposition to preceding orthodoxies, or by being seen in retrospect to be the premonitions or sources of ideas that were later to become widely accepted or influential. Those themes are the ones found among the items on our initial list.

On that initial list, we *named* a large number of doctrines. It might also be useful to indicate the general contents of the 'progressive thought syndrome' by a somewhat shorter list of actual formulated tenets.

There is, first and foremost, hostility to revealed religion: the world is knowable and known through human experience and thought, and its nature is *not* something contained only in an exclusive, privileged, and unimpugnable communication vouchsafed to some particular tradition or institution. Similarly, the bases of morality and politics are something to be sought in human experience and reason.

There is naturalism. By this I mean the denial of fundamental discontinuities in nature—for instance, the denial of the discontinuity between animal and human nature, or between the physical and mental aspects of man. This also involves the denial of supernatural intrusions into the realm of nature, and hence of the need or permissibility of invoking them in explaining the phenomena of nature.

There is materialism (in the narrower sense)—the insistence that there exist explanations of natural phenomena—including human and mental ones, in terms of the organization and activity of matter. It should be noted that this last idea can be seen as a corollary or justification or expression of the naturalistic and empirical vision of man, and it is in this capacity, rather than as an independent position, that it tends to be incorporated. For instance, La Mettrie's celebrated *L'Homme Machine* is concerned less with the thesis that gives it its name and notoriety than with the preaching of an empirical and medical, rather than an *a priori*, attitude to human phenomena, and with the establishment, on such a basis, of a continuity between man and the rest of nature; in other words it is concerned with the denial of the legitimacy of invoking some special principle or substance with regard to man's behavior. It should also be noted that if this interpretation is correct—if materialism in the narrow sense is, in the internal economy of the outlook, a corollary or support of empiricism and naturalism rather than an independent thesis—then the essence of the outlook contained in 'materialist' eighteenth-century works is *not* deeply shaken by certain features of modern science which are sometimes invoked against it—as examples, the recognition of psychogenetic factors in medicine, or the existence of irreducibly statistical laws in physics, or the shadowy nature of the modern physicists' equivalents of the notion of matter, or the possibility of its substitution by energy. Such phenomena would only strike at the heart of the characteristic eighteenth-century outlook under discussion *if* they were also incompatible with the empiricist, anti-revelational and antitraditional view of inquiry, and with the unitary view of nature. But it is doubtful whether there is indeed such a conflict

What is the significance, in the history of philosophy, of this outlook? Its formulations do not quite reach the first rank among the great philosophical works of history.[2] The individual ideas are generally not new, and their implications are not always worked out with the kind of thoroughness or rigor that, even if he inherits his premises from someone else, can place a thinker in the front rank.

Why then is the 'materialism' of the Enlightenment nevertheless of great importance? Its real significance lies in the fact that it crystallized, blended, articulated, and diffused an outlook which is still a part of the basis of the Western, educated man's vision of the world. Its achievement was the propagation of ideas and the sifting, fusing, and clear articulation of them. This is no mean achievement, even if not combined with the introduction of new ideas or with a truly rigorous exploration of the implications of old ones. And it should be added that if the outlook is with us still—if indeed it is the main constituent of our view of the world—then so are its difficulties and contradictions. We tend to be (not all of us, perhaps, but those professionally concerned with ideas) more clearly aware of the difficulties and inner incompatibilities of that outlook. There are two reasons for this: First, the mere passage of time, the accumulation of experience in trying to live with, or by, the ideas of the Enlightenment, have brought those incompatibilities or difficulties to light.[3] Second, the comparative decline in the intellectual and social significance of the opponent of the outlook in question—Christianity, and, in particular, Catholicism—has aided the emergence of oppositions *within* the Enlightened outlook. Ideas, like men, combine in opposition to external enemies, and their differences re-emerge when the external threat recedes. For instance, one of the striking and persistent inner strains within the outlook arises from the conflict between its radical empiricism, the insistence on the senses as the *sole* source of knowledge, and what may be called absolute materialism, the view that the structure and activity of independently and continuously existing matter is the only ultimate reality and explanation of other phenomena. The allegedly unique channel of information does not seem suited to convey information about the nature or even the existence of the allegedly unique existent. This difficulty remains inherent in the general modern outlook; empiricism in the sense that experience is the only arbiter of doctrines about reality (if not their source) is with us still, and so is the conviction that the paradigm of explanation is one in terms of the structure and activity of, if not always matter, then at least of something independently existing and possessing a structure. The opposition between the model of *information* (through *experience*) and the model of *explanation* (by means of a *structure* and activity of something existing independently of experience) is not easy to overcome and remains with us.[4]

The claim that the significance of the Enlightenment's philosophy lies in its having forged and formulated the main element of the outlook of the Western European secularized intelligentsia until this day and also to a large extent—even if it is not always officially recognized —of Western society at large, calls for some qualifications. But these qualifications do not contain any substantial emendation concerning that which was central to the men of the Enlightenment, their attack on religion. The view that historic, revealed religion is false and harmful when it obstructs nonreligious inquiries has been largely incorporated into the outlook of Western man. The fact that religious institutions, practices, and adherence survive in no way contradicts this, for the religion that has survived the onslaught of the Enlightenment has adjusted itself so completely that it tacitly recognizes the justice of the attack. The religion that was attacked by the men of the Enlightenment was, or contained theories concerning the nature of the world, of man, of society; these were either in conflict with empirical or naturalistic theories, or ruled out the possibility of such theories altogether. Contemporary religion no longer presumes to prejudge or interfere with the findings and inquiries of the sciences. Inquiries, not merely into inanimate and biological nature, but into man and society, or even into the sociology of religion itself, are no longer resented or resisted. They are tolerated or welcomed. It is unlikely that many contemporary investigators of, say, the applicability of the cybernetic model to psychology—and presumably there are Roman Catholics among them—felt that they were committing impious acts or undermining religion. (I doubt whether 'dabbling in cybernetics' has been the content of even a single confession.) Yet in the eighteenth century, men were driven to put forward something like the cybernetic hypothesis, partly just *because* if it were true, it would undermine religion and facilitate empirical inquiry into man and nature. Ascertaining the truth of the man-machine idea was deemed a necessary step in the liberation of inquiry.

The religion that has survived the onslaught of the Enlightenment is careful to restrict its claims to the realms, whatever they are (and their nature and locale vary), that do not prejudge the results of free and empirical inquiry; or to make quite plain that the truth it offers, whatever its subject matter, is different in kind and source from ordinary truth; or to restrict itself to the realm of values, where, admittedly, the outlook of the Enlightenment also made claims, but far less successfully. And even in the last field, it is noteworthy that the weightiest arguments—if not the only ones—in discussions of policy or legislation that affect moral issues, are utilitarian arguments. And note that this reduction of religion to noninterference was all that the Enlightenment really required; even that height of eighteenth-century impiety, *Le Système de la Nature*, which we shall examine in more detail as the quintessence of enlightened thought, does not demand more.

It is a truism to say that European society has undergone a process of secularization in the past two hundred years or so. This is not the place to examine the social significance of this assertion; but, on the intellectual plane, it means, roughly, that people have replaced religious ideas by others *largely drawn from the set that can be found, assembled, and systematized in the 'System of Nature'*.

Later thinkers who have set out to give secular answers to problems such as those of morality, of the relation of mind to body, or of the freedom of the will have generally drawn on some of the many ideas from the set found, ordered, and often succinctly and forcefully stated in the *System of Nature*. (To say this is not to say that the text itself has persisted in being influential; it has not. On the contrary, it has been rather unjustly neglected. But the complex of ideas of its time, which it summed up more forcefully than any other work, continues to be a kind of matrix from which secular thinking draws many of its crucial premisses.)

Many intellectual biographies in and since the eighteenth century have contained as their crucial episode the confrontation with the issue—to *believe* or not to believe? The precise nature of the tempting or beckoning *faith* does not here concern us. What do concern us are the beliefs of *dis*belief; the world picture which was generally assumed to be the alternative to faith was something rather like that of the *System*.

It has generally been assumed that the kind of residue or alternative that remains if faith is abstracted or abandoned must be something like the vision of the *System*—naturalism, determinism, empiricism, materialism, utilitarianism—fused as best one can.

It is easy and somewhat cheap—although also correct—to remark, as many have, that many of the ingredients of this outlook require as much *faith* as does religious belief. What is less obvious is whether the kind of 'materialistic' outlook found in the *System* is indeed the only, or natural, alternative to a conventionally religious view of the world. Roughly speaking, modern man tends to assume as obvious that if religion is false, then the world must be something like the picture of the *System*. This seems to me at least questionable, although it is very difficult to visualize what a radically different, yet seriously tenable, secular view would be like. But it is questionable nevertheless: one need only reflect on how much this particular secular alternative owes to the religion it combated. In its particular views, it owes it a great deal by opposition; and in its general structure it may well owe it as much by more or less unconscious emulation.

Modern themes not present in Enlightenment thought

The claim that the Enlightenment forged and first formulated the modern outlook as it manifests itself both in shared presuppositions and in formal philosophies does not, as indicated, call for qualification on the grounds that religion has survived its attack. If the characteristic eighteenth-century outlook fails to excite or stimulate today, it is partly because its exponents have done their work so well and successfully. What they preached has become common ground, shared even by the successors of their erstwhile opponents.

But the claim does call for some qualification on other grounds. There are certain prominent constituents of our modern climate of opinion which were either lacking or inadequately incorporated in the beliefs of the Enlightenment. It is their absence, as well as the success and hence the platitudinization of the outlook, which gives to the outlook of the Enlightenment that slightly stale and unexciting taste which, for many people, it has. It is worthwhile to specify the *lacking* constituents that were to be added later.

1. There is what may be called historicism and sociologism: a certain awareness of the continuity, unity, flow, and growth *in* the world. That awareness was later inspired by the consideration of either human or biological history, and is often lacking among the men of the Enlightenment, who were rather inclined to have what one might call a 'two basic states' view of the universe—*before* and *after*, as it were, the Enlightenment. (Before, there was darkness and superstition; afterward, there was light. The 'dual state' vision is perhaps itself something inherited from religion.)

With the replacement of the somewhat *simpliste* dual state view by theories of historical growth or evolution, there also came a more tolerant and, as it were, *functional* interpretation of those errors which the Enlightenment had fought. This made it impossible to see them purely as errors fathered on us by fear or imagination and exploited by priests and tyrants for their own ends. This greater sophistication or understanding and/or tolerance is reinforced by what may be called the 'sociological' outlook: If ideas are to be seen primarily as social, rather than individual, functions, then part at least of the weeding operation carried out by men of the Enlightenment was misguided. If societies or nations are supraindividual unities, they may well speak to the individuals who compose them through those seemingly absurd legends or dogmas or institutions that did not stand up to the Enlightened critique. Thus the relativism that *was* present in the Enlightenment, but which was not thoroughly followed up, received an impetus and development that led to the partial undermining of the critical Enlightened outlook itself.

2. Another notable constituent in the modern outlook was lacking in the Enlightenment, and indeed lacking among the views with which it grappled: a pessimism based, not on a religious doctrine of original sin, but on a quite secular view of man. This vision of man formulated metaphysically by Schopenhauer, aphoristically by Nietzsche, and clinically by Freud is something which is alien to Enlightened thought and which constitutes a grave problem for it. The Enlightenment was not necessarily given to attributing a fundamentally good moral substrate to man, as Rousseau did, but it saw man as at least morally neutral and capable of rational and indeed virtuous, behavior, once it could be freed from superstition; and even if motivated by self-interest, enlightened self-interest would lead to a rational harmony.

The idea that the enemy of rationality and happiness is *within* and deeply rooted, a kind of cosmic or biological or fundamental bloody-mindedness, is something which, if true, badly upsets the rationalistic and optimistic world-view of the Enlightenment. If true, it shows that enlightenment is not enough. The aims it offers humanity—rational, harmonized happiness—are in fact shown not to satisfy our real strivings; the means it offers—the removal of superstition and prejudice and tyranny—are shown to be inefficacious.

3. There is, finally, the Existentialist tradition, in a broad sense of the term. This arose in reaction, not to the Enlightenment itself, but to the 'enlightened', rationalist elements in Romantic post-Enlightenment philosophy—that is, to the belief that reason was the clue to nature, history and life and that the previous ideas of the priests, etc., and such people were not false but constituted a kind of lisping reason.

The essence of Existentialism is the attempt to shift issues of general and fundamental conviction from the realm of inquiry and objective truth to the 'subjective' realm of *decision* or *commitment*. It first did this either in the interests of religion—to save it from condemnation as false *theory* about the world, comparable to those of scientific inquiry—or as a reinterpretation of it, to save it from travesty in the hands of its rationalizing defenders.

This movement is of great significance from the viewpoint of understanding the subsequent history of the ideas of the Enlightenment, for it re-establishes the discontinuity which the Enlightenment attacked, and it does so in a new way that evades the arguments of the Enlightenment. The Enlightenment insisted on seeing man and things human as parts of nature and hence amenable to human reason and investigation: it concentrated its attack on dualistic doctrines which maintained that the human mind, destiny, or values were manifestations of something extra-natural and unamenable to unaided thought and scientific study. Existentialism re-establishes religious conviction, not by any dualistic ontology or superscience, or by claims of the presence of extranatural, spiritual stuff or whatnot, but by claiming that the manner in which our ultimate commitments are made is and must be different from the manner of empirical or scientific inquiry. Though Existentialists may sometimes express themselves quasi-ontologically, as though postulating a category of existence consisting of self-choosing or self-conscious beings, this does not really amount to the claim that there exists a special and further *stuff* in the world; the special existence is produced by the act of choice.

If this idea is valid—and it is hard to see how one could judge it—it turns the flank of the enlightened, naturalistic insistence on the unity of nature. It does so, not by saying anything about nature or by denying its unity as an *object* of observation, but by insisting that ultimate or most general convictions are not about *objects* but are a choice within a *subject*. Hence the dualism, the discontinuity denied by the Enlightenment and perhaps required by religion, reappears, but not as a rift *in* nature.

Existentialism has since assumed both religious and atheistic forms, but in either case it maintains this new rift and fundamental dualism between conscious subjects and objects of consciousness and this kind of dualism, unlike the old religious or Cartesian dualism, is something that evades the critique of the Enlightenment.

We are now in a better position to reassess the balance-sheet of the Enlightenment's conflict with religion—an aspect which, after all, was central to it. The religious doctrines that survive the onslaught of the Enlightenment among the educated tend to be, in the main, *re-formulated* religious doctrines—reformulated with the aid of either the socially functional view of knowledge or the Existentialist re-assessment of faith as something not cognitive or descriptive at all. (There are also more straightforward 'fundamentalist' and anti-rationalistic theologies; dogmatism or the denial of reasoning is easy.) So religion survives through certain ways of thought with which the Enlightenment was not familiar and which, in part, arose in order to evade its arguments. The old, forthright theology which dogmatized about this and another world is not much in evidence. Religious assertions are now made, not merely with regard to some 'other realm', but also in some 'other sense'. In other words, the unity and self-sufficiency of the natural world is not often seriously challenged. Sophisticated modern religion, when not simply dogmatic, tends to have either an Existentialist, a sociological, or a pragmatist coloring.

The essence of the 'materialist' outlook to be considered is, I think, to be seen in the insistence on the unity, continuity, self-sufficiency, and necessity of the natural world, and in the accompanying idea that human salvation is to be sought in that world, and that doctrines contrary to that unity are harmful. If this is indeed the essence of the outlook, then the subsequent additional ingredients of the characteristic modern *Weltanschauung*, which we have indicated, can be seen, first, as the extension of that continuity to social phenomena and to dualistic, transcendental beliefs themselves, the implications being that apparently irrational social forms and convictions also share in the general necessity of nature and cannot be discounted as mere aberrations; and hence, on quite irreligious (socio-epistemological) grounds, religion must be respected rather than exorcized; secondly, there is the realization that the unity and continuity of nature require one to see man, his aims, and conduct, as of a piece with biological nature, and the implications of this tend to be a pessimism in morals which in fact conflicts with the optimistic anticipation of secular salvation characteristic of the Enlightened outlook. Finally, there is the establishment of a new kind of discontinuity, based not on some kind of dualistic ontological claim, as hitherto, but on a kind of dual *aspect* of man, as object and also as a choosing (and, possibly, cognizing) agent.

The ideology and its impact

We have, so far, described the materialism of the Enlightenment as an outlook, a set of connected, but not necessarily consistent, ideas. We have also suggested that its importance lies in having first brought together, formulated, and disseminated the characteristic modern world-outlook, with the certain qualifications that have been indicated. A propagated general outlook which consciously incorporates certain values, and aims at an alteration of human life and society is sometimes referred to as an ideology. The work of the Enlightenment was certainly the promulgation and propagation of an ideology; indeed, the term originates from the period, and some of the later participants in the movement were known as the *Idéologues*.

But to say this is not to denigrate either the ideas or the work of the Enlightenment. The term 'ideology' is far too easily used in a pejorative way. What it properly designates is something which is indispensable to any society, and which is not, as such, necessarily bad or good. The men of the Enlightenment have, moreover, acquired a certain bad name as being the prototypes of thinkers who wish to remold man and society in the image of their own abstract ideas without regard to reality—to propagate the need for continuity in social life and for piecemeal rather than total reform. The term *philosophe*, designating the fashionable and influential thinkers of the period, is sometimes used as meaning an intellectual reformer of such a kind. The excesses of the French Revolution, or indeed the Revolution itself, are blamed on them and their teaching by those who do not approve of it.

The high valuation of the work of the Enlightenment, and indeed the claim that it is the source of our modern view of things, will of course not appeal to those who believe that philosophy can and should be detached and neutral. For such people, the philosophy of the Enlightenment must seem a travesty of philosophy; indeed, it is difficult to see how they can account for its existence.

But if the philosophy of the Enlightenment was an ideology or a propagated outlook calculated to transform society, it was *also* a philosophy in the narrower, technical sense. It contained doctrines on many matters, such as the limits of meaningful discourse, the criteria of morality, the relation of mind and body, which philosophers, who believe in the existence of a narrow, neutral, and ideologically uncommitted subject called 'philosophy', consider to be properly philosophical questions in their own preferred sense. The ideologies of the Enlightenment not only contained such doctrines, but contained them in an *essential* way. They were connected in many logical ways, as premises and as corollaries of the 'ideological' elements. The two aspects were quite inseparable, and indeed remain so.

My own view is that the separability of allegedly technical philosophy from questions of our outlooks on man, society, and the world—a separation which is sometimes claimed as an achievement and credit of the academic philosophy of our own century—is an absurdity. But if one took such a view, then indeed the claims made for the philosophy of the Enlightenment—that it was the first expression and powerful stimulus of the general modern outlook—collapse. What *is* true, perhaps, is that as 'pure' philosophy it is not quite in the first rank but as a *philosophy*, a way of looking at the world, it is in fact both of the utmost importance and of great merit.

Something further should perhaps briefly be said about the subsequent history of the outlook. Two fates can undermine the vitality of an idea: either success or failure. The 'materialism' of the Enlightenment has had to suffer both.

More specifically, the materialism of the Enlightenment has had comparatively little impact on Britain, and its immediate impact on Germany has been in the main to produce a reaction rather than to stimulate imitation. The failure to impress itself on Britain is still perceptible: the 'enlightened' complex of ideas does not operate as a unity within the Anglo-Saxon tradition. Its 'progressives', generally to the surprise of Continental observers, work for rational reconstruction of society on 'enlightened' lines—roughly, choosing ends by reference to human well-being and seeking guidance about the means from experience, without also being *ex officio* anticlerical. The explanation of why the complex of anticlericalism and materialism in the narrow sense did not fuse in Britain with utilitarianism, empiricism, and democracy is partly to be sought in the absence of a dominant Roman Catholic Church, and partly in the fact that the individual ideas of the Enlightenment were already present and were not imported from the *philosophes*. The land of Hobbes did not need to learn of materialism or egoism, the land of Hume did not need to learn of empiricism, nor the land of Bentham to be taught the consistent application of utilitarianism to social thinking.

But if, in the short run, the outlook of the Enlightenment either failed to impress itself on France's neighbors or produced a philosophic reaction, in the long run it provided the model or the main strand in the thinking of other societies when they in turn came to be shaken by the economic and political changes of the modern world. Fused with some later elements, with Marxist, romantic, and other ideas, the Enlightenment continued and still continues to provide the alternative world view in places where the local religious views lose their hold. This secular vision, evolved in the West when religion was being sapped from within the society, continues to be the paradigm of a secular alternative in those lands where religion is being undermined by the external impact of the West and by the emulation of it. The successors of the *philosophes* in the nineteenth century were men of the Western world[5] who turned away from their own local form of the religious *infâme* and sought salvation in mundane aims and by mundane means; their successors in our century are to be found among the agents and justifiers of modernization throughout the world. The ideas of the Enlightenment are not the only constituent in their outlook; there are also historical ideas, mystiques of the community, and other elements. Still, the notions of the Enlightenment are an indispensable ingredient.

It is not unusual to sneer at the outlook typified by *The System of Nature*, which will be examined in more detail, by saying that it expresses a religious *attitude* toward a nonreligious vision of the world. Enthusiastic rationalism of this kind is claimed to be out of date. It is not entirely clear to me why this combination—secular views held with religious fervor—should be so inferior to the alternative, the combination of religious formulas with nonreligious in-difference. It is often said that the retention of unenforced laws under-mines the respect for law as such, and it is at least possible that the respectful retention of the incredible beliefs may undermine intel-lectual curiosity and respect for truth, the drive toward understand-ing the world, without which much fundamental inquiry is unlikely to occur. The allegedly comic fervor implicit in the open adherence to a systematically secular view of the world may at least be credited with seriousness in its attempt to understand the world, and in its attempt at consistency. It may be better to inherit the all-embracing-ness and enthusiasm of faith without its content, rather than the reverse.

The system of nature

The eighteenth-century French thinkers were both numerous and prolific. A full account of the views even of those who can be characterized, in some sense or another, 'materialists of the En-lightenment', would be impossible in a limited space. It is customary and appropriate to take some writer or work as epitomizing the thought of the period. If one wished to concentrate on anticlericalism alone, without a total rejection of religious ideas, one might choose Voltaire. If one were to choose a single *work* as both typical and in-fluential, it would be appropriate, and customary, to take the co-operative *Encyclopédie*. But there would be obvious disadvantages in using a cooperative work of this kind, without the claim to con-sistency or restriction to general principles. For purposes of examin-ing a coherent, systematically expounded *philosophy*, it is best, from consideration of both merit and a kind of unity, to take Baron d'Holbach's *Le Système de la Nature*, and in particular the first of its two volumes. Its views are more radical than most of the publicly expressed views of the time; it is, however, essentially a coherent, frank, and passionate systematization of the largely shared ideas or of their logical conclusions of the most influential group of intel-lectuals of the time.

There is a sense in which *The System of Nature* can be said to *tell a story*. It is not merely a vision of the universe and man, and an exhortation, but it is a kind of dramatic presentation of a conflict of two forces: it is almost a narrative. The battle it describes is, of course, unfinished. The intention of the book is to make us see its true character, to make us understand the nature of the two contestants, and to enlist our support for good against evil and to aid its victory. We are conducted along the various points of the front line, the doc-trines of man, of knowledge, of morals, and so on.

The two forces engaged in this fundamental crucial conflict are two ways of thinking: the religious and the naturalistic (which includes materialism and empiricism). The former is both wrong and very harmful. The latter is both true and immensely beneficial to humanity.

The work consists of the delineation and demonstration of the true and beneficial view and style of thought, and of an analysis and refutation of the main features of the mistaken and harmful view. It also consists of a pathology of thought, a diagnosis of how the harmful type of thought comes to exist and have a hold on humanity; and, to a lesser extent, it also includes what may be called a rationalist theory of Grace—that is to say, an account of how the true, rationalistic, materialistic manner of thinking can be restored and establish itself amongst men. (This part of the doctrine is among its weaker aspects. So is the rationalistic doctrine of Original Sin—the attempt to account for how mistaken or meaningless and harmful doctrines have come to be so pervasive and powerful.)

The important features of the wrong and harmful type of thinking are: belief in God, in spiritual forces of any kind, in a nonmaterial element of man, in free will or any other exceptions to natural regularity, in innate ideas or any nonsensuous mode of knowledge, in the belief in divine creation or interference, and in the upholding of moral values other than those based on actual human needs and interests.

The particular object of attack is not merely the Christian, and in particular the Roman Catholic vision of the world, but also what the author considers its buttressing by 'modern' philosophers (above all, Descartes and his followers): the main dualistic doctrines to the effect that there is an independent thinking substance in addition to extended matter and that there are modes of knowing other than through the senses. In general, one might say that what is under attack is any doctrine that impugns the unity and exhaustiveness of nature—any doctrine that adds an extramundane religious realm to the totality of nature or that introduces some fundamental rift or discontinuity inside it (such as the discontinuity between matter and thought or between determined and free events).

The System of Nature is, of course, itself dualistic in its fundamental *sociology*, for it envisages two fundamental polar possibilities for man and society (though, of course, mixed, intermediate positions are possible and occur, and indeed may be the commonest fate of mankind): a state of rationalist salvation, when man, free or freed from superstition and prejudice, is guided by the trinity of nature, reason, and experience to happiness, and on the other hand the degenerate or unregenerate state when religious and spiritualistic superstition leaves man in misery under the domination of priests and tyrants. The most important social variable, so to speak, is the manner of *thought* (though this itself appears to be dependent on education and government). Materialistic, rationalistic, naturalist thought liberates man and society and leads him to happiness; religious thought leads him to error and misery.

In as far as *The System of Nature* distinguishes between the religious view proper and its more recent metaphysical supports, even if it classes them together as variants of the same basic intellectual sin, it can be seen as the anticipation of Comte's positivism and the distinction between the religious and the metaphysical stage which humanity passes through before attaining *positive* thinking.

The nature of the universe

The preface of *The System of Nature* opens with what is, in effect, the most central idea of all contained in the work: 'Man is unhappy only because he is ignorant of Nature.' The preface goes on to point out that man is so enslaved by prejudice that one might suppose him forever condemned to error. A dangerous germ has entered all his ideas and makes them unstable, obscure, and false: the pursuit of the transcendental, the desire to indulge in metaphysics rather than physics. Man despises realities in order to contemplate chimeras. He neglects experience and fails to cultivate his reason, but feeds instead on conjectures and systems; he claims to know his own fate in the imaginary regions of another life, and does not attempt to make himself happy in the world he inhabits.

In brief, the source of evil is ignorance, and ignorance is not accidental but the product of one pervasive error—extranatural beliefs and interests, and the inhibition of inquiry into nature by natural means. Hence, the author calls for a fight against religion and metaphysics in the interests of natural *knowledge* and the happiness it will bring.

One should note that this preface, which in its way sums up the book as a whole, quite unwittingly introduces a crucial ambiguity into the notion of that *Nature* which is its subject. One might have begun with a positive description of it—a unity, governed by laws, without inner repetitions, etc.—and proceeded deductively from its general features, imitating the procedure of Spinoza's *Ethics*, with whose vision *The System* has obvious affinities. But such a procedure, though orderly and logical, would obscure the fact that 'nature' here also has another meaning: namely, that which is found out by natural means, by the application of reason to experience, *whatever it turns out to be*. In other words, the main premiss of the *System* can also be seen to be an epistemological one rather than an ontological one: perhaps, one should say, the recommendation of a cognitive strategy rather than the postulation of a cosmological picture. (And more than this, the recommended epistemic strategy could itself in turn be seen as the corollary of an ethical premiss and a sociological one—of the exclusive valuation of happiness and of the conviction that it is furthered by naturalistic inquiry and hindered, above all, by religious and metaphysical conviction.)

The System, like most other systems of ideas, *can* be arranged as a deductive argument from premisses, but it is in fact more correctly represented as an interlocking system of ideas which support each other. Some of these ideas are, of course, more crucial than others, and can be singled out as premisses; but it is important to remember that they in turn can figure as conclusions inferred from other parts of the system, even if those other parts to some extent in turn depend for their proofs on them. The belief in the beneficial power of knowledge, and in the maleficent power, almost exclusively and predominantly, of ignorance, superstition, religion, and transcendentalism, is one such premiss within *The System*, and perhaps the most important.

The first chapter does in fact give us a positive description of that *Nature* which is the object of inquiry and, one might add, of reverence.

> The universe, that vast assembly of all that exists, nowhere presents us with anything but matter and movement: it displays nothing but an immense and uninterrupted chain of causes and effects: some of these causes we know because they strike our senses immediately; others we do not know, because they act on us only by effects far removed from their first causes . . . the sum total [of diverse matter, its properties and manner of acting, and the systems constituted by them] we call *nature*. . . . Thus nature, in its widest sense, is the grand total resulting from the assembly of the different materials, their combinations, and the different movements we see in the universe.

D'Holbach also uses 'nature' in a more special sense: 'Nature, in its narrower sense, or as applied to each individual being, is that which follows from its essence, that is to say, the properties, combinations, movements, and manner of acting which distinguish it from other beings.'

He thus distinguishes between *particular* natures and the general system (the *universal* nature) to which everything that exists is necessarily tied. A very significant *Nota Bene* ends the first chapter. It disclaims any interpretation that would seem to personify nature, which is an abstract being; the note explains how expressions frequently used in the book, such as 'Nature required . . .' or 'It is natural . . .' can be translated in a manner not suggesting a personified nature. It should be noted that these translations are not very convincing to a modern critical philosopher: they employ either the notion of essence or the legislative, 'compelling' idea of law of nature. So, indirectly, the reinterpretations of 'nature' offered by d'Holbach still seem tainted with the anthropomorphism that he strives to reject.

The second chapter concerns itself with movement. Movement is made central both to nature—being the agent of all the necessary changes which constitute it—and to cognition—being the only carrier of information. 'To know an object is to have felt it: to have felt it is to have been moved by it.' Two conflicts seem latent in d'Holbach's thought here, first, between his 'contact' theory of knowledge and his materialism, and secondly, between his essentialist manner of speaking (behavior seems to emanate from the essences of things) and the exclusiveness of communicated motion as the agent of change. For the emanation of all properties (including those of change) from the essences of things suggests an entelechy rather than a mechanism.

A distinction of great importance for d'Holbach is between external and internal movements. External movements are perceptible, consisting of the transfer of the whole mass of some body from one place to another. Internal movement is hidden and depends on changes in the essence, the molecular structure of a body. For his argument this type of movement is essential in helping to explain biological and psychological change and activities without recourse to some principle other than natural, deterministic movement.

D'Holbach also distinguishes between simple (one-cause) and complex (many-cause) movements. All movement is a necessary consequence of the essences and properties of things or of the causes that act on them. (One might, as indicated, suspect conflict between his Leibniz-like essentialism and his prescriptive notion of law, but interaction can also be covered by necessary laws that can be said to 'inhere', and perhaps this would be the solution adopted.) Everything in the universe is in movement; it is of the essence of nature to act. The notion of *nisus* (striving) is stressed, which is to bring harmony to the preceding thesis and the appearance of occasional rest in the world.

Movement is pervasive and inherent in nature; no impulsion external to the world is required. The supposition of creation from nothingness is but words without meanings attached to them. These notions become even more obscure if the creation is attributed to a spiritual being. Matter is sufficient. Matter and movement are facts and sufficient ones. He adds a doctrine of the diversity of substances, invoking Leibniz. Nature in its endless change is compared to a phoenix, ever reborn from its own ashes.

The third chapter expands his view of matter. What emerges again is both a sensualist view of matter—we distinguish substances by the various effects produced in us—and also a different theory only questionably compatible with the former, a specification of primary qualities called 'general and primitive': extension, mobility, divisibility, solidity, inertia. Moreover, all properties are claimed to inhere in their substances necessarily 'in the rigorous sense of the word', and yet *movement* is also said to be responsible for all change. (The problem of squaring the necessity of all truths with the existence of temporal change is not raised.) Mankind is castigated for having formed inadequate conceptions of matter in the past (that is conceptions calling for extranatural explanations of the properties of matter). An 'eternal circle' theory is put forward: the sum of existence remains the same, but everything changes.

The fourth chapter opens with some interesting observations on the psychology and logic of explanation: Men are not surprised by effects of which they know the causes (the implication being that only ignorance invokes extranatural explanations). But d'Holbach also makes the observation that men do not seek causes of effects with which they are familiar. 'It takes a Newton to feel that the fall of bodies is a phenomenon worthy of all attention.' This seems to be a sign of another latent tension in his thought, 'Is a sense of mystery, a need for further explanation, pathological or profound?' He wishes to say the former with regard to religious explanation or awe, and the latter with regard to scientific ones; but the differentiae are not adequately worked out. Natural, scientific explanations are of course, for him, those that are materialistic, monistic, and based on experience. But, one might object, their materialism and monism are not in fact things given by experience; and they are, in fact, frequently transcendent, though perhaps not anthropomorphically so. The chapter reaffirms that there can only be natural explanations.

He sketches a physics and a sociology ('*morale*') in terms of dispositions of matter and bodies in relation to each other: 'attraction and repulsion, sympathy, antipathy, affinities, and relations'. To exist is said to be the undergoing of the changes proper to some determinate essence.

Necessity is the infallible and constant connection of causes with their effects. (And, of course, it is claimed to be all-pervasive.) Man necessarily desires what is or what seems useful to his well-being, for instance. There cannot be independent energies, isolated causes (in other words, no extranatural interventions, no miracles). The examples given are, interestingly, one from physics and one from sociology—a whirlpool of dust and political convulsion.

The fifth chapter is concerned mainly with the notion of order. The real problem d'Holbach seems to face here is how to combine his orderly, deterministic view of nature, one that finds *inside* nature the explanation of all phenomena, with an avoidance of any possibility of a theistic argument from design. The main device employed for this end is the distinction between (real) order of nature, which is inherent in things, universal, and inescapable, and that which men *call* order, which is a subjective or relative notion men project onto things which have a certain conformity with their aims. This latter notion has a contrast, an antithesis, *disorder*, which men also project onto things.

This pair of contrasted notions is 'abstract and metaphysical', and corresponds to nothing outside us. (It is interesting to note that d'Holbach here considers the notion endowed with an antithesis to be metaphysical and meaningless, while the contrastless notion of order-of-nature, which covers *everything*, does, according to him, apply to reality.) Apparent disorder is (1) only apparent, (2) a transition to a new order (as in illness or death). Miracles and monsters are denied. *Chance* is but an illusion of ignorance.

Anthropocentrism and anthropomorphism are denied. It is ignorance that has led to explaining nature in terms of intelligence. But such an intelligence would require organs, etc. Intelligence is only a characteristic of organized beings. There is no need for nature (as a whole) to have it simply because it also produced it, as wine does not have the characteristics it produces in us. . . . It is but empty words and anthropomorphic inferences which lead to attribution of intelligence to the universe. (And how about the attribution of order and necessity? One might ask, is *that* not anthropomorphic? D'Holbach attributes both more and less to nature than the theists do. He *gives* it power so as to eliminate the need for extramundane interferences, and *denies* it constituents that destroy its unity and which could appear to be intrusions from some other realm. For him, explanations must be both intranatural and materialistic.)

The nature of man

The sixth chapter deals specifically with man; it explicitly sets out to apply the general ideas, which are claimed to have been established earlier, to the 'beings who interest us most'. Notwithstanding some nonfundamental differences, we shall see *man* falling under the same rules as those to which everything is subject. D'Holbach's special kind of 'essentialism', the view referred to earlier that everything has an 'essence' which *is* its special manner of acting, and the determinism associated with this are both applied to man. There is reference to the hiddenness and complexity of the human manner of acting.

This (hidden operations) is the origin of mistaken—voluntaristic, spiritualistic—views of man which are rooted in the idea that he moves himself, that he can act independently of the laws of nature. Careful examination will remove this illusion. There are two kinds of

movement, inner and outer; and in a complex machine, the inner
ones may be well hidden. Spirituality, immateriality, immortality—
those vague words—are then invented to account for hidden movements. Thus, according to religious, spiritualist theories, man becomes double—gross matter and simple pure spirit. This dualism
d'Holbach denies. But has man existed for all time? he proceeds to
ask. We don't know, but probably not. Man is tied to the particular
conditions which have produced him.

There follows an attack on dualistic theories. These are but the invention of words to hide ignorance. The dualism that most philosophers accepted in d'Holbach's time is based only on unnecessary
superstitions. Man is a material being organized to feel, think, and be
modified in a manner suitable to himself, to his organization, the
combination of substance assembled in him. And why suppose
nature sterile and incapable of creating new beings?—In other
words, why invoke external or 'spiritual' agencies to account for
them? Then follows an invocation to man: Accept your ephemeral
nature! All is change in the universe. Nature contains no constant
forms. The conclusion is that man has no reasons for supposing himself privileged (unique) in nature.

The seventh chapter continues the assault on the 'spiritualist
system' (the religious and Cartesian doctrines of the soul). It stresses
the uselessness of the gratuitous assumption of duality, of differentiation of inner and outer activity, of the notion of an imperceptible, indivisible, unextended inner stuff. This is an unintelligible and merely
negative idea. Only material causes can act. One has invented an infinite intelligence in the image of a finite one, and explained the union
of the latter with body by reference to the former, failing to see that
neither can move matter. (Here he gets close to admitting that we do
at least have an image of the finite intelligence at any rate.) But, he
asks, how and where is this extensionless body located and connected
with matter? It is through failure to respect experience and reason
that men have obscured ideas, have failed to see the soul as a part of
the body, and have created a being in the image of wind. But politically the idea is useful to theologians, for it makes the separable part
of man available to punishments and rewards. In fact, the 'soul' is the
body seen relative to certain functions.

The paradoxes of general dualism are elaborated by him: Can
God not endow matter with thought? And if not, are there then two
eternal beings? Primitives explain what they do not understand
animistically. We have done this for man and nature.

Chapter 8 proceeds to carry out the program of a unitary vision
of man by establishing the thesis that all our intellectual faculties are
derived from sensing. (We thus see that sensationalism plays a double
role in the system—a positivistic one, eliminating empirically un-

cashable ideas, and also an antidualistic one in philosophical anthropology.)

The faculty of *feeling* (in a broad sense) may seem inexplicable, but it is not different in this respect from gravity, magnetism, electricity, elasticity. He proceeds to define feeling in terms of physiological modification and to argue for the importance of the nervous system: the sensibility of the brain derives from its *arrangement*. Milk, bread, and wine become the substance of man. He repeatedly remarks on this point. (D'Holbach's materialism has its own doctrine of transubstantiation.)

Sensation is defined as the impact made on our senses; *perception* as its transmission to the brain; an *idea*, the image of the object causing the sensation. (Thus the theory is both causal and sensationalist.) This is then worked out with regard to the individual senses.

This is the only way in which we receive sensations, perceptions, ideas. These modifications produce further ones in our brain, which we call thoughts, reflections, memory, imagination, judgment, will, actions; these all have sensation as their basis. To have an accurate idea of thought, reflect on what happens in us in the presence of any object: we combine impressions. Thoughts have beginnings, ends, duration, a history like all other events; how, asks d'Holbach, can the soul be indivisible? Memory, imagination, judgment, and will are defined in conformity with this. Understanding is the capacity of apperceiving outer and inner objects. The sum of faculties is intelligence. One manner of using them is reason.

Everything is in the brain, which is sufficient to explain mental phenomena. Invoking spiritual beings of which we have no idea does not help. (Everything is thus reduced both to sensation and to brain —empiricism and materialism—thus doubly exiling spiritualism as unintelligible and as alien stuff.)

The soul is affected by events—hence it is material. (The connection of materialism with causality and intelligibility is that materialism is made to follow from possibility of explanation, as well as from possibility of experiential contact, of sensation.)

The ninth chapter begins with a reaffirmation of diversity, necessary diversity. There are no two strictly identical beings. Hence men differ: hence they are unequal, and this inequality is the basis of society. Mutual need is the consequence of inequality and diversity. Our diversity leads us to be classified according to our moral and intellectual characteristics. These are physically caused. Parentage and nurture determine us. Man's temperament is but the arrangement of his parts. Then follows another attack on dualistic spiritualism. (Not even man himself may be seen anthropomorphically. Existentialism later, and Kant at the same time, maintain dualistic, non-naturalist views of men at the price of at least partially opting out of science.)

Spiritualism makes *morals* (d'Holbach rightly uses this in a broader sense that includes the whole study of man and society) a conjectural science. Materialism, on the other hand, gives us knowledge and control. Man is alterable. The theologians will always find man a mystery, attributing his behavior to a principle of which they can have no idea. Our discoveries, in terms of the materials that enter into man's constitution, will lead us to improve him. There follows a phlogiston theory of the psyche along with an electrical theory of nervous communication. Fire and warmth are indicated as principles of life.

Science is based on truth, and truth depends on the fidelity of our senses. Truth is conformity between objects we know and the characteristics we attribute to them. It is attained by well-constituted senses with the aid of experience. How can one check on defective senses? By multiplied, diversified, repeated experiences. In brief, truth is the just and precise association of ideas. Error is faulty association of ideas. (Thus we have both a coherence and a correspondence theory of truth. The checking-by-accumulation-of-experiences is of course compatible with both.) Prediction also is based on experience and analogy. (D'Holbach does not ask how this is squared with his doctrine of necessary diversity.)

Our faculty of having and recalling experience, foreseeing effects so as to avoid harmful ones or to procure those useful to our survival and happiness (our sole aim), constitutes *reason*. (A very pragmatic and utilitarian definition—but one which is not open to a Humeian critique!) Sentiment, our nature, may mislead us, but experience and reflection lead us back to the right path. Reason is nature modified by experience, judgment, and reflection. It presupposes a moderate temperament, an *esprit juste*, a controlled imagination, knowledge of truth based on sure experience, prudence, and foresight. Thus few men are indeed rational beings! Our senses are the only means of telling the truth of opinion, the usefulness of conduct. Man's only aim is happiness and self-preservation. It is important to know the true means: his own faculties. Experience and reason show him he needs other human beings.

Moral distinctions, all manners of judging men and their actions, are based on utility and diversity, not on convention nor on the chimerical will of a supernatural being. Virtue is what is constantly useful to human beings in society. Our duties are the means that experience and reason show up to our ends. To say we are obliged is to say that without those means we shall not reach our ends.

Happiness is the state in which we wish to persist. Pleasure is transient happiness. It depends on a certain inner movement. Hence pleasure and pain are so close. Happiness cannot be the same in all men; hence moralists disagree. Ideas men form of happiness also depend on habit. Most of what men do depends on habit. A footnote illustrates this by expanding a learning theory of criminality: *'c'est le premier pas qui coûte'* ('it is the first step that counts').

We are so modified by habit that we confuse it with nature. This is the origin of the fallacious theory of innate ideas. But the physical and moral phenomena are explicable by a pure mechanism. Hobbes is quoted in support. Habit explains the almost invincible attachment of men to useless and harmful usages. (No facile refutation of the *philosophe*, as failing to see the importance and force of *habit*, is possible. He is fully aware of it—he just does not like what is contemporaneously habitual.) Education is inculcation of habit at an early age when organs are flexible. A theory of conditioning, of transmission of culture, is put forward.

Politics is in fact so vicious because it is not based on nature, experience, or general utility but on the passions, caprices, and particular utility of those who govern. To be useful, politics should operate according to nature, that is to say, it should conform to the essence and aim of society. (An empiricist essentialism?)

Men have, formally or tacitly, made a pact to help and not to harm each other. But given their pursuit of temporary and selfish caprices and passions, force is necessary, and it is called the law. As large societies cannot easily assemble, they are forced to choose citizens to whom they accord confidence. This is the origin of all government, which to be legitimate must be based on free consent of society, without which it is only violence, usurpation, brigandage. These citizens are called sovereigns, chiefs, legislators, and according to form, monarchs, magistrates, legislators. (Thus the attempt is made to derive a moral, critical theory of politics from a neutral naturalism.)

Society can revoke the power it has conferred when its interest so requires. It is the supreme authority, by the immutable law of nature which requires that the part is subordinated to the whole. Thus sovereigns are ministers, interpreters, trustees, and not absolute masters or proprietors. By a pact, be it tacit or expressed, they have bound themselves. (Thus d'Holbach has a double 'contract theory'— among citizens themselves, and between them and government.)

To be just, laws must be for the general good of society and ensure liberty (pursuit of one's happiness without harming others), property (enjoyment of the fruits of one's work and industry), and security (an enjoyment of one's person and goods under the protection of the law as long as one keeps one's pact with society). Justice or equity is essential for society's happiness; it prevents exploitation.

Rights are what is allowed by equitable laws. A society that does no good has no rights over its citizens. *'Il n'est point de patrie sans bien-être: une société sans équité ne renferme que des ennemis, une société opprimée ne contient que des oppresseurs et des esclaves.'*[6]

Through failure to know this we get absolute government, which is nothing but brigandage. A man who fears naught soon becomes evil. (*This* diagnosis of the current corruption of those in power is not in harmony with d'Holbach's optimistic prognosis, expressed elsewhere and implicit throughout, of the social behavior of Enlightened man. The political implications of d'Holbach's views inevitably fluctuate between democracy and paternalism.) Hence one must limit the power of chiefs. Also, the weight of administration is too great to rest on the shoulders of one man. Power corrupts. Sovereigns must be subject to laws and not vice versa. (Thus, in effect, we get a double diagnosis of such ills: ignorance and concentration of power. D'Holbach assumes, too easily perhaps, that the removal of the one and of the other will go together.)

Government affects the physique and morals of nations. Government affects all other social variables. *Mores* are the habitudes of people. No habit, however abominable, is without the approval of *some* nation. Some religion is found to consecrate even the most repulsive usages.

The passions of the governors are reflected in the governed. One cannot destroy passion in the hearts of men, but let us direct them toward objects useful to them and society. Let education, government, and the laws habituate and fix them within limits set by experience and reason. Nature as such makes us neither good nor evil. Man is a terrain on which weeds or useful grain can grow. Education and other environmental influences mold him.

For man to be virtuous, he should have a motive for virtue; education must give him reasonable ideas; public opinion and example must show him virtue as estimable. In fact, the reverse is the case. Man must pursue his own well-being and hence the means to it. It is useless and perhaps unjust to ask a man to respect virtue if only harm comes of it. Some savages flatten the heads of their infants, thus distorting nature. So it is with institutions. Religion leads men to seek happiness in illusions. Public opinion gives us false ideas of glory and honor.

Authority generally believes itself interested in maintaining established opinions. Prejudices and errors which it holds necessary for its maintenance are supported by force, which never reasons. Princes, puffed up by false ideas of grandeur, are surrounded by flatterers. Courts are the real centers of people's corruption. This is the real origin of moral evil. Thus all conspires to make man vicious. Habit reinforces this. Thus most men are determined for evil.

The tenth chapter attacks the doctrine of innate ideas. Our inner organ, which we call our soul, is purely material, as was shown by the manner in which it acquires ideas through impressions made by material objects on our senses, which are themselves material. All faculties we call intellectual spring from sensing. Moral qualities are explicable by laws applicable to a simple mechanism.

The ideas of Descartes and Berkeley are attacked. To justify their monstrous opinions, they tell us that ideas are the only objects of thought. But ideas are *effects*. Though it is difficult to reach the causes, can we suppose that there are none? If we have only *ideas* of material objects, how can we suppose that the causes of our ideas are immaterial? To suppose that man, without aid of outer things and objects, can have ideas of the universe is like saying a blind man could have a true idea of a picture he had never heard spoken of.

It is easy to see the origin of these errors. Forced by prejudice or fear of theology, men start from the idea of a pure spirit—and then fail to see how this can interact with body. And seeing that the soul does have ideas, they conclude that it draws them from itself.

Yet there are certain phenomena supporting these views: *dreams*. D'Holbach then gives a casual account of dreams. Dreamers are compared to waking theologians. But dreams prove the opposite from the spiritualist dogma. The soul of a dreaming man is like a drunk or delirious man.

If there were a being in the world capable of moving itself by its own energy, it would have the power to arrest or suspend movement in the universe—to be an exception to general determinism. (D'Holbach as usual fuses his determinism with an essentialism—his view that causal and other properties flow from the very nature of beings— or an essentialist mode of expression.)

The difficulty of understanding the capacities of a human soul causes attribution of incomprehensible qualities. For instance, our thought and imagination can survey the vast universe. In reality, it is only as an effect of our senses that we have ideas: it is only through modifications of our brains that we think, will, act. (Sensationalism and physical determinism are fused by him.) From this, a verification principle, in effect, of meaning, is extracted and declared to be but the inverse of Aristotle's dictum about what is found in the mind being first in the senses. If a word or an idea refers to nothing sensible, then it is meaningless.

The profound Locke has brought this principle to light, to the regret of the theologians. Others, too, have seen the absurdity of the system of innate ideas. How is it that he and they have failed to see that their principle undermines theology? But, alas, prejudice— especially of the sacred kind—is strong. Moralists should have seen the absurdity of innate moral sentiment or instinct.

D'Holbach offers an empiricist theory of geometrical and logical truth in order, again, to avoid the theory of innate ideas. He applies the denial of innate ideas to abstract ideas—goodness, beauty, order, intelligence, virtue, etc.—and offers an empiricist theory of their significance. All men's errors and disputes spring from abandoning the evidence of experience and the senses, and allowing themselves to be led by allegedly innate ideas. To think of objects that have not acted on our senses is to think of words (only), to use imagination (in a void)—for example, the word *God*. Theology, psychology (i.e. the contemporary study of a psychic stuff), and metaphysics are pure sciences of words. They infect the study of morals and politics. But men have need of truth. This consists of knowing the true relation they have to things that can influence their well-being. Those relations are known only with the aid of experience. Without experience there is no reason; without reason we are but blind men who act by chance. But how to acquire experience of ideal subjects never known or examined by our senses? How to know their effects on us? By making morals depend on these transcendental things, one makes morals arbitrary, abandoning it to the caprices of the imagination.

Men vary, but beings of the same species are roughly similar, though never identical. Here the book develops an individual relativism. No proposition, however simple, evident, and clear, can be the same in two men. (Thus, the isolation of the individual is arrived at from his 'organized-matter' nature, rather than from sensationalism.)

To ask that a man thinks like us is to ask that he be organized as we are. Men must vary. Their chimeras and religions also vary. Men kill and persecute each other for words devoid of sense. But man devoted to experience, reason and nature would only occupy himself with objects useful to his felicity. If man must have illusions, let him leave others to theirs. Thus tolerance is derived from determinism, relativism, and positivism. (But this relativism is not turned back upon d'Holbach's own position.)

The eleventh chapter discusses the doctrine of liberty. The notion of freedom (from laws of physics) it holds to be a corollary of the spiritualist view of soul. The self-origination view of ideas and of action are tied up. He goes on to remind us that the soul is but the body envisaged relatively to some functions more hidden than others, and stresses determinism. Our life follows a line decreed by nature.

Yet people believe in the notion of freedom, a notion which is a basis of religion and is allegedly required by society for responsibility. For man to be free would require that all things lose their essences (natures) for his sake (in other words, that they should not be governed by necessary laws. This shows, incidentally, that d'Holbach's terminological 'essentialism' can really be seen as a manner of affirming a determinist, law-bound view of nature, and no more). Man is determined by his pursuit of well-being and survival, and is informed by experience. The will is, as indicated, a modification in the brain which disposes to action. Thus will is ever determined. The will is, for instance, determined by thirst and water, and by the knowledge of the water being poisoned. This model, he claims, helps explain all phenomena of will.

When will is in suspension, we deliberate. To deliberate is to love and hate alternatively. We are often in balance between two motives. Our manner of thinking is necessarily determined by our manner of being. The errors of the philosophers are due to seeing will as a first cause rather than going a step further back in the inquiry.

The partisans of liberty have confused constraint with necessity. Thus man can be free of constraint without being (metaphysically) free. Saying that man is not free is not to say that he is always like a thing moved from outside. He can be moved from inside. It is only the complexity of our inner movements that obscures the truth of determinism.

Education is necessity displayed to children. Legislation is necessity displayed to members of the body politic. Morals is the necessity of relations subsisting between men, shown to reasonable men. Religion is necessity of a necessary being, or necessity shown to the ignorant and pusillanimous. The theologian and tyrant necessarily persecute truth and reason. Education is generally so bad because it is based on prejudice. When it is good, it is then unfortunately contradicted or destroyed by the evil there is in society. The great art of the moralist would be to show men and those who regulate their wills that their interests are the same, that their reciprocal happiness depends on the harmony of their passions. Religion would only be allowed if it fortified this, if indeed a lie could be of real aid to truth. It is religion and power which make men evil. This shows we must go to the roots if we wish to effect a cure. (Government and religion appear to be the roots of reform.)

Fatalism (i.e. d'Holbach's position) is the necessary, immutable eternal order of nature. The theory of liberty only springs from the fact that in some cases we see causes and in others we do not. In man, liberty is but the kind of necessity enclosed within him. He quotes in support of this, '*Volentem ducunt fata, nolentem trahunt*' ('The fates lead the willing, and drag the unwilling')—which gets very close to a theory of freedom as recognition of necessity.

The twelfth chapter examines the view that the system of fatalism is dangerous. For beings whose essence is to conserve themselves and make themselves happy, experience is indispensable; without it, there is no truth, which is, as indicated, the knowledge of the constant relations existing between man and the objects acting on him. Truth itself we desire because we hold it useful; we only fear it when we suppose it will harm us. But can truth really harm us? No, it is on its utility that its value and its rights are based. It can be disagreeable to some individuals and contrary to their interests, but it will always be useful to the human species, whose interests are never the same as those of the men who, being dupes of their passions, think it in their interest to plunge others into error. Utility is thus the touchstone of systems, of the opinions and the acts of men. It is the measure of the esteem and love we owe to truth itself: the most useful truths are also the most estimable. Those we call sterile and despise are those whose usefulness is limited to being the amusement of men who do not have ideas, manners of feeling, and needs similar to our own.

Utility is also the measure of *this* system itself. Those who know the harm done by superstition will recognize the value of opposing it by truer systems, founded on nature and experience. Only those interested in established lies will see it with horror. Those who do not perceive—or only feebly—the misery caused by theological prejudice, will see it (our system) as sterile.

Let us not be surprised by the diversity of judgments, for men's interests vary. But let us look at the system with the eyes of a disinterested man, free from prejudice and concerned for the happiness of the species. We shall then assess it more correctly. (The argument then proceeds from the premiss that control requires knowledge of true causes.)

The argument from freedom to responsibility is mentioned. But, it is claimed, we *can* impute an act even to determined beings. We can still distinguish useful from harmful acts and we cannot but approve and disapprove. Laws are made to maintain society and to prevent the associated men from harming each other. The tools of punishment are to society as drains are to a house. A utilitarian deterrent theory of punishment is expounded.

The system of fatalism would not leave crimes unpunished, but would mitigate the barbarism of punishment—which is inefficacious anyway, only wasting criminal lives (more usefully employed on forced labor) and making criminals more cruel and so on. The facility with which one deprives men of life is an index of the incapacity of legislators. The paradox of determinism is avoided by stressing that we do not have the freedom to choose to be passive. Let it not be said that man is degraded by being compared to a vegetable or a machine. A tree is a useful and agreeable object. Nature herself is a machine.

Everything is necessary. Nature distributes (what we call) order and disorder, and pleasure and pain. She provides remedies for ills. Evils are due not to wickedness but to the necessity of things—a neutral nature from which all emanates. Let us submit to necessity! And a paean to determinism follows.

The thirteenth chapter deals with the doctrine of the immortality of the soul, with the dogma of a future life, and with the fear of death. The soul grows and declines with the body—in other words, it is identical with it. Origins of 'soul', i.e., of reduplication-of-the-self theories, are discussed. The illusoriness of immortality is shown from the fact that soul is sensation, and from the notion of organism. An organized being is compared to a clock. Once broken, it cannot work. Similarly, we cannot exist without our bodies. As Bacon says, 'Men fear death as children fear darkness.' Even deep sleep gives us ideas of death. Death is sleep, the cessation of ideas. Fear of death is an aid of tyranny. But it does not frighten the wicked, only the good. The effect of religious fanaticism is that men show themselves at their worst. For the wicked also apparently go to heaven: Moses, Samuel, David, Mahomed; Saints Cyril, Athanasius, and Dominic, and other religious brigands. (A footnote points out maliciously that Berkeleyans and Malebranchists do not need Resurrection.)

The foundations of morality

The fourteenth chapter maintains that education, morals, and laws suffice to restrain men. It is not in an ideal world, but in the real world, that one must seek solutions and cures. It follows from what has been said earlier that it is education, above all things, that provides the cure. Good government has no need of lies.

Men are bad because government is bad. Society is the war of the sovereign against all, and of all against all. In a footnote d'Holbach remarks that he is not saying, like Hobbes, that the state of nature is a state of war; men are by nature neither good nor bad, but can become either.

The fifteenth chapter continues these themes: Man cannot be happy without virtue. Utility, as already said, should be the unique measure of human judgments. To be useful is to contribute to the happiness of one's fellows. This being so, let us see whether our principles are advantageous.

Happiness is sustained pleasure. For an object to please us it must be in harmony with our 'organization'. Our machine has need of continuous movement—hence the taste for (theatrical) tragedies, excitement, coffee, alcohol, spirits, executions, etc. (In a footnote he remarks that religion is the *eau-de-vie* of the people.) To be happy without interruption would require infinite forces. For d'Holbach, this follows from his view that sensations are functions of inner activities.

Interest is what each of us deems necessary to his felicity. Interest is the unique motive. Hence no one is disinterested. Sometimes we do not know enough of a man's motives to see this, or do not ourselves attach value to the same object as he does. We admire interest which results in benefice for humanity. A good man is one whose true ideas have shown him his interest in a manner leading to action that others love and approve in their own interest. This is the true basis of morality. There is nothing more chimerical than interests placed out-side nature or innate instincts. Psychological egoism is thus postu-lated. Morals would be a vain science unless it showed virtue to be in one's interest. Obligation can only be based on interest. Harmony is shown to obtain through the existence of mutual need. We need other people, require their affection, approbation, and so forth. Virtue is but the art of making oneself happy through the happiness of others. Virtue and happiness are thus connected. Virtue is essential to society, and so is interest. But in fact (that is, in our bad times) virtue is not recompensed. The explanation of this is that society corrupts, and the good man retires out of its way. (The virtue-is-recompensed view is thus altered and made to hold only in a rational society.) Yet even now there are some virtuous men.

The sixteenth chapter discusses the errors of men concerning (the nature of) their happiness and the true source of their ills, as well as the remedies that others have wished to impose on them. Happiness is only the fruit of the harmony of desire and circumstance. Power, supreme power, is useless without knowledge of how to use it for happiness. Princes and their subjects are so often unhappy only be-cause they lack knowledge. Hence, ascetic declamations—against power, riches, and pleasure—are frivolous, ineffective, and beside the point. The power of man over man must be based on the happiness that the power provides. Without it, it is usurpation. Rank and power are justifiable (only) by utility.

If we consult experience we see that the source of human ills is to be found in illusion and in sacred opinion. Ignorance of natural causes produces the belief in gods. And men have prejudices no less dangerous and harmful concerning government. They dare not demand happiness from kings. Nations adore the origin of their miseries.

We find the same blindness in the science of morals. Instead of being based on the real relations among men, it is based on imaginary ones, and on relations between man and imaginary beings. The notion of a 'supreme good' is a chimera. Diverse ills require diverse cures. Those who combat human desire have mistaken the natural state of man for a disease. Yet there are some happy men—even among the poor. The world is not, even now, so very terrible. Do not men cling to life?

The seventeenth chapter maintains that 'true ideas founded on nature' are the only remedy against human ills, and contains a re-capitulation of Part One of the work and a conclusion. It is when we cease to take experience as our guide that we fall into error. Our errors become particularly dangerous and incurable when they have the sanctions of religion. We then refuse ever to retrace our steps, and suppose that our happiness depends on closing our eyes to truth. If moralists have failed, it is because their remedies have ignored nature, reason, experience. (This is d'Holbach's Holy Trinity. Note that the second is but a systematic regard for the third, and the third is the revelation of the first, and the second and third are somehow *specially* legitimate parts of the first.)

Only passions are the real counterweights of passion. Reason, fruit of experience, is but the art of choosing what passions to listen to for our own happiness. Education and legislation is their canalizing to useful ends. Religion is the dissemination of chimeras.

Reason and morality have no hold over man unless they show him his true interest. Man is only wicked because he feels it almost always in his interest to be so. Make men more enlightened and happy and you will make them better. An equitable and vigilant government will soon fill its state with honest citizens by giving them motives for doing good. A footnote quotes Sallust: *'nemo gratuito malus est'* ('no one is bad for no reason'), and adds: *'nemo gratuito bonus'* ('no one is good for no reason'). If we seek the origin of our ignorance of morals and motives we find it in false ideas of speculation, such as the dualistic theories of man which have supposed the soul free.

The conclusion is that all human error follows from having renounced experience, the testimony of the senses, and right reason, and from having allowed oneself to be guided by frequently deceitful imagination and ever suspect authority. Man will always misunderstand his true happiness so long as he fails to study nature, learn its immutable laws, and seek only in it the remedies of the evils that follow from his present errors.

'The System of Nature', Volume II

It is impossible, in a limited space, to give the same kind of summary for the second volume of *The System of Nature* as we have of the first; and it is also less necessary. The second volume does not add to the positive picture provided by the first. It concerns itself largely with further diagnosis and refutation of theological, spiritualistic, dualistic doctrines, and with the social conditions and consequence of both truth and error. The general themes are often restated (Ch. VI).

> Nature is self-existent; she will always exist; she produces everything; contains within herself the cause of everything; her motion is a necessary consequence of her existence; without motion we could form no conception of nature; under this collective name we designate the assemblage of matter acting by virtue of its peculiar energies.

Or again, elsewhere

> The simplest observation will prove [to man] incontestably that
> everything is necessary, that all the effects he perceives are
> material; that they can only originate in causes of the same
> nature. . . . Thus [the human] mind, properly directed, will
> everywhere show [man] nothing but matter, sometimes acting
> in a manner which his organs permit him to follow, and others
> in a mode imperceptible to [our] faculties. . . . [Man] will see
> that all beings follow constant, invariable laws, by which all
> combinations are united and destroyed . . . the great whole
> remaining ever the same. Thus [he will be] cured of idle notions
> with which he was imbued . . . [and of the] imaginary systems;
> he will cheerfully consent to be ignorant of whatever his organs
> do not enable him to compass. . . .

The passages which discuss the psychological and social possibility
of atheism, and which concede that so philosophical an outlook is
unsuited (at any rate, at present) for the generality of men, are interesting as expressions of the state of mind of an enlightened intelligentsia which is confident of the truth of its vision but does not feel
that it can share it—for a long time, at any rate—with the common
run of humanity. Truth *is* salvation; but not as yet, it appears, for
everyone.

Towards the end of the second volume there are a number of
declamatory passages that well convey the spirit of the work, even if
they are stylistically atypical. Thus, the penultimate (thirteenth)
chapter contains the following *confessio fidei*, to be made by the
devotee of nature to the theologians:

> We only assure ourselves of that which we see; we yield to
> nothing but evidence; if we have a system, it is one founded
> upon facts; we perceive in ourselves, we behold everywhere else,
> nothing but matter; we therefore conclude from it that matter
> can both feel and think; we see that the motion of the universe
> is operated by mechanical laws, that the whole results from the
> properties, is the effect of the combination, the immediate
> consequence of the modification, of matter; thus we are content
> we seek no other explication of the phenomena which nature
> presents. We conceive only a unique world, in which everything
> is connected; where each effect is linked to a natural cause,
> either known or unknown, which it produces according to
> necessary laws; we affirm nothing that is not demonstrable. . . .

The final chapter repeats the doctrine of the utility of mundane
truth before giving us the celebrated 'Code of Nature', another

declamatory passage (sometimes, on stylistic grounds, attributed to Diderot). What is false cannot be useful to men, and that which ever harms them cannot be founded on truth, and should ever be proscribed. (This authoritarian Utilitarianism was not brought into harmony with d'Holbach's earlier tolerant relativism.) So it is a service to the human spirit to lead it out of the labyrinth of imagination where it cannot find certitude. Only nature, known by experience, can lead him out and give him the means that are at our feet.

But men defend their own blindness, for light hurts them; and they defend themselves against their own liberation. But the friend of nature (i.e., the enlightened man) is not the enemy of men!

Listen to nature, who says (and here follows the *Code of Nature*, which I reproduce only in very abbreviated form):

> Be happy, seek happiness, without fear. Do not resist my law.
> Vain are the hopes of religion. Free yourselves from the yoke of
> religion, my proud rival. In my empire there is freedom.
> Tyranny and slavery are ever banished from it. Follow my laws
> —human sensibility should interest you in the fate of others. Be
> just—equity is the pillar of humanity. Be a citizen—for a
> homeland is necessary for security, pleasure, well-being. In brief,
> be a man. Do not indulge in self pity or be tempted by the
> transitory pleasure of a crime. Vengeance is mine[7] [says *nature*!
> —once again reminding one of someone else]. Do not doubt my
> authority. See the miserable ones [the ambitious ones, or the
> indolent rich]. . . .

How preferable this is to the dogma of supernatural religion, which harms man, which covers itself with a cloak of utility when attacked by reason, claiming to be linked to morality while in fact it is at war with it. It is this artifice that has seduced the learned.

The morality of nature is the only morality offered by the disciples of nature. The friend of man cannot be the friend of the gods, the scourges of man. (In other words, atheism is a condition of humanism. Does it follow that the majority, unfit as yet for atheism, cannot be true 'friends of man'?)

Nature—the sovereign of all beings! And you, its adorable daughters—virtue, reason, truth! Be our sole divinities. Be man's teacher.

The final passages of the *Code of Nature*, as well as the prose that follows it just before the end of the book, have a kind of stoic rather than (or as well as) a 'progressive' ring: they invite man to accept his condition bravely without seeking spurious consolation, rather than stressing the hope of mundane salvation and improvement.

Thus the final passage of the book invokes nature to 'console thy children for [the] sorrows, to which their destiny submits them, by those pleasures which wisdom allows them to partake; teach them to be contented with their condition; to banish envy from their minds; to yield silently to necessity: conduct them without alarm to that period, which all beings must find, let them learn that time changes all things, that consequently they are made neither to avoid its scythe nor to fear its arrival. . . .'

This type of stoicism is perhaps a more logical corollary of the worship of nature—seen as an all-embracing and exhaustive, self-sufficient, and necessary unity—than the 'progressive', happiness-through-enlightenment-and-secularism outlook that is more generally characteristic of *The System*. (Indeed, in earlier periods, an ethic of acceptance had been characteristically associated with the kind of vision of nature preached by *The System*.)

In these final passages of the book, the emergence of such an alternative moral outlook alongside the main, progressivist, Enlightenment one, can perhaps be seen partly as a survival and/or as a perception of the consistent moral implications of the general vision, but mainly it can be seen, no doubt, as a defense against an expected counter-attack by the adherents of religion—a counter-move which would attempt to seduce man into illusory consolations by stressing his mundane ills and mortality.

Conclusion

In essence, *The System of Nature* is a recipe for salvation: the progressive, secular salvation of man through understanding and acceptance of a unitary and physical nature of which he is a part, and a part like any other; a salvation by positive knowledge. Fused with this progressive panacea, as a kind of minor supporting theme, there is also an older recipe, salvation by acceptance, the avoidance of false hopes.

The two are fused in that they both militate against religious, dualistic, anthropocentric or anthropomorphic views of the world. *The System* is, of course, not merely the recommendation of a positive remedy, it is also the diagnosis of the disease: the source of all human ills is ignorance and false and meaningless beliefs, religion and nonmaterialist doctrines in general.

In elaborating this simple vision, *The System* formulates, as indicated at the beginning, many if not all of the themes that have become familiar and have been elaborated in modern thought. For instance, the verification theory of meaning, the behaviorist analysis of mind, the view that religious assertions are meaningless, that religion is an intoxicant of the people, and many others are found clearly stated. Moreover, the manner in which these ideas, which individually may not be original, are made interdependent has a characteristic modern ring.

The System does not really deal adequately with the problems that his modern outlook has to face. For instance, at its root there are two premises that are used alternatively and which are perhaps not consistent: *materialism* in a narrow sense—the all-exhaustiveness of matter, a theory about the world—and *empiricism*, the view that all knowledge and indeed all psychic life is based on sensation, a theory about cognition and about mind. Both ideas are used as sticks with which to beat religion and metaphysics, but their mutual compatibility is not explored sufficiently. As formal philosophy, this fails to reach the level of Hume or Kant. The compulsive insight of materialism—that what exists must exist in space and occupy a part of it, and that all else can only be an aspect of it—is made use of, but it is preached rather than critically explored.

This might be expressed by saying that no harmony is brought about between the paradigm of *explanation*—in terms of structure of matter—and of *information*—in terms of sensing (though sensing is defined in part in terms of impact, modification, etc., the activity of thought, and hence of explanation, is in turn derived from sensing).

There are other (to us) obvious conflicts within the system— between its determinism and call to arms and its hope of human liberation by human effort. One might say that both its theory of Grace and its doctrine of Original Sin are weak: it does not succeed in explaining how, in a determined universe, men will free themselves from the religion and tyranny that have poisoned their lives; nor does it convincingly explain how, in a world in which truth (materialistic truth), virtue, usefulness, and happiness are so closely connected in the very nature of things, the unspeakable and pervasive evils of spiritualistic doctrines could have gained the hold over man that they appear to have. It is, of course, easy to analyze the outlook of *The System* as an all-embracing religion turned inside out; it is also, I think, correct. But this, as such, is not something of which the author or authors need be ashamed—nor would they have been. It is indeed, in a sense a 'religion'; but that by itself does not prove it to be a false one.

The System has other weaknesses still: not only does it oversimplify the roots both of evils and of salvation, but it naïvely overestimates the prospects of human harmony and reasonableness once the chains of superstition have been removed. There are in it, mixed up with its anticipations, some views that now seem, or are, archaic, such as an empiricist theory of mathematical truth, the phylogistic theory of psychology, and the doctrine of the qualitative differentiation of all objects. (This is used only as a premiss for relativism, and *not*, as some others have used it, as a premiss for the impossibility of scientific understanding of the world.) There is, again, a curious gap between its positivistic and deterministic scientific program on the one hand, and, on the other, its essentially normative, prescriptive, evaluative sociology. (Its statements about man and society hover uncomfortably between analysis and prescription.) There is a tension between the democratic-liberal and the progressive-paternalistic implications of its politics.

There are other conflicts still: Between the empiricism on the one hand and the determinism and the essentialist manner of speaking on the other; between the doctrine of the irreducible diversity of things and the doctrine of the intelligibility of nature; between its relativism and the absoluteness with which its own central doctrines are maintained. There is a conflict between the optimistic view that truth is not only useful but also manifest, and the more pessimistic view that the truth is not something acceptable to humanity at large, in view of the tyrannical power of habit. This conflict between Enlightened truth and the power of antiquated popular custom perhaps brings out most clearly how the men of the Enlightenment were the prototypes of later, similarly alienated intelligentsias throughout the world. Professor Réné Hubert, in his excellent *D'Holbach et ses Amis*, remarks at the end (Paris 1928, p. 99) that the diffusion of d'Holbach's views has endowed France with its dogmatic village atheists. Perhaps so. But a more important consequence of the diffusion of those views has been the endowment with them of a wider world, the 'men of two worlds'; the men who bring a new Enlightenment, fashioned in large part from the ingredients present in *The System*, with which they attempt to reform and reeducate populations whose ingrained and habitual beliefs are of the kind which *The System* combated.

1964

Notes

1 This is similar to the division into tough- and tender-minded suggested by William James, whose dichotomy in fact seems to owe something to the contrast described here.
2 For instance, they receive no discussion in Bertrand Russell's *History of Western Philosophy*.
3 For instance, the political history of the twentieth century makes it less tempting to suppose that when freed from transcendental religious prejudices, men will thereafter co-operate rationally and harmoniously in the interests of general human happiness.
4 It would of course be incorrect to say that it was only the passage of time that brought the conflict to light. In eighteenth-century *British* thought, the awareness of the conflict was

crystal-clear and central: No one could accuse the tradition of Berkeley and Hume of being oblivious of it. The fact that British eighteenth-century thinkers could devote themselves to clarifying this issue and working out its implications is presumably connected with the fact that they did not have to be concerned with combating Roman Catholicism.
5 Including its marginal lands.
6 'There is no nation without well-being: a society without equity includes only enemies, an oppressed society contains only oppressors and slaves.'
7 'Car, ne t'y trompe pas, c'est moi qui punis, plus sûrement que les Dieux, tous les crimes de la terre; le méchant peut échapper, aux lois des hommes, jamais il n'échappe aux miennes.'

Part four   Philosophy in particular

Chapter 11

Thought and time, or the reluctant relativist

R. G. Collingwood (1889–1943) did not much care for seeing the label 'Idealist' attached to himself. Commenting on the reception of his *Speculum Mentis* (1924), he observes in *An Autobiography* (1939) 'any one who had been intelligent enough to see what I was trying to say would have realized, had he not been grossly ignorant, that it was neither "usual" nor "idealistic".'

In an interesting recent collection of essays on Collingwood,[1] Professor Alan Donagan castigates this repudiation of Idealism as 'fantasy' on Collingwood's part. But whether or not Collingwood welcomed or deserved the characterization 'idealist', be he 'usual' or exceptional, he displayed no reticence whatever in making clear his feelings about realism and realists:

Realism . . . the undischarged bankrupt of modern philosophy. . . .

The tailless fox preached taillessness. I have already said of 'realism' that its positive doctrine was nugatory. . . .

The 'realists' discredited themselves with their pupils before their lessons could take effect. This self-stultification was a gradual and piecemeal business.

The 'realists' . . . destroyed everything in the way of positive doctrine they had ever possessed. Once more, I am concerned only with the effect on their pupils. It was . . . to convince them that philosophy was a silly and trifling game, and to give them a lifelong contempt for the subject. . . .

The fox was tailless, and he knew it. But this mental kind of decaudation, when people part with their morals, their religion, the learning they acquired at school, and so forth, is commonly regarded by the tailless as an improvement in their condition; and so it was with the 'realists'. . . . They were proud to have

excogitated a philosophy so pure from the sordid taint of
utility that they could lay their hands on their hearts and say it
was no use at all. . . .

The men who best understood the ideas of the original 'realists',
and tried hardest to remain loyal to them, . . . stumbled from
one temporary and patchwork philosophy to another in a kind
of intellectual nightmare.

All these splendid passages of denunciation are taken from
An Autobiography. Collingwood's autobiography has been accused[2]
of being a falsification of history:

The first obstacle to understanding Collingwood's later
philosophy is his own narrative of its development, which
beyond doubt is untrue. Collingwood's narrative . . . affords
melancholy evidence of the power of an intellectual temptation
he had himself exposed. . . .

Be that as it may, Collingwood's attitude to realism at any rate was
long-standing and consistent. Donagan's book-length study refers to
it as his 'King Charles' head'. Already in *Speculum Mentis*, Collingwood wrote (p. 281) 'realism itself is as old as thought, being in fact
identical with dogmatism or error in general. . . .' His comments on it
in his *An Essay on Metaphysics*[3] are no less brutal: 'This theory of
knowledge is called "realism"; and "realism" is based upon the
grandest foundation a philosophy can have, namely human stupidity.' He goes on to observe that realism may offer a tolerable account
of 'the lowest type of low-grade thinking' in which 'thinking almost
at zero-level efficiency, we say "That is a clothes-line" "What I am
looking at is my hand" . . .'. The allusion here is obvious to anyone
familiar with the folklore of contemporary philosophy. The story of
G. E. Moore 'establishing' the reality of the external world by looking at his own two hands and noting that at least two material objects
exist, occupies a place in the mind of the apprentice philosopher
comparable to that which, say, Alfred and the cakes holds in the
nursery.

This realist account of low-grade, routinized thought, 'so casual
and haphazard . . . that [it] is hardly thinking at all', could be
tolerated, Collingwood observed in *An Essay on Metaphysics*:

if this were all it professed to be: a study of the way in which
anchors get foul, the twists in their cables . . . in calm weather
and at neap tides an anchor in that condition may actually hold
the ship. . . . [But] a whole library of books about foul anchors

will not replace one page of Descartes or Kant, who knew well enough that anchors get foul, but cared enough about making them hang the right way up, so that even in a tideway or a gale the ship would be safe.

This is indeed the crux: the theory of knowledge is about the recovery of confidence in gales and tideways, not about the slipshod methods used, or corrected, in calm weather and neap tides. The realists liked to indulge their theorizing about knowledge with the help of examples drawn from low-grade thinking, 'so casual and haphazard . . . that [we are] hardly thinking at all', and they like to treat this condition as the paradigm of our cognitive experience. Sir Karl Popper has often made the same point—trivial knowledge makes bad epistemology. This helps to explain why Collingwood should have felt so strongly about the realists: their theory of knowledge expressed a complacency about our cognitive predicament which is an insulting travesty of the real situation. The trivial cases are taken to be paradigmatic. Collingwood, from his historical knowledge, his practice of the historian's craft, and his human experience, knew full well that this was indeed a dreadful travesty, and hence chose not to restrain the expression of his contempt.

Yet the general reader may still feel surprised that so much passionate feeling should be aroused by the holders of—what?—a technical opinion in the theory of knowledge? Is it decorous that there should be so much anger and denunciation in the cloisters? Why can't they debate these technicalities in a quiet and decorous manner? And who are these realists, that they should be so vehemently denounced?

Their central doctrine, Collingwood tells us, is that 'knowing makes no difference to what is known'. One objection he had against this view was that it expressed a howler:

Any one who claimed . . . to be sure of this, was in effect claiming to know what he was simultaneously defining as unknown. For if you know that no difference is made to a thing θ by the presence or absence of a certain condition c, you know what θ is like with c, and also what θ is like without c, and on comparing the two find no difference. This involves knowing what θ is like without c; in the present case, knowing what you defined as the unknown (*Autobiography*, ch. VI).

Philosophical errors of importance are seldom pure howlers. The complacency, the insensitivity to our cognitive precariousness, and to the intellectual transformations which took place in recent centuries, which underlie the whole 'realist' attitude, are more important than the technical error (if such it is) which expresses that attitude. The realist is indeed a man who compares his own ideas with his own ideas and finds, to his satisfaction but without surprise, that they tally. What drives him to the contradiction noted by Collingwood is his prior lack of serious doubt, his unwillingness even to suppose himself radically and pervasively mistaken, indeed his outrage at such an offensive suggestion, at any impugning of his own cognitive status. He is blissfully free of anxiety on this score. Much of recent philosophy starts from this most un-Cartesian state of mind, the outrage at the solecism of even being placed under suspicion of fundamental error. What—*we* be mistaken? Whoever heard of such nonsense! This excessive self-confidence is not a very healthy starting-point.

On formal grounds, it is possible to defend those who perpetrated the alleged howler. Donagan attempts it in his book, claiming that 'the reasons . . . [given] for the proposition that "what is known exists independently of being known" . . . were not empirical. [The realist] did not claim to have compared the state of any object as known with its state as unknown'. Indeed not. Collingwood did not suppose that they had claimed anything of the kind. People on the whole do not consciously, openly, knowingly propound self-contradictions, or articulate them in a manner which would highlight their self-contradictoriness. Collingwood merely pointed out that any doctrine which claims that two things are identical, presupposes some measure of information about the two things, and that the realists had defined one of the two things in a way which precludes our possession of such information. Talking about the difference between knowing and seeing, as Donagan does, does not overcome the difficulty. Donagan is more persuasive when he invokes the realist's conviction that 'knowledge is essentially discovery, or the finding of what already is'.

Quite so. It would hardly be 'knowledge' if we just made it up. There must be something extraneous, not under the control of the explorer himself, if he is to be credited with *discovery*. This is an overwhelmingly important point; this is the idea which underlies the weightiest consideration on the realist's side, and it remains to be seen whether it can be made compatible with Collingwood's insights.

This issue is central. Donagan makes an illuminating observation in *Critical Essays*, in connection with Collingwood's early work: 'Just as logical positivism is grasped most clearly as the rejection of metaphysics as the logical positivists understood it, so the idealism of *Speculum Mentis* is best approached through its negation—realism as Collingwood understood it' (p. 8).

Yes, indeed, and the observation really applies to the whole of Collingwood's work. But what is so terrible about realism, that it should provoke both his anger and such strenuous efforts at constructing an alternative? Let us leave aside the question of that logical howler. Whether they did or did not commit it will depend on what they 'really' meant when they asserted the formula about that which is known being independent of the fact that it is known, and how we interpret them—whether favourably to them or to Collingwood—will depend, I suspect, on our appreciation of his other griefs against them. They were complacent; they concentrated on dead, routinized, unproblematical instances of 'knowledge', rather than dramatic, innovative, difficult, doubt-haunted ones; hence their image of knowledge is dreadfully static and in the end passive, the co-presence of 'mind' and its 'object'; hence it ignores or underestimates all the active, questing, questioning aspects of knowledge, and the manner in which this active and questioning aspect depends on the shared intellectual stock of the thinker's culture, society or period, a stock which may in large part be opaque to him; and hence, in this crescendo of related sins, they are insensitive to history.

Thus there is an intimate connection between Collingwood's detestation of realism (which he combated with the help of ideas and terms borrowed from the Idealist tradition), and the fact that he was one of the very few academic philosophers of his general background to take history seriously. (Professor Bryce Gallie is another such.) And he has a genuine point when he equates a specific philosophy, realism, with human stupidity and dogmatism in general. Realism is in the end a blindness to the manner in which one's own mental activity and conceptual equipment contribute to one's view of things, and hence of the way in which that background may be historically specific and problematical. The realist has an unshakeable conviction that things must be as they seem *to him*, and that to doubt this must be pathological—and of late, he has possessed philosophical premises which enabled him to say just this, in so many words. Realism differs from ordinary flatfooted complacency only by being elevated into an overt system, with the help of formulae such as that 'the known is not affected by being known'. . . .

So Collingwood has a point when he equates realism with human stupidity as such. But, apart from Nature's Own Realists, who cannot bear to see their own cognitive status questioned, there occasionally arise rather more specific reasons for being attracted by the realist vision. Collingwood was aware of these, and was also capable of speaking of individual realists with respect, whatever he felt about the species as a whole): 'One of them, Bertrand Russell, a gifted and accomplished writer, has left records of his successive attempts at a philosophy. . . .' Collingwood saw with great clarity just what specific ideas lay behind certain forms of realism which were influential early in the century (*Autobiography*, ch. V):

> Here I parted company with what I called propositional logic. . . . According to propositional logic . . . truth or falsehood . . . belongs to propositions as such. . . .
>
> It seemed to me that this doctrine was a mistake due to the early partnership between logic and grammar. The logician's proposition seemed to me a kind of ghostly double of the grammarian's sentence. . . .
>
> This attempt to correlate the logical proposition with the grammatical indicative sentence has never been altogether satisfactory. There have always been people who saw that the true 'unit of thought' was not the proposition but something more complex in which the proposition serves as answer to a question.

And in a really devastating footnote, he goes on to say:

> Hence that numerous and frightful offspring of propositional logic out of illiteracy, the various attempts at a 'logical language', beginning with the pedantry of the text-books about 'reducing a proposition to logical form', and ending, for the present, in the typographical jargon of *Principia Mathematica*.

What is fascinating about these passages is that they contain, in a lucid, forceful, elegant, and succinct form, whatever is valid in Wittgenstein's 'later' philosophy, in his onslaught on the 'logical atomism' (in effect—propositional atomism) of his own and Russell's youth, on the belief that the World is obliged, in the interest of making itself intelligible to us, to construct itself in the image of the notation of *Principia Mathematica*, so that the secret of the universe is in the keeping of the type-setters of the Cambridge University Press.

It is important to note that, whatever accusations are made against Collingwood to the effect that he re-wrote history in his autobiography, this central insight, the rejection of 'propositional logic' and its replacement by a logic of question and answer, was demonstrably present in his thought from the very start, as was his hatred of realism which is so intimately linked with it. *Speculum Mentis* already contains a section entitled 'Knowledge as Question and Answer', and in it we can read:

> A crude empiricism imagines that knowledge is composed wholly of assertion. . . . Knowledge as a past fact, as something dead and done with . . . does consist of assertion, and those who

treat it as an affair of encyclopaedias and text-books may be forgiven for thinking it is assertion and nothing else. But those who look upon it as an affair of discovery and exploration have never fallen into that error. People who are acquainted with knowledge at first hand have always known that assertions are only answers to questions.

The rejection of the philosophical assumptions of propositional logic is central to Collingwood, as it is to the 'later' Wittgenstein. In *Critical Essays*, Professor W. H. Walsh notes some aspects of the similarity (ch. VII):

> [Collingwood] . . . arrived at something like the Wittgensteinian conception of autonomous language-games. . . . He differed from Wittgenstein in thinking that individual games were constantly changing their rules. . . . But his position in other respects was surprisingly similar to the one Wittgenstein was developing. . . .
> Like Wittgenstein, the later Collingwood thought that philosophy cannot judge or explain; at bottom it can only describe. But we may well wonder if Collingwood lived up to his own professions in this matter. . . .

Very much to his credit, Collingwood did not live up to his professions in this matter, and did not resign himself to relativism and merely 'describing'. If Collingwood and the later Wittgenstein shared an insight about the inadequacy of propositional logic and the passive view of knowledge, the most interesting way of comparing them will be by seeing how they cope with the corresponding problem, the realist insight that knowledge must be *of* something that is independent of the knower or of his conceptual system, in other words that *relativism won't do*.

But the historical question which now also imposes itself is this: if the emphatic denial of the grammar/logic/thought parallelism was already available, vigorously expressed, in Collingwood, as was the alternative to it, the view that thought is a concrete activity dependent on a historically specific framework (a system of questions and answers, or a 'language game' that is a part of a 'form of life', as you prefer)—then *why* did philosophers need to wait for Godot/Wittgenstein, when it was all already available in Collingwood? Why?

The answer to this question will become manifest if we compare the two thinkers in more detail, and in particular at the way they handle or fail to handle the issue of realism, of external checks on knowledge.

At one or two minor points, the comparison of the two thinkers goes in Wittgenstein's favour. First, Collingwood's manner of formulating an alternative to 'propositional logic' has certain dangers: those who are deeply wedded to the implicit Platonism of propositional logic, and its timeless, ahistorical entities, may be tempted by Collingwood's 'logic of question and answer', not to replace it, but to *expand* it. The population of the Platonic realm will then grow beyond mere 'propositions', being augmented by further inhabitants called 'questions', and 'presuppositions', including a special aristocratic élite known as 'absolute presuppositions', who, it seems, can do no wrong, are accountable to no one, and are beyond the reach of any laws. . . .

Second, Collingwood's stylistic *élan* and panache rather carried him away: when explaining the logic of question and answer, he gives the impression of describing terribly neat and elegant pyramidal structures, in which propositions, questions and presuppositions sweep up towards the sky, with 'absolute presuppositions' in the place of the highest spires. . . . The logical edifices which we actually inhabit are most unlikely to be quite as neat and elegant as this, or if they are, Collingwood has certainly failed to show that it is so. Moreover, the implicit suggestion that all these systems of question-and-answer have a similar structure seems to reproduce, in new form, one of the fallacies built into the old 'propositional logic'—namely, that when men think, they are always doing roughly the same kind of thing. By contrast, it is a merit of Wittgenstein's notion of 'language games' that he insists on their most varied and, often, very humble nature. If some of them resemble cathedrals, others are like hovels.

But in more important ways, the comparison is favourable to Collingwood. The really crucial issue is the handling of the one central insight of realism—that belief systems ought not to be, and sometimes indeed escape being, judges in their own case, that what makes *some* of them genuinely cognitive is that they stand in relation to something other than themselves. It is not so much, as the realists would have it, that the known is unaffected by being known, as that the knower is not always autistic. The task facing the theory of knowledge is to combine the idealist insight, concerning the active, context-bound, historically specific nature of mind, with the realist awareness of the non-autistic nature of genuine knowledge. Neither of the two thinkers in any way solves this problem and reconciles the two insights: but it is enormously to Collingwood's credit that he continued to be tormented by it, whilst Wittgenstein's failure lies in his easy willingness to accept the collective-subjectivism inherent in his view that 'forms of life' are ultimate, and cannot be accountable to anything. He was all too willing to exchange his earlier view that thought was subject to the constraints of propositional entities, in the keeping of the type-setters of the Cambridge University Press, for a new view which confers ultimate cognitive sovereignty on each culture and its linguistic custom, without any further checks or constraints whatsoever.

Collingwood, as the contributors to *Critical Essays* and in particular Professor Stephen Toulmin remind us, continued to struggle with this. He knew that constellations of absolute presuppositions replace each other in history, that this is the very life of thought, and that this is what philosophy is about. He would never have accepted the option mentioned by the editor, Professor Michael Krausz, in his own contribution to the *Essays*, p. 222): 'the historian of ideas could account for such change only in non-rational terms [e.g. economical or sociological]'. Collingwood was acutely sensitive to the fact that these fundamental conceptual changes were to an important extent intellectually endogenous. This is what makes history interesting. But at the same time, he had defined absolute presuppositions as absolute and logically terminal. If such, there is an obvious contradiction—ironically similar to the one for which he blames the realists —in *also* explaining in any rational way the self-transformations of those presuppositions; *rational* explanation of such change involves an appeal to some more ultimate criteria of rationality. . . . If the realists implicitly claimed to know that which they had defined as the unknown, so Collingwood found himself driven to seek *reasons* for changes in those very ideas which, on his own definition, stood at the very end of and beyond the regress of reasons. . . .

Facing this dilemma, Collingwood falls back, as Toulmin reminds us in *Critical Essays* (ch. X), on metaphor (*Essay on Metaphysics*, ch. VII):

> The essential thing about historical 'phases' is that each of them
> gives place to another; not because one is violently destroyed
> by alien forces impinging . . . from without . . . but because each
> of them while it lives is working at turning itself into the next.
> . . . . The metaphysician's business, therefore . . . is . . . also to
> find out on what occasions and by what processes one of them
> has turned into another. . . .
> The dynamics of history are not yet completely understood
> when it is grasped that each phase is converted into the next by
> a process of change. . . . One phase changes into another
> because the first phase was in unstable equilibrium and had in
> itself the seeds of change, and indeed of that change. Its fabric
> was not at rest; it was always under strain.

Collingwood could hardly pretend that he had thus overcome the dilemma between intellectually endogenous and hence somehow rational change ('seeds' which determine not merely *that* change must come, but *the* specific change which is to come, as the above quotation makes plain), and on the other hand the logical ultimacy of 'absolute presuppositions'. But he did not pretend that the problem does not arise. By contrast, 'forms of life' or 'language games' really were claimed by Wittgenstein to be ultimate. And there was a most curious double strategy in making them appear so. The rules of language games were final because they were ultimate, because there was nothing which could stand beyond them either to validate them or to place them under strain; *and*, at the same time, they were also binding because they were humble, trivial. Games will be games.

George Santayana observed somewhere that our nationality is like our relations with women—far too implicated in our moral nature to be changed honourably, and far too accidental to be worth changing. This corresponds exactly to the Wittgensteinian double basis for the legitimation of the hold which conceptual custom has over us: the rules of language are far too implicated in our whole way of life to be changeable without deep disruption, and at the same time they are far too contingent to deserve reform. They bind us because they are oh so ultimate *and* because they are ever so trite and ordinary. They are too ultimate to be changed and too optional to be worth changing. This is the double vindication: they stand both beyond and beneath the compliment of rational opposition. . . . Santayana was being half facetious: Wittgenstein, alas, was not. But concepts at any rate are a serious matter. Loyalty to ideas cannot be justified as Santayana justifies loyalty to women—that they are not worth swapping because it doesn't make much odds anyway. *Outlooks* we are sometimes *obliged* to change, and for rational reasons. Collingwood, professionally concerned with the profound conceptual revolutions which make up western history, knew this full well. Wittgenstein was ignorant of it, because he equated all philosophy with the appeal of what Collingwood called 'propositional logic', and with the overcoming of that appeal. As Professor Norman Malcolm reports:[4] 'Wittgenstein . . . told me once that . . . in the *Tractatus* he had provided a perfected account of a view that is the *only* alternative to the viewpoint of his later work.' In other words, where Collingwood equated philosophy with the history of human ideas, Wittgenstein equated it with his own personal development.

Through this difference in the way they faced their biggest problem, we can now answer the intriguing question of why Collingwood did not receive the full recognition which was his due. The ideas which were acclaimed two or three decades ago as a great revelation —the rejection of propositional logic, of the grammar/thought parallelism, and their replacement by an active, context-sensitive theory of thought—could *also* be found in Collingwood, in a form which was both earlier and expressed in clearer and more vigorous prose. Why then did he not receive credit for it?

In *Critical Essays*, Toulmin propounds some interesting but basically extraneous reasons for why Collingwood should have been under-estimated in his final years. But the main, most interesting and ironic reason, which is also internal to his ideas rather than related to his personal situation, escapes Toulmin. Where Collingwood's thought contradicted the spirit as well as the letter of the realists, Wittgenstein *perpetuated* their spirit. In a cock-eyed sense, Wittgenstein's achievement was quite remarkable—the serving of realist ends by idealist means.

It is not surprising that the old realists were blind to history. If knowledge is the co-presence of 'mind' and its object, well then the historic dating of the first occasion of each such blissful encounter is quite external to the inner meaning of the encounter itself. Thus realism naturally leads to ahistorism. But if one holds the 'active' theory of mind (presented here as the 'use' theory of meaning, in contrast to the 'echo' theory presupposed by realists), and a contextual theory of concepts (each tied to its 'language game', a term which conveys both the idea of system and that of activity), then, one should have supposed, one would naturally be led to an interest in the concrete historic incarnations of 'forms of life' and 'language games'.

But, oddly enough, this was not to be. Through the quite mistaken doctrine that the *only* thing which leads people to seek extraneous validation for the ideas of their 'form of life' (i.e. to escape relativism), was that one error about grammar/thought parallelism enshrined in 'propositional logic', Wittgenstein was led to the facile, doubly-based vindication of all and any 'form of life'. Overcome the illusions of propositional logic, under competent guidance of course, and you will find yourself happy and content in your own 'form of life'. . . .

It was *thus* that his philosophy could serve so admirably all the requirements of the realist spirit—cognitive complacency, blindness to history and change, ethical smugness. The slogan that philosophy leaves everything as it is replaces the one about the thing known being unaffected by knowledge, and the two slogans fulfil *perfectly* analogous roles in generating or confirming the curious realist ontology—the view that everything in the world is much as the realist always thought it was. One might suppose, superficially, that the slogan about *philosophy* leaving everything 'as it is', might be a bit narrower in its application than the view that *knowledge* does not tamper with its objects. But no: the operational force of the slogan about philosophy is that any counter-commonsensical view is *ipso facto* both philosophical and mistaken, and by this curious *via negativa*, all commonsensical views are automatically vindicated at one remove, through the elimination of their rivals.

So the realists are alive and well and kicking, trading under a new name and from new premises. Their views on the irrelevance of thought to concrete choices, ensuring that their philosophy was and is 'so pure from the sordid taint of utility that they could lay their hands on their hearts and say it was no use at all' spring not merely from the general realist compulsive instinct that thought must not have the power to reform anything, but also more specifically from the work conditions of the don: it would be a dreadful solecism for a philosophy teacher to say to his pupil, 'the proofs of the existence of God are valid, so you'd better attend chapel', or equally to say, 'they are invalid, don't bother to attend'. The separation of roles which, for historically specific reasons, obtains here and now, is perceived by these thinkers as a universal logical intuition. Collingwood reports asking himself about 1920: 'Why is it that nowadays no Oxford man, unless he is about 70 years old or else a teacher of philosophy . . . regards philosophy as anything but a futile parlour game?' Things have changed: there is little need now to put in that qualification about men of seventy and teachers.

Still, it was a *tour de force* of a kind to bring about the realist ends by idealist means. It could only be done if the relativism remained unqualified: for it was the relativist endorsement of all cultural outlooks as such which now did the job of realism, of reassuring the temperamental realist that whatever he had believed was indeed so. But this was precisely the message. 'Philosophy leaves everything as it is' —i.e. things are the way you thought they were, before you started worrying about it.

By contrast, Collingwood, though also in full possession of the premises rejecting 'propositional logic', disqualified himself from performing this service of re-endorsing realist expectations, simply because his flirtation with relativism was open and explicit, tormented and incomplete, and highlighted rather than obscured the problems of relativism. His thought was rooted in history, rather than systematically blind to historic diversity and the problems it raises. Collingwood also never stooped to use the double vindication, from both ultimacy and triviality; he did use the argument from ultimacy, but was so honest in his use of it that he had great trouble with it, being driven, as we saw, into the metaphorical language of 'strain' and 'seeds of change', when he had to explain how presuppositions which were, each of them, logically ultimate, nevertheless *also* had logical links with each other. . . . So with him, the problems of relativism remained undisguised. On the contrary, they were highlighted.

It was quite different with Wittgenstein. His relativism, and above all its difficulties, were largely camouflaged, by its negative formulation (it concentrated on the removal of supposed obstacles to the acceptance of any given local 'common sense', rather than on a direct positive vindication of it); by its rapid alternation between the argument from ultimacy and the argument from triviality (we *could* speak differently if we so chose, but why bother?); and by its total lack of concrete historical identification of those allegedly ultimate 'forms of life' which were such a central idea for it (preferring instead to use *ad hoc* imaginary tribes, or fragments drawn from ordinary speech, which of course leaves unanswered the question concerning the identity and limits of the 'form of life' from which those fragments are drawn). Being so half-camouflaged and formal, his relativism was not pressed to face the problems of relativism, and it made no attempt to face them. Thus it remained both serene and unqualified, and delivered the realist goods at a minimal cost in worry or anxiety—and cheap at the price it was.[5]

In *Critical Essays*, there is no consensus about Collingwood's relativism. Walsh thinks he should have been a relativist, but did not live up to his professions in this respect. Toulmin refers to 'Collingwood's ultimate relativism', but also notes that 'Collingwood never took the final step, of replacing "reasons" by "causes" completely'. Professor Nathan Rotenstreich refers to 'Collingwood's ... confessed historicism', and does not think he can escape from the well-known paradoxes which follow if relativism is applied to itself. Krausz on the other hand thinks that Collingwood *could* escape the pitfalls of irrationalist relativism, if only he adopted certain modifications proposed by Krausz himself. Professor Errol E. Harris, whilst he concedes that in the *Essay on Metaphysics* 'Collingwood ... at least appears to be advocating a relativistic type of historicism'—it would indeed be hard to deny this—wishes none the less to clear him of this charge on the grounds that it 'is not typical of his philosophy at its best'. This would seem a somewhat circular principle of exegesis. Harris would have Collingwood be an idealist first, and a relativist on the surface only. Could one not claim the opposite? Had he ever found his apparent erstwhile escapes from the relativist predicament through Idealism really satisfying, might he not have mentioned this in the *Autobiography*, if only with a sigh of regret? He did not hesitate to record in it the defects of Idealist logic. Was it really only the abuse of a reviewer, as Donagan suggests, which by the 1930s led him to resent the label 'Idealist'?

Harris, like his predecessor Professor Sir Malcolm Knox, values Collingwood the idealist above Collingwood the relativist. Donagan would fuse the two into a man awaiting salvation from religion (see pp. 15–18 of his book). But where Knox blamed Collingwood's later relativism on his illness, Harris, in truly idealist spirit, blames what he alleges is a mere *appearance* of relativism on the interpreters, on their failure to see Collingwood's later thought in its full context, on being misled by looking at the part not the whole. It is amusing to see these members of an Idealist pressgang trying firmly if kindly to take Collingwood by the scruff of his neck and frogmarch him back to the Idealist encampment. To do so they have to discount his later work, notably the superb *Autobiography*, either by invoking ill health or by crediting its manifest and brilliantly expressed meaning to the supposed projection of non-Idealist readers, who have a predilection for parts rather than wholes. . . . 'How came Collingwood to fall from the heights of the *Essay on Philosophical Method* to the depths of his *Autobiography*?' It is with these words that Donagan in his book (p. 12) sums up Knox's attitude to the problem, without making clear to what extent he himself shares it.

Many contemporary readers might well invert this assessment of what constitutes the heights and the depths, and attempt a *tu quoque* reply to Harris. Is it so obvious that the *Essay on Philosophical Method* (1933) is lily-white idealism untainted by relativism? It culminates in an eloquent passage which says, in effect, that philosophy *is* conceptual self-exploration:

> Every piece of philosophical writing is primarily addressed by the author to himself. Its purpose . . . is . . . to fasten upon the difficulties and obscurities in which he finds himself involved, and try . . . at least to understand them better. . . .
>
> Philosophical writing [is] essentially a confession, a search by the mind for its own failings and an attempt to remedy them by recognising them.
>
> Their [philosophers'] only excuse for writing is that they mean to make a clean breast, first to themselves, and then to their readers, if they have any.

This view of philosophy as self-knowledge, which being conceptual self-knowledge must of course be of a largely shared set of ideas rather than of personal idiosyncrasy, really, is *not* so very far removed from the brutally expressed but uneasy relativism which came soon after. So who is it who mistakes a part for the whole?

Had Collingwood's relativism been facile and evasive, like that of his more influential contemporary, he would have been much less interesting. But equally, as against his Idealist friends, one can say that he would have been even less interesting if he had not been a relativist at all. He used idealism as an idiom for his relativism, not as an escape from it. It is unfortunate for these Idealists that, in order to make their claim, they have to discount the *Autobiography*, which happens to be a literary masterpiece, and one which will continue to be widely read and to carry conviction—which cannot always be said of its detractors. It is the works of Collingwood that 'lack serenity' and are 'marred by febrility' (Knox, quoted by Donagan, and which record his relationship with relativism, which have a claim on our attention. Had he really found serenity in the cloud-cuckoo-land of Absolute Idealism, we might well be tempted to endorse that early and dismissive reviewer, who had made such a permanent dent in Collingwood's ego, and speak of 'the usual idealistic nonsense'.

So, in the end, was he or was he not a relativist? There is no straight Yes or No answer. His sensitivity to the implications of the 'questioning' theory of mind, and to the historic specificity of the questions, impelled him towards relativism. His awareness of its difficulties was equally strong. So he wobbled. What is important is that he saw relativism as a difficult problem, not as a facile solution.

1973

Notes

1 *Critical Essays on the Philosophy of Collingwood*, ed. Michael Krausz, Oxford, 1972, 8.
2 A. Donagan, *The Later Philosophy of Collingwood*, Oxford, 1962, 1.
3 Oxford, 1940, ch. V.
4 *Ludwig Wittgenstein*, London, 1958, 69, italics in the original.
5 Even his erstwhile admirers do not doubt his relativism, de-emphasized though it was. Cf. S. Toulmin in *Human Understanding*, London, 1972, 17: 'If Wittgenstein's position is at all sound, it means that the very image through which our enculturation is achieved is itself only intelligible to men who share enough of our own modes of life.'

Chapter 12   Poker player

Philosophy of the past three centuries is concerned basically with two questions: which world are we in?—and, who the devil are we? These questions arise in the following way. Traditional societies possess reasonably rounded-off and self-maintaining world-pictures. But the advancement of learning and the broadening of horizons have dealt these pictures some devastating blows. So rival worlds, most of them sound by their own lights, make their mutually incompatible claims on our belief, our cognitive loyalty. Though one may temporize, one must also choose: after all, we must needs be *some* place, and our various decisions must be taken against *some* background picture.

The modern theory of knowledge developed in response to this predicament. It was and is an attempt to chart the nature and limits of knowledge, and thereby tell us how to choose between the competing world-pictures. As political philosophy set out to give the criteria of legitimate authority, so the theory of knowledge was concerned, primarily, with the principles of cognitive legitimacy. Various theories of cognitive legitimacy were elaborated, and constitute the mainstream of modern philosophy. One of the most important ones is empiricism, the doctrine which, in its radical form, asserts that the only ultimate legitimation of any belief is *sensation*.

The other great problem of modern philosophy concerns the moral identity of man. This preoccupation arises in a manner similar to the epistemological one. The advancement of knowledge utterly disrupts the old balance of beliefs: we find we know much more, and much less, than we had supposed. Unsuspected knowledge, and unsuspected ignorance, both loom large. In traditional society, men take their own selves and their own powers as self-evident. They act as owners of a smooth-running car who take the functioning of its controls totally for granted, and do not worry about the mechanisms under the bonnet. But suddenly, unexpected new models, unsuspected breakdowns and performances, quite beyond the range of the familiar controls, force one to think in a more fundamental way about what may or may not be expected of a vehicle, what it could or should be used for. That is moral philosophy.

J. L. Austin was a very influential academic philosopher, who died prematurely and tragically in 1960. The nature and circumstances of his death created an atmosphere in which it was felt indecent to criticize him harshly. Even criticisms written and published before anyone knew of his illness were considered, as another professor observed in print, 'tainted'. Enough time has now elapsed since his death to discuss his thought, and the manner of its presentation and influence, without further reference to the tragic end of the thinker.

Austin's thought tended to circle around a limited number of themes. Two of the most persistent ones among them are closely relevant to these two central preoccupations of modern thought. In fact, *if* what Austin has to say about the problem of perception, and about 'excuses', were true and to the point, the two crucial issues would now be solved, dissolved, or transformed.

There is an irony in this admission that his work *does* relate to these problems. A common charge against him, as Mr G. J. Warnock, a warm admirer, reports, is that 'he appears at times to be dealing directly with no standard, identifiable problems of philosophy'. Warnock admits this charge, but deems it a merit. Merit or not, it is not so. If what Austin has to say in *Sense and Sensibilia* is sound, it follows that there is no epistemological problem. Those who wanted to defend (or reassess) our knowledge of the world were basically misguided in failing to notice, according to Austin, that there was no case to answer. He is very explicit about this:

> There *could* be no *general* answer to the questions what is
> evidence for what, what is certain, what is doubtful, what needs
> or does not need evidence, can or can't be verified. If the Theory
> of Knowledge consists of finding grounds for such an answer,
> there is no such thing.

If there is neither room nor need for a theory of knowledge, *then* the ordinary, unquestioning world of 'common sense' acquires a kind of absolute status. This is the really crucial argument underlying Austin's type of philosophy. The premiss (no theory of knowledge) is asserted, as we have seen: the conclusion (daily world made absolute) is *used*, both as a covertly fed-back assumption for supporting the premiss itself, and as a kind of general *weltanschaulich* conclusion which made this outlook so attractive to its adherents. But, conveniently, it need not be defended, and can be and is disavowed if it comes under fire, for it is conveyed through the premiss rather than directly. The real truth of the matter is quite different: the ordinary world has only a kind of interim validity, it is a temporary compromise, sometimes a shabby one, and we cannot but invoke the theory of knowledge in order to scrutinize and possibly revalidate it, as a whole or in part.

So, contrary to the claims of his admirers that he held no general views, he did in fact hold a negative general view of breathtaking importance, if true or even remotely plausible: there is neither room nor need for a theory of knowledge, for a formulation of criteria enabling us to tell just which world we inhabit. We neither have it *nor* need it, he argues.

The presupposition of this is: we know, without any need to revalidate, just which world we are in. Austin's own examples, of course, are trivial: he insists that when a pig 'stands . . . plainly in view . . . the question is settled'. But as he does not, and on his own account cannot, offer any general criteria for delimiting these happy cases of cognitive certainty about the presence of pigs, so the same must by symmetry apply to jinns, witches, sanctity, salvation, the dialectic, alienation, the Oedipus complex, in whose putative presence some people are known to feel as confident as others are about pigs. More important, the pig we see is not the same pig, according to which world it inhabits. Various objects, pigs and the rest, come to us as parts of wider styles of life and thought, each of which internally validates itself, most of which are mutually incompatible, many of which we can empathize and learn to operate, but between which we are forced to choose.

This is really the crucial clue to Austin's influence. He and those he influenced were totally blind to the real source of epistemological inquiry: *cognitive legitimacy is very seriously in doubt.* We do *not* know which world we are in, and we have to decide as best we can. The epistemological theories by means of which we do so are far from a rigorous science, but they are far, far better than pretending the problem does not arise. But if you assume that there is a unique, unambiguous, and straightforward world available to us, you can then amuse yourself, if you have no better employment for your time, by pointing out that *in* this unproblematical world we know all kinds of things in all kind of ways, and that no general criterion of knowledge is required. An admirer of Austin has credited him, in print, with the opinion that the crucial mistakes of philosophers are the tacit assumptions hidden in the first few pages of their books. This observation certainly applies to Austin himself. His supposed overcoming of epistemology—'the main thing is not to get bamboozled into asking [the epistemological question] at all'—is entirely circular, question-begging and hollow, and hinges simply on missing the point of the question. We were never *bamboozled* into it. It happens to be a genuine and inescapable problem.

How did anyone fail to see this? The tired, weary, narrow, claustrophilic, yet also smug, complacent, and self-congratulatory academic climate of the time, now so happily distant, must be part of the answer. Some of the more critical contributors to the volume under review[1] are also puzzled. A. J. Ayer can only think of personal magnetism as an explanation. He asks why Austin 'was able to persuade so many philosophers that he had succeeded' in disposing of empiricist epistemology, when in fact he failed to give any sound reasons (a good question). Ayer wrily observes that this achievement is 'a tribute to his wit and the strength of his personality'. R. J. Hirst is more illuminating:

> It seems to me one of the tragedies of recent English philosophy that . . . Austin and Wittgenstein have been so blind . . . to the importance of scientific findings. 'Philosophy begins in wonder' . . . but these latter-day exponents have conspicuously failed to wonder. . . . As a result there is a brittle superficiality. . . .

It must be said that some recent formulations of empiricist epistemology made Austin's task easier, by starting with trivial versions of the 'Argument from Illusion'. If the theory of knowledge were really about how we distinguish bent sticks from straight sticks that appear bent in water, then Austin would be welcome to his alleged overcoming of the subject. But the significant forms of the argument from illusion run quite differently. How can we be sure of anything within our belief system, given that we see other societies or groups embrace blatant absurdities with sublime confidence? And if we cannot be sure that they are as wrong as they seem to be, what can we be sure of? Descartes used the argument in this form. It is anything rather than an idle academic exercise. A society, such as Descartes' or Austin's, which faces drastic alternatives of belief, cannot evade it. But the reality of the question clearly never crossed the threshold of Austin's mind.

The problem is how, if at all, we can rationally choose between rival world-pictures, and how we must revise our vision of man in the light of radical scientific advance (determinism is but an aspect of this issue). Austin's work makes no contribution to either, but much of it consists of cheap derision of both, and a comic, totally unwarranted claim that he can somehow by-pass them, or even that he has already done so—a delusion resting on a complete misunderstanding of what is at issue. Yet he has left behind a cult whose members, as visible from a number of contributions to this volume, seem confident that in practising this style they are on the right lines.

Austin's admirers like to maintain that he did not commit himself to any far-reaching view. 'Austin . . . held no views whatever about *the* proper objective or *the* proper method of philosophy' (J. O. Urmson). He did not like being close to identifiable problems, and did not hold those views which alone make sense of his procedures (G. J. Warnock). The reader may well wonder what it was that he did do or hold. In fact, these disclaimers do not stand up to examination. For instance, Austin's own and italicized, endorsed commendation of the certainty of the presence of chairs or pigs only makes sense on the assumption that ordinary language is sovereign, because it determines the meaning of expressions such as 'seeing a real chair'. If he qualifies this view elsewhere, the qualification remains indefinite and uncircumscribed, and hence worthless, a pure insurance. If the qualification applies to *all* cases, it is in blatant contradiction of the premiss he uses elsewhere. If it only applies to *some* cases, we must conclude that it is a mere insurance, unless we are given at least some indication of how these exceptions are to be identified and delimited, and distinguished from the cases in which the qualification does not apply. Here one can only quote Austin's own observation, made with unconscious irony about other philosophers: 'There is the bit where you say it and the bit where you take it back.'

The book under review contains some 26 articles about Austin, most of them previously published in journals. Though there is some criticism, on the whole the volume takes Austin with great seriousness. Professionals who are of a like opinion will find the volume useful as an alternative to chasing up individual articles. It is doubtful whether non-specialists will gain anything other than bewilderment from it. Ironically, though the intention of this kind of philosophy is to defend common sense, its operational assumptions are so far removed from common sense that the uninitiated reader will generally miss the point.

'It is unlikely that the philosophical genius of the late John Austin will ever be adequately appreciated by those who have merely read his words in print . . .' (Roderick Firth). Even less likely, I fear, is it that they will get the point from this collection of essays. But Professor Roderick Firth is too pessimistic. All in all, the curious should turn to Austin's published lectures, *Sense and Sensibilia*. Despite the cold print, they do most remarkably convey the relentless softening-up process which Austin used to achieve his effect. I find it terribly hard to locate any intelligible arguments in it, as opposed to the unsubstantiated assertion that the presence of pigs is certain: basically of course there is no argument, it is all a kind of inverted mystical exercise, which by repetition, wearing-down, and bewilderment produces a state of mind in which anything other than the alleged common-sense view is made to seem absurd. This then appears as a conclusion, when in fact it is only a premiss and an induced state of mind. But even in print one is more than half intimidated by the endless castigation and derision of the stupidity, or worse, of anyone who does not agree.

At the same time, there is the terrible playful girls-school wit. (Did you get the joke about the title, *Sense and Sensibilia*? His name was Austin, like *Austen*, you see . . .) The combination of scholastic pedantry, a tendency to miss the point and to silence without convincing (in brief: browbeat), a coy don's old-womanish humour, a blindness to what is important and a passion for the trivial, all these make him a less than attractive thinker.

His admirers claim that his supreme preoccupation was truth. His work, with its sad conjunction of extraordinary cunning in presentation with very thin content, leaves rather the impression of a man who had little sense of real problems but who liked winning arguments and dominating people in the course of them, and who was well equipped to gratify this taste. He was the supreme dialectical poker player, unsurpassed at making people believe that their bluff had been called when in fact they weren't bluffing, and at stonewalling any attempt to call his own. It would be hypocritical not to say all this. Hypocrisy might not matter, but it would also be unfair to all those students who are still being conned into supposing that this kind of philosophizing has much in common with serious intellectual endeavour.

1969

Note

1   K. T. Fann, ed., *Symposium on J. L. Austin*, London, 1969.

Chapter 13   Ayer's epistle to the Russians[1]

It is always a great and genuine pleasure to be able to disagree with Professor Ayer. It is a pleasure because, whether one agrees or not, one finds his positions stated with admirable lucidity; and one faces an opponent actuated by a genuine concern with truth, one who adopts positions and employs arguments because they appear to him true, rather than uncritically accepting current fashion, and who does not stoop to evasion, trickery, or cloudy formulations intended to give the impression that they hide a transcending insight. . . .

My first and perhaps main disagreement is with Professor Ayer's assertion at the very beginning of his paper, and which indeed is crucial to his general argument: 'philosophers have theories, but their theories do not enable them to make predictions'. This seems to me false, and false in a very important way.

It is true that Professor Ayer goes on to qualify this: he goes on to add that 'they cannot be empirically confirmed or refuted *in the way that scientific theories can*' (italics mine). In the interpretation of his position, much depends on how this crucial phrase is to be construed. For his position could be saved, at the price of being made trivial, by interpreting him to mean that philosophical theories *do* entail predictions, but that these predictions differ in some way or other from scientific ones. In as far as most probably *some* 'differentia' could always be found to distinguish between any two sets of predictions, e.g. between scientific and philosophical ones, this would make Professor Ayer's thesis quite irrefutable, but also most uninteresting and empty. I shall assume, on the contrary, that what Professor Ayer intended, or what he would maintain if this ambiguity had been pointed out to him at the time he wrote his paper, would be one of two positions: (1) that philosophers as such do not make predictions *at all*, or, (2) that if they do make predictions, or if their theories entail predictions, these predictions are radically and fundamentally unlike those of science. Position (1) is certainly false, and I think the somewhat weaker position (2) can also be shown to be mistaken.

Curiously enough Ayer attempts to cover himself, not against a possibility that it might be claimed that philosophers *do* make predictions, but against the alternative possible objection to his positions, namely that some scientists do *not* make them (e.g. palaeontologists). This objection against his position is not one that I should like to raise. The answers that can be made to it in turn seem to me quite adequate.

Let us begin by simply giving counter-examples to position (1).

It is hardly open to dispute that Immanuel Kant was a philosopher. Moreover, although his views differed significantly from those of Professor Ayer, he was one whose general view of the nature of philosophy was not all that radically different from Ayer's: like Ayer, he conceived philosophy to be a 'formal' discipline radically distinct from the sciences which provided the 'content'. If, by citing Kant's theories, we can find counter-examples to Ayer's thesis about the lack of predictive power of philosophy, this will be more striking than if we achieved this by examining a thinker whose conception of his own work was radically unlike that of Ayer (though this, too, would be legitimate, for Ayer did not qualify his generalization so as to make it apply only to philosophers of a certain limited kind).

Amongst Kant's philosophic views there were the following: that Aristotelian logic was a complete and definitive system, not open to further correction; that Euclidean geometry was similarly definitive and that it provided the necessary form for our experience of the extended physical world; and that causality provided a necessary form for our experience and understanding of the processes of the physical world. (Ayer discusses this last example, but not, alas, in the form it was put forward by the real philosopher Kant, but in an emaciated form attributed only to an unspecified, hypothetical 'philosopher' whose mode of thinking is designed to conform to Ayer's thesis.)

These are all clearly philosophic theories, and what is crucial here, *they entail predictions*: they entail the predictions that the subsequent developments of logical theory (if valid) would at the very least not contradict Aristotelian logic, if indeed they went beyond it all; that the subsequent developments of geometry (if valid) would not contradict Euclidean geometry, and that subsequent developments in the natural sciences such as physics would remain within the framework both of Euclid and of causal explanation. Each of these predictions have in fact either been falsified by the subsequent developments of the relevant sciences, or at least it can plausibly be maintained that they have been; and I have no doubt but that Professor Ayer would accept either that some or even that all of them have in fact been falsified. If falsified by subsequent events, these propositions or theories must have been predictions. Something which is falsified by subsequent events *is*, or contains, a 'prediction', in virtue of the very definition of that term.

One might indeed object that interpreting philosophical theories and analysis as predictions mistakenly assimilates the work of philosophers to a kind of sociological forecasting. It might be objected that, characteristically, philosophical theories are not predictions about the future course of intellectual history as such (though *some* philosophers perhaps aspire to just this: but this is not what I wish to stress); and that I only managed to interpret ordinary philosophies as predictions by adding, in the case of each such prediction of a future form of science or thought, the qualification '*if valid*'. It might then be argued further that this qualification shows that what is at stake are not future events in the history of science as such, but the implications of *doctrines*, and hence that no *historical* prediction is intended (though, of course, the unfolding of the truth or falsity of a theory will take place in historical time). Quite so: but it is not my point that philosophers as such characteristically make *historical* predictions. For Kant's theory would not become true again if, through some relapse into barbarism, all modern developments in physics and geometry were eradicated from human culture.

But what this *really* shows is that a philosopher's theory cannot be interpreted as a prediction about men or societies *holding* a theory; and that it must, on the contrary, be interpreted as a prediction about the occurrence of *evidence*, of one kind or another, which will make them hold or reject the theory, provided they behave rationally and choose theories sensibly on the available evidence. And all this is another way of saying that, albeit indirectly, philosophers' theories *are* about the world and do contain or imply predictions: which is precisely what is required for the argument.

Or let us come closer to home in the search for counter-examples. In his youth, Professor Ayer himself maintained a position which can briefly be summed up as the doctrine that 'material objects are logical constructions from sense data'. This theory is the revival, in other words, of the old doctrine that material objects are really collections of sensations: that when we speak of them we are really speaking of the collections of sensations we have or did have or shall have or might have.

In more recent years, Professor Ayer has either abandoned this doctrine, or has come to feel much less sure of its truth. Why? The main reason is that, since he put forward this theory, certain predictions which are entailed by the theory and which he expected to be fulfilled, have not been fulfilled. The relevant prediction was that translations of statements about material objects into statements about sensations would be found. This, notoriously, has not happened. It is worth noting that the abstract reasoning which led Professor Ayer to formulate and adopt that position, and to expect the predictions to be fulfilled, are as valid now as they were then: these abstract reasons were, in substance, that unless such translations were possible, it would seem that we must postulate a double reality, one of material objects as they are, and the other as we experience it through our senses, and that we must also postulate some strange power of the mind to apprehend that reality which is not accessible to our senses. These theories, which would seem to be the only alternatives to adopting the position which Ayer once held, were repugnant to him then and, I have no doubt, are repugnant to him now. Nevertheless, he has either abandoned his earlier position or at any rate lost some of the confidence which he once felt about it. The reason for this appears plainly to be the non-fulfilment of the *prediction* entailed by his earlier theory. Why, then, does he now maintain that philosophers as such make no predictions, when the fate of his own predictions has played such a significant part in his own development?

I do not imagine that my objection to his doctrine of the absence of predictions in philosophy will convince him as it stands, for certain counter-objections could be made. These counter-objections in turn seem to me invalid, but they will have to be examined in detail. I can conceive of two main answers which he might offer.

(1) It might be maintained that the reason why the doctrines of Kant referred to entailed predictions was just because they were *false* philosophic theories. Kant, it might be said, incorporated in his idea of a kind of universal and permanent form of human thought and sensibility, features which in fact only characterized the science of his time. No wonder that, as the sciences developed, contradictions were observed between the later state of the sciences and the Kantian doctrine. (Ayer offers his hypothetical holder of the 'principle of causation' a way out: to make his principle quite vacuous. But we must deal with philosophers as they really are. The philosophic reaction to Heisenberg has been not to water down Kant, but to elaborate 'statistical' interpretations of physics.)

A *true* philosophic doctrine, on the other hand, which did not mistakenly incorporate in its analyses bits of contemporary and transient science, would never come up against subsequent discoveries in a similar way. It would in a sense be *exemplified* in subsequent scientific theories or language, as it was exemplified in its own day, but it would never be contradicted by them. It was, it could be maintained, precisely the unwarranted incorporation of current bits of science which led to the falsification of parts of the Kantian theory of knowledge.

I shall not insist, in opposing this way out, on the awkwardness of distinguishing between 'predictions', which can be falsified in the future, and mere 'exemplifications' which whilst holding both for the present and the future are not open to falsification. The real objection to this approach seems to me that it causes 'philosophy' to become something whose contents could only be determined at the very end of time, when truth and falsity have been finally and definitively sorted out. But such an end of time, a kind of scientific Day of Judgment, there never will be. The disastrously inconvenient consequence of this approach would be, that we should never know whether something does or does not fall under a certain discipline until *after* we knew it to be false (when we should know that it was *not* a part of it). The differentiation between philosophy and science, which is so central to Professor Ayer, would be something that could then only be done *ex post*, or indeed at the very end. . . . But whilst the endless growth of human knowledge, and the fallibility of all theories, seems to be something that one may gladly accept, it seems to me that the delimitation of disciplines and fields of inquiry, whilst also not fixed for all time, is something which must on the whole precede and not follow the determination of the truth or falsity of given theories.

(2) The second possible answer to my objections is one which is more important and also more likely to be actually used by Professor Ayer. The answer would run something as follows: the examples provided show not that philosophers make predictions properly speaking, but only that they do make predictions, not about the world, but about the forms of other people's pronouncements. Kant's views, it would be argued, were falsified not by events or experiments which have taken place since his death in 1804, but by the *form* of theories or *propositions* which people had formulated since that date.

This position would in effect be a very considerable modification of the original position found at the beginning of Professor Ayer's paper. It might be claimed that the original formulation had been over-simplified in the interests of presentation, and that it should really be interpreted along the present lines, as excluding from philosophy not predictions *as such*, but predictions *about the world*, while allowing predictions about the sciences and the forms of human thought or language.

This argument is of considerable importance, for at its root there is the division between thought about the world, and thought about thought or language, a division which is an extremely important and persistent theme in the wider philosophic tradition of which Professor Ayer is a part.

Let us go back to a Kantian example. Some of Kant's views can plausibly be held to be refuted by the sheer *possibility* of Einstein's physics, and others of his views can similarly be held to have been refuted by the *possibility* of the physics of Heisenberg. This is perhaps a consideration supporting the view with which I am crediting Ayer: that it is the *possibility* rather than the *truth* of these physical theories which is relevant to the philosophic issue—for it seems to show that the *possibility* of a form of thought, and not the *actuality* of an event, is at issue.

And yet, one is left highly uncomfortable. The physics of Einstein or of Heisenberg find confirmation or support in experimental evidence. If they had no experimental relevance (as distinguished from being experimentally false) they would hardly have the hold over practising physicists which they appear to have. But if it is their experimental relevance, and the fact that the experiments have not gone against them, which lend them authority, and if in turn it is their conflict with Kantian epistemology which is a crucial factor in the undermining of that epistemology, then, indirectly, has not empirical or experimental evidence turned out, after all, to be relevant to the philosophic doctrine? Has not that philosophic doctrine turned out to have contained implicit predictions, and has not the existence of those predictions been brought to light by their falsification?

The position with which Ayer begins his paper (that philosophy contains no predictions) can only be made even plausible by being modified in this way into a somewhat different position which maintains that philosophy contains no predictions about the *world* (for it cannot be denied that it does contain predictions about the general aspects of human beliefs and the sciences), but that it *does* make them about *thought about* the world. But this view in turn presupposes that the form and content of human thought, or of its expression, are clearly separable. It was Kant himself who said that concepts without experience are empty, and that experience without concepts is blind. But many modern philosophers have, to my mind mistakenly, inferred from this insight that the properties of concepts can be investigated independently of the properties of things. It is conceivable —though controversial—that this should be true in certain disciplines, properly called 'formal', notably logic and pure mathematics. (Though it is significant that many of those competent in these disciplines deny this.) But it certainly isn't true in those many disciplines which are not 'formal'. Yet on *any* definition of philosophy, even on the rather puritan kind of definition favoured by Professor Ayer and by many whose views are similar to his in this respect, philosophy cannot but concern itself with human thought even in these disciplines, tainted though the concepts in them might be with actual 'content'.

Examples could be found in various regions. For instance, there are many live issues in the philosophy of the social sciences. These issues are 'conceptual' ones, they are concerned with the analysis of concepts, and are of the kind such as would be recognized by Professor Ayer as characteristically philosophical. They tend to be centred on the analysis of notions such as 'social causation', 'social structure', 'function', 'social law', 'social whole', and so forth. In a superficial and immediate sense, the theories or analyses which are intended to provide answers to these problems are not predictive, and in this immediate and superficial sense they conform to Ayer's characterization of philosophy. But in practice, the really crucial evidence in support of one analysis or another is the practical success of the methodological strategies adopted under their inspiration. Analyses which seem sensible when first formulated in the abstract may turn out in practice to have no fruitfulness in the actual working of the science concerned; they tend then to be abandoned, with or without the *ex post* discovery of theoretical weaknesses in them. Others turn out to be fruitful, and although there may have been theoretical weaknesses in their initial formulation, the practical success of their application provides a stimulus for attempts to iron out such theoretical difficulties as exist.

There isn't really a sharp separation between the verification of the proposition and the validation of a concept, and in turn between the validation and the analysis of a concept, such as Ayer presupposes, and which underlies his sharp separation of science and philosophy. To validate a concept is, in the end, to try out the usefulness of the propositions in which it can occur. To analyse it is to give an account which makes sense of it, which validates it. To test the usefulness of a proposition in a science often is not so much to test its truth as to test the sharpness and adequacy of the concepts occurring in it. (Many propositions are true and yet lack other characteristics, such as sharpness of definition, which they would require to be incorporated in an advanced science.)

Thus Ayer's theory holds neither for the advanced nor for the backward sciences. In the backward sciences, the 'analyses' are really the *forging* of satisfactory concepts, and this activity is at the very heart of current endeavour in these studies. There are here no stable or accepted concepts *to* analyse, and all the philosopher really can usefully do or ought to do is to discuss the merits of rival concepts or 'analyses'. (There is not much difference between the two activities: an analysis in such a field, if adopted, simply fixes the use of some word or other.) But if a philosopher cannot stand outside and be neutral in the case of backward sciences simply because, as it were, there is no established order with regard to which he could be neutral (just as a visitor *cannot* be neutral in a totally anarchic country), so also he cannot be detached and neutral in the case of the advanced sciences, for there he has to be, more or less, a recognized citizen to have a right to speak at all. So, in neither case is there much merit in the idea of a detached and neutral philosophy.

Professor Ayer makes the interesting and characteristic observation that 'often what starts as a problem of justification (in philosophy) turns out to be a problem of analysis' (p. 14). My disagreement with him could be summed up by the contrary contention: what may seem at first to be a problem of analysis generally turns out to be a problem of justification.

Moreover, the type of activity, research and consideration relevant to justifications of concepts is not so dissimilar in philosophy and in science. One fears that somewhere at the back of Professor Ayer's position, if not of his own mind, there lurks a naïve view of science as consisting simply of the discovery of facts and testing of propositions. But the crucial advances in science are not the blind accumulation of facts: they tend to be the discovery or refinement of new concepts, which order facts better and lead to further discoveries. Similarly, philosophy cannot, in a kind of puritanical way, simply be concerned with concepts and not with the (unpredictable) consequences of their use. So the *apartheid* of philosophy and science turns out to be untenable.

It is true that some philosophic problems are more general than scientific ones in the sense that they arise in and for all the sciences, irrespective of their particular problems and subject-matter. Professor Ayer's own example of the problem of induction is a very apposite one. Yet could it be maintained that anyone can nowadays profitably discuss the general problem of scientific inference and extrapolation without familiarity and understanding of the procedures and theories developed by statisticians for coping practically with various specific types of inferential situations? I think not.

Ayer is quite clear about this difficulty in connection with philosophizing about the concepts and procedures of physics. He himself observes that in order to make any useful contribution in this field, one has to be at the very least familiar with the procedures of physicists. But the conclusion he draws from this is a strange one: he concludes that the consequence is that philosophizing about physics will have come from 'within physics'—and not from philosophy. But if the philosophy of physics, the most impressive and advanced of all the sciences, is not philosophy proper, then *what is*? It would in any case be a very strange view of philosophy indeed which excluded from philosophy proper the discussion of questions such as whether or not physics must be rigidly deterministic, or what the role of alternative geometries is, and so forth. My disagreement with Ayer here is terminological, but it is a very important one: that which, in his terminology, is something that must come forth from 'within physics', in my view *is* philosophy, though admittedly not the whole of it.

It is at this point that the social roots or the basic mistake in Ayer's position become evident. What underlies Ayer's position is the assumption that there must be a subject called 'philosophy' which, in its central part, if not in its entirety, is independent of the sciences. I have no wish to deny that there may be problems which are independent of any of the existing sciences, in the sense that these cannot help towards the solution, and that familiarity with them is of no particular assistance. To deny such a possibility would be an unjustifiable piece of dogmatism. What I do wish to deny is the assumption that there *must* be such problems (on some formal grounds), that they have some common feature which would warrant classing them together as the subject-matter of a special discipline, and finally, and of some practical relevance, that a discipline and academic specialism can usefully be defined in terms of them.

The main social root of this mistake is fairly simple and obvious: this view is attractive to a specialized intelligentsia which once had had a transcendental area as its main field, and which (partly owing to Professor Ayer's own most distinguished efforts) has lost faith in the existence or importance of that area and wishes to find a new one without having to migrate to a field already occupied by others with prior claims and expertise in it.

Ayer's attachment to the doctrine of the separation of philosophy and science is odd, because this doctrine is the fragment of two positions, one of which he no longer holds and the other (as far as I know) he never has held. First, it can be seen as a fragment of naïve positivism: naïve positivism saw science as an accumulation of data collected by the senses, with theory merely a kind of abbreviated summary of those brute and given data. The main defect of this theory is that data are not brute and given, that on the contrary the kind of data we get depends on the kind of theory and concept we employ. Ayer is perfectly clear about this now, as is shown by his use of the striking analogy of the cognitive 'net'. If the naïve positivistic theory *were* true, then indeed the separation of philosophy and science would be both possible and mandatory. If facts were totally independent and given, we could examine the shorthand tools employed in summarizing them quite independently.

But the theory is not true, as Ayer himself stresses. The fish we catch depend on the kind of net we use. But if philosophy is the postulation of theories about the 'nets', as Ayer himself implies, then the main way of testing those theories about nets is by seeing the nets in use and seeing what kind of fish they bring up: the philosophic theory will contain assertions about the kind of fish a given net is liable and likely to bring up—and this is, implicitly, *to make predictions*—and the theory is tested by seeing whether, indeed, those fish and no others, or *any* fish, do turn up.

The analogy, incidentally, does not altogether fit, for philosophic theories are not merely the making of statements *about* nets, but—and this is their most important aspect—they are the making and designing of nets.

Alternatively, Ayer's doctrine of separation can be seen as a detached fragment of another position, recently held by many other thinkers close to his tradition of thought (but not, I believe, by him): this position recognizes the interdependence of nets and the fish caught, but nevertheless consigns the study of nets to a wholly different discipline from the study of fish, on grounds such as that the nets we have are perfect, and that the study of nets (our concepts) requires wholly different methods from the study of fish: whereas fish have to be studied by generalizations, our nets, being infinitely various and *sui generis* in each case, have to be studied only by *individual* case studies, so to speak. This seems to me quite false. The study of 'nets', as of things, can only proceed by the formulation of general ideas and the use of general concepts. It does not, in this respect, differ from the study of 'things'. Views of this kind are associated with the later development of the 'linguistic movement', but Ayer himself has never gone all the way with it.

Two related dogmas haunt the wider philosophic tradition with which Ayer is associated: one is the dogma of the neutrality and passivity of philosophy, and the other is the dogma of the *apartheid* of philosophy and science. In his interesting paper, Ayer rejects the first of these two dogmas. It is strange to find him still so close to the second, as the two doctrines are intimately and necessarily linked. Once it is admitted, as he does, that philosophy may be (and indeed must be) concerned with a criticism and reform of concepts as well as with giving accounts of them, the doctrine of apartheid is hardly tenable, for science proceeds as much by the invention and refinement of concepts as it does by mere accumulation of facts. Science is much more like philosophy than the dogma allows. Moreover, giving 'accounts of concepts' is no passive business either: it is a matter of choosing the second-order classificatory concepts, and the choice of these cannot but be guided by pragmatic considerations which in turn often depend on subsequent events. Philosophy is also more like science than the dogma allows.

Moreover, there is no residual region which could in principle be guaranteed to provide the field of such a 'pure' philosophy. The yearning for such a region is the natural reaction of those who for some reason or other fear the impact of scientific advance on their lives. Some have thought that the area of daily life and its concepts is such a redoubt, such a residual area of refuge.

Ayer describes and expresses this himself when he says about 'concepts which are current property' that 'with *these* the philosopher feels entitled and equipped to deal' (italics mine). Only or even especially with these? Why? Such philosophers have even thought that the application of scientific concepts to this area, or the drawing of implications borrowed from the sciences, is in general a mistake, and that the specific task of philosophy is to combat this very type of error. Nothing seems to me less true. *If* we cannot apply the concepts of, for instance, psychology to our daily life, this, it seems to me, is due to the fact that the concepts or theories of this science are not sufficiently advanced to be reliably applicable, and not because they are in principle inapplicable. If the concepts really fitted, and the theories formulated with their help really were true, whether we like it or not I cannot see how we could avoid reordering our daily lives and relationships in terms of them, any more than we can avoid utilizing those aspects of scientific technology which have revolutionized the patterns of production.

Adam really had no choice about leaving the Garden of Eden once the crucial information was available. Once we are reliably told, for instance, about a connection between some type of behaviour and its causal antecedents, we cannot but reorder the concepts which have covered that behaviour and which may have been based on the assumption that this behaviour had different or no specifiable antecedents; and we must reorder them in a way which takes note of the new evidence. (Of course, someone may insist on going on using the old concept from a kind of determined clinging to the past, as someone may go on using antiquated tools in the presence of more powerful and efficient ones: but the sheer fact that the motive here *is* a *deliberate* archaism makes such a romantic persistence quite different from the previous and natural use of the notion or of the tool in the earlier period. So, in either case, the past is irrevocable. . . .)

It is true that the concepts of daily life may continue to differ from those of science in precision, explicitness, and so forth, just as, for instance, our measurements of space and time in daily life do not have and do not need to have the precision of those made in the laboratory. This, however, does not affect the principle that conflicts and cross-implications between the sciences and daily life do exist and must exist. Professor Ayer does not himself adopt this particular argument in support of the separation of philosophy and science, but as it exists and is influential, it is worth mentioning it.

Professor Ayer's own case seems to rest rather on a certain special kind of generality. But will this do either? The case of induction has already been mentioned. But take other very general categories: the notion of time and of temporal succession is general enough, by any criterion. It occurs in all or virtually all sciences and in daily life. Yet again, could it be maintained that the 'analysis' of this notion can now be carried on independently of any awareness of the implications of the work in physics, concerning the interdependence between chronological succession and the position of observers ́and the speed of signals?

Behind the two dogmas of the passivity and purity of 'philosophic analysis', of which Ayer still seems to uphold one, there lie two main kinds of justification—the positive and the negative. I think Professor Ayer's adherence to this position or a part of it is based mainly on the negative justification, but it is worth mentioning both of them as both play a prominent part in the wider philosophic tradition of which Ayer is a part.

The positive justification arises from a theory of language, a theory which maintains that actual language is perfect or very nearly so, and which concludes from this that therefore the philosopher's task is to observe and understand it, but not to pass judgment on it or try and improve it, nor to confuse his accounts of *language* with the statements made about *things* within the language. (This theory itself in turn has two different kinds of justification which are sometimes confused: one is that language is perfect, or very nearly so, in virtue of a long process of natural selection—not a very subtle argument— and the other is that it is perfect in virtue of the non-existence of any standard in terms of which it could be *im*perfect. This latter justification of the perfection of language has certain affinities with the 'negative' justification of the separation of philosophy discussed below.)

The negative justification of the separation of philosophy is really a kind of scepticism. The ultimate reason why 'philosophy is the *analysis*, and not the *justification* of concepts' is that justification is held to be impossible. It is this negative view, rather than any positive idolatry of language, which underlies, I believe, Ayer's particular position.

Two comments seem to be called for in connection with this 'camouflaged scepticism'. One is that in the case of very many concepts undergoing 'philosophic analysis', the scepticism seems to be simply unwarranted. In the case, for instance, of the disputes in the philosophy of the various sciences, we *can* justify an analysis in terms of the practical fruitfulness of it, and we are more concerned with justification, and the prediction of pragmatic validation, than we are with the analysis in the abstract: indeed, in the abstract, both (or neither . . .) of two competing analyses may be acceptable.

With regard to some other and more general concepts, it may well be true that ultimate justification is just impossible. It may well be true that ultimate judgments of value, or the faith in the possibility of scientific extrapolation at all, simply cannot be justified without circularity. But if this is so, it seems to me far more illuminating, more forthright, and less misleading to assert it in some such wording, rather than to camouflage it under philosophic doubletalk. If no justification can be offered, why then, let it be bluntly asserted. No merit attaches to renaming the 'impossibility of justification', and calling it 'the discovery that the demand for justification is really a demand for analysis'.

1963

Note

1 This article was originally written in response to a Russian invitation and for the Russian *Voprosy Filosofii*. It has not in fact been published by that journal. The present version has not been rewritten.

Chapter 14   Ayer on Moore and Russell

The rationale for writing a book about these two authors[1] appears to be offered on the very first pages: 'For the recovery of the empiricist outlook . . . and for the flowering of this tradition in the first half of the present century, we have mainly to thank the University of Cambridge: and among Cambridge philosophers, in the first instance, Bertrand Russell and G. E. Moore.' This, then, would seem to be the general plot—the rescue by two brave knights of British thought which 'had fallen very largely under the spell of Hegel' (which we also learn on the first page of the first chapter).

This, however, is an odd book, for a number of reasons. For one thing, if this were the plot, it is by no means obvious that it constitutes a correct account of what really happened. It is only about as true as the opinion that every child born alive must be either a little liberal or a little conservative: it is tied to the supposition that Hegelians and empiricists between them exhaust universe. *Only* on such an assumption is it plausible to say either that British academic philosophy was recovered *for* 'empiricism'—it was indeed recovered from Hegelianism—and only on such an assumption is it possible to claim Moore for empiricism. Russell is a different matter.

In fact, if one is to understand what happened, a rather more complex scheme is required. Three themes seemed to float in the Cambridge air at the time the rescue operation was being mounted:

(1) Empiricism.

(2) A respect, or reverence, for 'Common Sense'.

(3) Hardest to define and convey, something that might be called 'logicism'—the view that the structure of the world can be inferred from the structure of thought (or perhaps language), so that the minimal kind of language we need to employ gives us a clue to 'what there is'. To articulate what we know, can we dispense with (say) universals, definite descriptions, irreducible moral characterizations, etc.? If the answer is No, it is then held that it follows (according to this particular approach) that the type of entity referred to is an ultimate piece of cosmic furniture.

This is the briefest, though no doubt formally unsatisfactory, way of summing up the general approach which pervaded much of the strategy, and literary style, of academic philosophy, and still pervades some of it.

Now the really important thing, which does not emerge from the book with sufficient clarity, is that Russell held both (1) and (3), but not at all (2). Much of what is central to his thought consists of elaborating an empiricist philosophy with the tools of logicism. For (2), so-called common sense on the other hand, he had little reverence, or none. This may be obscured by the fact that in our age, 'common sense' has itself absorbed so much empiricism that it resembles it in some respects; and also because, in the simplified two-party system which Ayer uses on his first page, common sense and empiricism are classed together as fellow non-Hegelians. Nevertheless, they are in other ways profoundly different from each other.

Moore, on the other hand, did consciously and passionately embrace (2); he also shared (3) with Russell, but more from a kind of mimesis, as a more or less tacit though general assumption that this was *the*, or the only, way to talk, than from any lucid and conscious commitment, such as he displayed for (2). As for (1), he did not appear wedded to it at any level, either conscious or tacitly operational.

This shuffling of three themes between two enormously influential thinkers needs to be specified if one is to understand how they set the scene for the main development in British academic philosophy. (By 'main development' I mean not the greatest achievement in terms of objective merit, but the most conspicuous intellectual change of style, in the estimation of the professional practitioners themselves.)

Now despite all the careful, attentive discussion of individual doctrines, this general pattern does not emerge with sufficient clarity from the book. Perhaps Ayer would not agree that this *is* the crucial pattern (though there is nothing in what he actually says to indicate that he would so disagree), but if so, no alternative really illuminating pattern emerges either. A certain pattern *half* emerges: but more of this anon.

The second odd thing about this book is that it is primarily an essay in the history of ideas. Now no-one will, I fear, be tempted to say that this is Ayer's best book. Historical reconstruction for its own sake is not at all his genre. It is a genre which requires that one should be fascinated by questions such as why a problem or a solution, which does not tempt us now, arose and seemed plausible in a given historical context, or how the choice of one option at a given intellectual cross-roads contributed to a later situation, and so forth. Ayer is not much interested in this kind of question, and what he does towards answering them is brief and perfunctory. Basically he is interested in the truth or otherwise of the ideas and arguments considered in a rather timeless way, which treats all doctrines as contemporary and as denizens of the same universe of discourse. This is a perfectly legitimate approach (and when it is wholly displaced by a purely historicizing interest, it is disastrous); but nevertheless, when applied, and applied almost exclusively, to an historical situation, it leads to a kind of catalogue of theories plus discussions of their merit, which seldom fully comes to life. One can only wonder why Ayer chose a genre which cannot be congenial to him and which does not suit his particular gifts.

When Ayer does sketch in the historical background, he is not very profound. For instance, he on the whole accepts the authorized and self-propagated image of Moore as a spirit so pure, unpretentious and straightforward that he would not allow himself to be bamboozled, as others were, by philosophical departures from common sense—the child who bravely cried that the emperor was naked. The *faux naïf* style is taken at more or less face value. Now this is odd, as Ayer himself cites the piquant evidence that in Moore's earliest published paper, he held that 'the arguments . . . which . . . prove the unreality of time appear to me perfectly conclusive'. In other words, far from having always been the virgin of common sense, who clearly sees the one untainted truth which philosophical impurity prevented others from recognizing, he must on the contrary have made a decision, at some time in or after 1897, that this game of philosophy could be played by at least two different kinds of convention—either the one commended by Socrates which bids us follow the wind of argument wherever it may lead, or the other consisting of never allowing it to stray outside the bounds of 'common sense'. By what processes, rational or other, did he come to make this deep choice to which he subsequently remained loyal? Moore clearly preferred to let people think that he had sprung into the world complete with the expression of total surprise at philosophers' counter-common-sensical absurdity, and that it had never left him. (Similarly, J. L. Austin at one stage believed that sense data were the one thing of whose existence we could really be sure, but also did not care to inform his later audiences of the extraordinary reasons required to turn a firmly held view, not merely into a rejected one—there is no mystery about that—but into—allegedly—a *self-evidently* absurd one.) This reticence concerning his most interesting conversion away from the unreality of time contrasts with his ever-present willingness to confess to most trivial common logical errors, thus highlighting both his own logical fastidiousness and an apparent lack of undue amour-propre. But that there had to be such a leap of faith is significant, for it is one of the ways of showing the falsity of one of the assumptions on which the 'common sense philosophy' rests—namely that one set of conventions for thought, known as respecting common sense, is somehow unique and *manifestly* privileged.

But to return to Ayer: if imaginative historical reconstruction is not his forte, his strength does lie in the lucid organization of complex material from some one definite viewpoint—and organization concerned with the truth, rather than the psychological or historical role, of the ideas concerned. It is this particular kind of approach, most conspicuous in his early work, which shows him at his best. Now the central organizing idea'or issue which underlies this book is half hidden, and emerges only obliquely and intermittently. And the idea is *not* the rescue of the maiden of British thought from the Hegelian dragon by two parfit knights.

Why not? Simply because Ayer is *so* sure that Hegelianism was a paper dragon, that no excitement or interest can possibly be obtained from rescuing anyone from him. On the contrary, whenever Ayer introduces some Hegelian doctrine, he is visibly embarrassed at being seen in such company at all. He hastens to reassure the reader that though the view is plainly absurd (no need even to say why), it nevertheless did mislead even quite intelligent people, and though the issue itself cannot really be in doubt, there may be at least some intellectual interest in locating the precise point at which the error occurs. Well, if that is your view of Hegelianism, you cannot extract much drama from the rescue of British thought from it.

Yet clearly, something about Moore's and Russell's approach does fascinate Ayer. It is not the intrinsic interest of a historic reconstruction, and it is certainly not the drama of a battle with Hegel. Well, what is it?

One of the clues is to be found in the final passage of the book. 'It is a . . . serious mistake to bracket Moore with the later Wittgenstein. Though we have seen that he differed from Russell in many ways, he agreed with him in thinking that philosophical problems are genuine and that they are capable of being solved.' Here and elsewhere, the underlying driving force which inspires the argument, in as far as the argument is inspired at all, is laid bare: it is not what unites Russell and Moore and distinguishes them jointly from Hegel, but it is what in Ayer's view unites them and then distinguishes them from the later Wittgenstein. It is when it deals with questions related to this theme that the book comes to life. Unfortunately, the theme is not clearly avowed and allowed to organize the material, and the interest of the book suffers in consequence.

It is necessary here to spell out what the 'late Wittgenstein' stood for, in terms of the three themes which Russell and Moore revolved around—(1) empiricism, (2) reverence for 'common sense', and (3) the logicist idiom. Russell and Moore shared (3), but Russell alone was devoted to (1), whereas Moore alone was addicted to (2). The 'mature' Wittgenstein, nurtured on both thinkers, had his great illumination when he firmly repudiated (3): henceforth, he would no longer look for the underlying structure of thought and language, which was to have revealed the structure of the world; instead, he would see language as an activity *in* the commonsensical world, that world itself to be taken for granted, as is.

One can have much sympathy for Wittgenstein's repudiation of the logicist idiom and assumptions. But he went further, much further, and disastrously so. He assumed that the logicist error (if such it be) underlay *all* other philosophy, including (1), empiricism. So empiricism went out. Further, he inferred that because (3) was false (i.e., there is no underlying logical structure of thought and reality), *therefore* (2) was true: there being no underlying structure to discover and to correct our opinions, things were to be accepted as they are. Ordinary opinion remains as the residue of truth when error has been eliminated. All philosophy is based on logicist error, on this view, and when this is eliminated, common sense will inherit the earth. (This is absurd, for in fact most philosophy is *not* based on the logicist error, and there are many varieties of common sense.)

Things 'as they are' are but another way of referring to common sense. So Moore was right after all, on this view, though he had not known *why* he was right.

Ayer, it seems to me, is wrong in overstressing differences between Moore and Wittgenstein. This hinges, as the final passage quoted shows, on the distinction between saying that there are philosophic problems and solutions (though the latter may be bound by the limits of common sense, as Moore held), and saying that there are no real problems, only misunderstandings of how language works, and that when these are obviated, everything remains as before. In the one case, common sense is asserted, as an official solution; in the other, it merely inherits the earth, as the residual legatee, and the only possible one, all other claimants to truth having been eliminated. The difference between the two positions seems to me minimal and verbal.

Apart from overstressing this basically verbal distinction, Ayer also attempts rather unconvincingly to exonerate Moore, but not his followers, from the consequences of his position, by invoking the fact that in one of his works, written early but published long after, he allows room for basic categorial doubt 'under the covering of analysis'. This is unconvincing, barely compatible with the other things Moore was doing and, as Ayer notes, really takes most of the sting and point out of his defence of common sense.

Now why is all this of burning interest to Ayer (unlike the Hegelian denials of common sense)? If common sense is beyond all challenge, it would seem to follow that philosophy can 'analyse' it, whatever that means, but cannot sit in judgment on it. Ayer tells us that unlike some other philosophers, he personally does not find the reduction of philosophy to analysis emotionally repugnant, and it seems to me that this self-characterization is quite correct. So the trouble is not the deprivation of philosophers of the status of those who bring positive information. What then is the trouble?

The trouble is that Ayer (rightly) feels that the debate concerning the justification of various kinds of knowledge must be a genuinely open one if it is to be serious. There is something plain comic in a painstaking logical investigation of whether some kind of reasoning is or is not valid, if, whichever way the argument goes, you *must* in the end ratify that style of reasoning anyway, simply in virtue of its being part of the holy corpus of common sense. If that really were so, the only question one could really take seriously would be why indeed common sense (variant reading: ordinary language) should claim such infallibility. No wonder so many academic philosophers have indeed found it hard to tear themselves away from this question, despite the fact that they upbraided themselves to *practise* their craft, rather than merely talk about its fundamental principle. For if that is the principle, the detailed practice is of little interest, for everything is already pre-judged.

Now Ayer himself never really accepted this Infallibility Doctrine of Common Sense, but he did not firmly repudiate it either. In an interesting broadcast discussion with Mr B. Magee,[2] Ayer made the fascinating confession that in some of his more recent work on the theory of knowledge, the *arguments* in fact favoured a sceptical conclusion, but that he, as author, arbitrarily deprived scepticism of its victory, as this would have violated common sense. But if common sense cannot sin, then philosophy is in the comic position of some pious medieval thinker, who is allowed to exercise his reason, but only on condition its conclusions always tally with what orthodoxy lays down anyway. Under such conditions, why bother? Ayer is clearly worried by this pointlessness, as well he might be; at the same time, he cannot quite bring himself to commit the solecism of doubting common sense outright. Moore and Wittgenstein and their followers have done their job too well, and what they preach also fits in too well with the actual contemporary work situation of professional philosophers: cut off from positive knowledge, they feel silly in seeming to sit in judgment on it.

In consequence, Ayer seems to have been driven into a kind of awkward compromise position, in which what is endorsed is not some ill-defined common sense as such, but *logical* truisms, whose tautological nature is not immediately apparent and had to be brought out, and which moreover have consequences unpalatable to some people. 'As Hume puts them these statements are not obviously tautological; but they become so when it is seen . . . what he is really saying. . . . What is difficult is to make the consequences of such truisms palatable, to discover and neutralize the motives which led to their being denied.' (*The Problem of Knowledge*, Pelican ed., pp. 29 and 30.)

If this were the heart of the matter (and Ayer is careful to refrain from claiming that all philosophy fits this mould), it would give him what he wants: the legitimation of the philosophical conclusion would lie in its logical status (a tautology) and not in its incorporation in some authorized common sense; yet at the same time, the philosophic job would be the analysis and elucidation, rather than the bringing of new truths, for the truths in themselves, as opposed to the neutralization of difficulties accompanying them, would be very simply and easily accessible to all. This would avoid treating 'common sense' as an oracle, and at the same time also avoid any risk of contradicting it. In the trade, *The Problem of Knowledge* is often considered Ayer's best book, just because it comes closest, among his writings, to the trendy thought of the post-war period.

It is fairly evident that this unconvincing and rather strained compromise no longer satisfies Ayer, if indeed it ever really did. (And in fact it is not defensible: the principles of knowledge are *not* simple tautologies, which have for some mysterious reason become unpalatable and questionable for some people. Philosophy is not at all like making a child eat wholesome food which it misguidedly rejects, the overcoming of a misguided reluctance.)

And from this also clearly springs the attraction which the exegesis of Russell and Moore now has for him. What they have in common, and what clearly is significant for Ayer, is that they do philosophy in what might be called a 'propositional' way: theses are propounded and their truth or falsity considered. This is in marked contrast to the style of the later Wittgenstein, which is conspicuously unpropositional, and which is meant to leave us with a cure, not a doctrine. And if indeed there are propositions to be accepted and rejected, this frees us from the triviality of merely indulging in an exercise which 'leaves everything as it is', which merely returns us to common sense after liberating us from our misguided temptations to stray from it, without ever presuming to judge it.

He is of course right to be attracted to the propositional way of doing philosophy, if this means the formulation of clear theses, as opposed to some supposedly therapeutic activity, the most hypothetical removing of alleged errors or obstacles, meant to leave us with truth as an unspecified and obvious residue, whether that residue is to consist of Holy Common Sense, logical tautologies or anything else. But if it meant returning to the logicistic idiom characteristic of some of Russell and Moore, I fear this would be a mistake. (The way forward lies in quite another direction.) Ayer is also mistaken, as indicated, in classing Moore with Russell, rather than with Wittgen-stein. Though formally a propositional philosopher, in the sense defined, nevertheless the terms of reference Moore imposed on the game takes much of the substance out of it. If the truth is known before ever we start, then the game is not worth the candle. And, in fact, the truth is emphatically *not* known when we start. (Ayer is formally aware of the arguments which support this, but appears to have some difficulty in accepting their weight, a bit like those people he wrote about who find the consequences of a truism hard to accept. Perhaps one needs a sense of social and historical diversity to be properly sensitive to this point.) There is not one common sense but many, and the childish philosophy of common sense was possible only as a result of a social insularity, which extrapolated from one particular rather strange and circumscribed consensus, and supposed it to hold for all men. Whether one attempts to codify it, as Moore did, or whether one leaves it as an unspecified chaotic and boundless residue, as did Wittgenstein, makes little difference. Mankind in fact did *not* enter the world with the norms of cognition clearly available and manifest. They need to be found or agreed, and there is nothing (other than the historical insularity so characteristic of Moore and of much academic philosophy) to suggest that the job is complete. Moore of course talked as if the job need never have begun.

It is from this angle, and with this contrast in mind, that Russell and Moore are now of interest to Ayer. When themes relevant to this issue come up, the book comes alive. But unfortunately, the book is not consciously and openly organized around this question, and hence much of it does not come to life very much. Ayer has now written about the pragmatists and about Russell and Moore—one can only hope that he will also grasp the nettle and write about the 'mature' Wittgenstein, and do so openly from the viewpoint of the impasse which Ayer's own thought has now reached.

1972

Notes

1   A. J. Ayer, *Russell and Moore: The Analytical Heritage*, London, 1971.

2   Bryan Magee, *Modern British Philosophy*, London, 1971, 61–2.

Chapter 15　The belief machine

Alasdair MacIntyre's collection of essays[1] falls into two groups, those which had previously appeared in literary/political journals, and those which had graced the philosophers' trade press. The stylistic difference between the two kinds is considerable, corresponding roughly to that between charismatic and routinized utterance. The routinized ones are much longer. The idea underlying their joint publication is an entirely sound one—namely, that issues of fundamental belief, and the so-called technical concerns of philosophers, are not logically separable.

The essays have two connecting threads—the denial of the demise of ideology, and the author's own development. This is a rather personal book. It is not merely the very large photograph of the author on the dust jacket, looking menacingly pensive, which conveys the sense that one is being invited to observe a spiritual pilgrimage.

Professor MacIntyre's position amongst professional philosophers is an unusual one. Taking them all in all, they are a dull lot, and MacIntyre is not. Their dullness, in most cases, springs from the belief that they operate a technical specialism, when in fact their techniques amount to very little, and merely sacrifice substance for the trappings of rigour. MacIntyre is one of the exceptions. He always seems to be involved, publicly and passionately, for or against, (usually both in succession, and it doesn't make much difference these days), with the major belief systems of our time.

The book under review will provide much useful documentation for a comprehensive study of contemporary faiths, but it will be insufficient, for it is rather selective, and with a definite bias in its selection. The bias is already conveyed by the title, which promises that the book will be *against* the self-images of the age. Why *against*? What distinguishes Professor MacIntyre is not the number of beliefs he has doubted, but the number of beliefs he has embraced. His capacity for doubt we share or surpass; it is his capacity for faith which is distinctive and perhaps unrivalled. In his youth, he wrote a book on Marx for the Student Christian Movement, and if he did not at the same time write one on Jesus for the Young Communist League, it must have been a very close thing. It is no secret that he was, for many many years of adult life, a paid-up, card-carrying Christian. As for Marxism—like other important historical developments, it has made its appearance twice, the first time as tragedy, the second time as farce. This second coming of Marxism, the mystical soteriology of 'alienation', was in its time much heralded by MacIntyre, and in fact a good deal of this survives even in the present volume. In addition to this attempt at Christian/Marxist synthesis, there have also been most curious attempts to marry Marx and Wittgenstein, and so forth.

It is this spiritual omnivorousness, and not the occasional *recul*, which is distinctive and interesting—even if it is a case of *reculer pour mieux croire*. One would have preferred the positive declarations of faith to be more fairly represented, if one is to understand that inward movement of thought which the book appears to promise. The denials are parasitic on the affirmations and a return to an affirmative stance is strongly indicated.

Still, quite enough survives of the characteristic and rather priestly believer even in this volume, and he will not be obscured by the thinner and less plausible sceptic. The believer tells us (p. 86) that what really matters is whether you are concerned with God's existence, not whether you affirm or deny it—an observation strikingly similar to the kind of modernist theology which he elsewhere denounces, with its Instant God generated tautologically from the mere existence of a central concern, and its indifference to the object of that concern. Freud is vindicated (p. 37), though in a strikingly Wittgensteinian manner, as essentially an observer of detailed facts, whose significance is that he 'broke all conceptual schemes—including his own'. There is a rebuke (p. 43) for 'those for whom the whole project of the revolutionary liberation of mankind from exploitation and alienation is an absurd fantasy', and a defence of the concept of alienation (p. 66). (This is combined with an historical account of the manner in which this notion originally acquired its psychological content, which is excellent and in my view entirely correct.) So the word 'against' in the title must be read in a rather relative way. The author is not so much in favour of current faiths as he was at the apogee of his enthusiasms, but he is still a great deal more so than most of us.

As for shrines, he seems to have moved from Trotsky's to Guevara's. He is contemptuous of R. H. Tawney's 'cliché-ridden highmindedness', exemplified by observations such as that 'capitalism . . . corrupts human relations by permitting the use of man by man as the instrument of pecuniary gain . . .'. (As the Polish schoolboy said, capitalism is the exploitation of man by man, and socialism is the other way round.) But for some reason, Che's very similar remarks are treated with reverence and seriousness: 'Essentially, nothing has changed, except that I am much more conscientious, my Marxism has struck deep roots and is purified.'

The author's stance and style are remarkably pastoral—earnest, stern, admonitory, but understanding. He gives us to feel that he comprehends and sympathizes with our doubts, but that we can take comfort from the thought that even a mind such as his, as familiar as we are with the grounds of doubt, can nonetheless recognize the need and the possibility, nay the necessity, of a much, much more complete conceptual fulfilment, if only we are big enough to overcome our inner impediments. His Marxism was truly episcopal, and it was an achievement of a kind to get on a soapbox and sound like a bishop. If anyone objects that the star we are asked to follow changes with bewildering rapidity, one may reply that these terminological changes do not matter much anyway, for apparently Christ, Marx, Freud and Wittgenstein all very often point the same way, and even if at this moment some of them are *out*, no matter—a new vision of similarly gratifying richness is not far away, waiting to be found and revealed in, of all places, the philosophic analysis of moral and social concepts (p. 94).

The contemporary ideologies with which the flirtation is most persistently and openly carried out are indeed Christianity, Marxism and psychoanalysis. There is also a fourth, much used and invoked, but which, for some reason, is not classed with the others—Wittgensteinianism. Why not? Is it because it is not of comparable historic importance (correct), or because he does not wish to group it with faiths he has currently 'overcome'? It seems to me to deserve inclusion, as much as the pragmatic liberalism with its doctrine of the end of ideology, which he does include (without so visibly flirting with it). Here some points need to be made.

There is a curious affinity between the pseudo-technicians' tendency to be interested in almost nothing, and MacIntyre's inclination to believe in almost everything (in succession if not simultaneously). The same premiss, surprisingly, can justify both, and in each case it constitutes a total misreading of our real intellectual problem situation. The narrow range of the would-be professionals springs from the view that all's well, and cannot but be well, in the sphere of belief. This *carte blanche* warrant for all faith they use, however, with most remarkable restraint. (In fact, in the main they used it only to disconnect their subject from questions of faith.) One is tempted to speculate whether the secret of MacIntyre is that he makes really full use of that utter conceptual permissiveness which is inherent in Wittgenstein's views, and which the other followers have used so modestly. This, as well as some deep ultimate lack of seriousness, would help explain the author's remarkable rate of ideological growth, or should one say rate of circulation of faiths. These faiths are always so to speak secondary, in the sense of being accompanied by insurance meta-beliefs about the very nature of faith, which at the same time constitute a justification of faith as such, quite independently of its content. Such secondary faith is then invulnerable to the ordinary objections to which literal, straightforward faith is vulnerable. It is not clear why such secondary faith need ever be lost, except through a kind of ideological fidgetiness. But it cannot be hard to regain either. MacIntyre speaks scathingly of the lack of agony in Dr Robinson's prose (p. 14), with his 'cheerful, even brisk style'. But the only sign of anguish conspicuous in this book is in the cover photograph of the author, which looks as if he were suffering from indigestion. Well, to lose one faith could happen to anyone, to lose so many looks like carelessness.

MacIntyre also takes too narrow a view of the 'end of ideology' doctrine, which he repudiates. Under that blatant name, it was the way in which a New York ex-Trotskyist, doing well in the cold war, repudiated his youth, and with splendid *chuzpah* treated his own development as the paradigm for humanity at large. (I have in mind a species not an individual.) But the very explicitness of that doctrine made it vulnerable. Elsewhere, the same end was achieved, though perhaps not consciously aimed at, with greater finesse and less candour. Wittgenstein taught that the supposedly big questions were fruits of conceptual confusion; if these confusions were eliminated, a residual reality would remain. This would be endlessly various, lacking a general justification, constitute its own legitimation, be incarnated in the local custom, and be quite viable when not disturbed by overgeneral questioning. It could also be spiritually luscious or soberly grey according to taste. Now this was a conservative end-of-ideology thesis if ever there was one, and a damned sight cleverer than putting everyone on their guard by calling it by that name. Though MacIntyre notes the blindness of this tradition to history and change, he does not really seem to see how close a variant it is of the soporific evasion which he attacks.

In fairness to MacIntyre, it must be said that he is now quite clear, as the more technical essays show, about the logical error behind that universal *carte blanche* for faith, at any rate when abstractly formulated. So it can no longer be used to oil the dialectic. But the debt is repaid: the technicians are invited to return to interesting topics, by an argument which at the same time treats their erstwhile reasons for ignoring them as deserving of full and continued respect. So if they heed this sermon, they can retrace their steps without loss of face.

Instead of pursuing, as would seem logical, the local forms of the 'end of ideology' thesis which is under attack, MacIntyre puts forward the entertaining idea that the philosophic analysis of the *concept* of action is an important prerequisite of action itself, notably such as would hope to bring about socialism with a human face. Unity of theory and practice could hardly go further, and this is clearly a new variant of his old aspiration towards a Marx/Wittgenstein synthesis. I relish the thought of socialist revolutionaries storming the barricades, having first fortified themselves by a careful analysis of their own concepts. *Charge! You have nothing but your confusions to lose! Hurrah!*

The main thing is, I suppose, that doubt of a secondary faith (in the sense indicated) is itself secondary, and thus subject to much laxer rules than primary conviction or doubt, and liable to go into reverse gear at any time. The Introduction does indeed tell us that the quest for a new vision is on, and it will evidently retain the gratifying properties of the old ones. It will answer the 'key question', and either find or vindicate 'a language in which we can say what we sometimes desperately want to be able to say'. I do not anticipate that he will have any inhibitions about saying it. This dialectic in double quick time, like some old film, will surely not come to a stop. (Though it is piquant to find him complaining of the eclecticism and lack of coherence of the new romantic young.) A heart so avid will not be denied, and though prediction is normally perilous, we can feel absolute confidence that, in the end, we shall see the reunion of Father MacIntyre and Mother Church.

1971

Note

1 Alasdair MacIntyre, *Against the Self-Images of the Age: Essays on* *Ideology and Philosophy*, London, 1971.

Part five   Psychologists and others

In his *Tractatus*, Wittgenstein said (4.1122): 'The Darwinian theory has no more to do with philosophy than has any other hypothesis of natural science.' When, later, Wittgenstein stood the philosophy of the *Tractatus* on its head, and thereby provided a basis for the dominant philosophy of the mid-century, he still retained *this* part of the earlier position. In fact, nothing could be more false: there is no realm which can enjoy such total *apartheid* from the contents of the sciences. Yet the example is well chosen to illustrate the mistaken point. Amongst scientific theories, some do and some do not have philosophical implications, and they have them in varying degree. But in the front rank amongst claimants to our philosophic attention are the biological doctrines connected with the notion of evolution.

Of course, Wittgenstein had not chosen his example at random. When Darwinism appeared and came to be accepted, it made, and was logically entitled to make, an enormous impact on man's vision of the world, of himself and of human knowledge. (If this is not philosophy, what is?) To begin with, it was in manifest conflict with some rival views of the origin of man. But even if it were not in conflict with parts of other world-views, it would still be extremely fertile in providing the crucial images and concepts for our view of ourselves and the world. There are, to begin with, the implications of the doctrine concerning the alleged mechanics of evolution—natural selection: which, if true, implies either that a higher value must be placed on competitiveness and ruthlessness, and a lower value on charity and compassion, than might otherwise be the case, or, alternatively, that an ethic differing from the ways of nature, must be conscious of being a rebel and a deviant against the order prevalent in the rest of nature. There is, again, the possibility of avoiding the argument from natural order to purposive design.

There is the continuity between human and other biological phenomena—a diffuse idea but perhaps one richer and even more important in its consequences than the others. There is the intoxicating idea of evolution itself, providing a kind of theodicy, a justification of the ways of nature to man, a kind of new purpose for life, a cosmic story in the image of the manner in which middle-class people see and justify their lives—a career with rung after rung after rung, each step up justifying the tribulations of the preceding rung.

After an enthusiastic exploration of these and other possibilities, the whole business of building philosophies around notions inspired by biological evolution went out of fashion, for reasons sometimes good and often bad. The fallacies inherent in drawing ethical conclusions from natural trends became familiar and were indeed overstressed, providing a rationale for the anti-scientific formalism of academic philosophy. The application of evolutionary ideas to social studies proved to be not nearly as fertile as had been hoped. Evolutionary schemata did not fit, and even if they did, did not provide explanations comparable in power and relevance to those obtainable by other means. So, in one way and another, this particular interest came to be comparatively eclipsed; though there must still be enough interest in the matter to enable a piece of evolutionist *naturphilosophie* to become a best seller if it is sufficiently edifying and obscure. (With time, evolution can be enlisted on the side of the angels.)

The time has no doubt come for a revived philosophic interest in biological theories, differing from its predecessor in avoiding its errors and enthusiasms and in working on the much more sophisticated biology of today. This is the need which Professor Goudge tries to meet in his systematic and sober book,[1] amongst whose epigraphs there is a quotation from Bertrand Russell, which should be read in juxtaposition with the quotation from Wittgenstein at the beginning of this review: 'A philosophy which is to have any value should be built upon a wide and firm foundation of knowledge that is not specifically philosophical. . . . Philosophy which does not draw nourishment from this soil will soon wither and cease to grow.'

The author's purpose is 'to outline in a reasonably clear, nontechnical way some major features of the new (biological) conception of evolution; and . . . to investigate some philosophical questions which arise in connection with these features.' He classifies the philosophical problems in which he is interested into three groups: first, there is the *language* used by biologists in expounding the theory of evolution. Here he has in mind the technical meanings assigned to words such as 'adaptation' borrowed from ordinary speech. Secondly, he is concerned with the *logic* of evolutionary theory. Here for instance he is concerned with a feature of the theory of evolution which, as has often been pointed out, does rather single it out amongst scientific theories: it is both theoretical and *historical*. Thirdly, there are the metaphysical implications of the theory, by which he seems to mean simply the wider issues raised by it which are not a matter of either its internal vocabulary or internal logical structure.

There are passages where the author seems drawn towards the conclusion that it is metaphysical to assert that evolution 'really happened'. He is impelled towards this conclusion by the kind of view of scientific theory which holds that theories are somehow devices, conveniences, artifacts of the theorists for the purpose of collating and manipulating observations, and that consequently the things mentioned in them have no reality outside the life of the theory in the context of scientific activity. Such a view has its appeal in the context of, say, physics: I am not repelled by the idea that it makes no sense to ask whether an 'electron' really exists, and that this entity has no reality outside the theory within which this term performs an essential function.

But I find it almost impossible to adopt this kind of sophistication in the face of the biological theory of evolution, perhaps because it deals with macroscopic objects, and perhaps because it *is* an historical theory. Apart from anything else, one feels that historical events either *did* or *did not* occur. Somehow one feels that one's past, even when extended to include one's biological ancestry, though indeed it may be interpreted in the light of this or that concept or framework, nevertheless is something which in the main occurred in the way it did independently of the activities of the scientific interpreter— perhaps because large parts of it were, at one level or another, experienced by the participants in it. It seems to me that Professor Goudge is misguided in classing such a 'realism' about evolution with metaphysics (even although he does not use that term pejoratively), and also in linking the question of whether such realism is justified with other, more properly metaphysical issues, such as the existence of purpose in evolution. The permissibility of such questions about purpose and progress does not seem to me to depend, one way or the other, on a 'realistic' attitude to evolution. On the one hand, it seems to me quite possible to adopt the 'realistic' viewpoint —'it really happened'—and yet reject all notions savouring of purposiveness and evaluation as unsuitable for inclusion in a science: and on the other hand, if one does adopt a non-realistic viewpoint, this could yet give one great freedom in using *any* concept whatever, provided one found it useful in manipulating the theory. But it is an interesting reflection that the kind of subjectivism which sees the objects of scientific inquiry as constructs made by the theorist, is much easier to adopt in physics than in biology.

The reasons which make Professor Goudge tie up the realistic approach to evolution with other more properly metaphysical issues arising from it, becomes clearer in an extremely interesting section on 'evolution and knowledge of evolution'. Here he faces the fascinating problems in the theory of knowledge arising from the fact that man is connected with the theory of evolution twice over; as its author and as one of the objects of it. (If evolution were just a construct of a theory, these problems would not present themselves with such force, if at all. One of the implications, and perhaps the tacit motive of the 'construct' view of science, is that it provides us with a justification for not treating the content of scientific theories with undue seriousness when it is disagreeable to do so.) The author notes and rejects the kind of dualism, represented above all by Kant and in our time by Schrödinger, which starts from the insight that a 'pandemonium of disastrous logical consequences' (Schrödinger's phrase) follows if the subject, the thinker *qua* thinker, is treated at the same time as one of the objects of his own thought.

The dualistic way out is to conclude that the thinker as such must never be seen as part of the world he is investigating: he is a kind of pure visitor to the world, observing it but not a part of it. This view has the merit of solving some of the problems, and the demerit of leaving one with a most profound sense of implausibility. Professor Goudge rejects it. He is tempted by an alternative solution: 'Is it utterly fanciful to regard the theory of evolution as a means whereby certain members of Homo sapiens achieve an "intellectual adaptation" to the universe?' Thus the discovery and elaboration of the theory of evolution becomes itself an event illustrating that very theory. Moreover, Professor Goudge's own tentative suggestion that this is indeed so, *itself* becomes one further such event: and so does my observation that this is so, and my observation in the preceding clause, and this one in turn, and this, and . . . etc., etc. We have a lovely and possibly not even a vicious regress here. It is of course like the girl in the photograph holding a photograph of herself holding a photograph of herself . . . etc. I am just a little suspicious of the possibility that we can speed up one part of the process of evolution by reflecting on our own cleverness, first of all in having the theory at all, and then in seeing it as a piece of adaptation and so on. Yet, perhaps there is no harm in this.

But in general I am not too happy about this kind of solution. I am quite aware of the difficulties of the 'pure visitor' theory which Professor Goudge strives to avoid. But the theory which he tentatively suggests is a version of the 'pre-established harmony' approach in the theory of knowledge: the visitor is not pure. His thought and perception are governed by laws similar to those governing other parts of the world. But providentially, somehow, these laws are such as to ensure that his conclusions correctly reflect the rest of the world. Perhaps I am suspicious and untrusting by nature, but I feel ill at ease when such benevolence towards our cognitive aspirations is ascribed to the universe, even when it is made more plausible by assuming this benevolence to be the product of a mechanism such as natural selection.

Incidentally, in supporting his 'adaptive' view of theoretical activity itself, the author quotes a remark of Wittgenstein's which, as it stands in isolation, does seem to support him, but which in fact had quite another meaning for its author. 'A philosophic problem has a form "I don't know my way about" ' (Wittgenstein, *Philosophical Investigations*, Oxford, 1953). Wittgenstein certainly did not view philosophic theorizing as part of an evolutionary adaptive process. He seemed to view it as the restoration of a stable equilibrium inside a language system, which had been disturbed by thinkers using its terms to ask questions for which there was no habitual role within it. His view of language systems was, if anything, pre-Darwinian. Professor Goudge immediately comments: 'Not knowing one's way about is a kind of absence of adaptation.' But Wittgenstein did not mean philosophy to be a part of a groping towards new hitherto absent adaptations. He thought it merely the restoration of a previously existing adaptation, whose perfection was guaranteed by the consideration that there was no possible standard, in terms of which the actual use of language *could* be philosophically imperfect.

In his final conclusion, Professor Goudge invokes man's good evolutionary record in the past, in order to justify optimism concerning man's prospects in coping with the present crisis arising from the availability of means of collective self-destruction. I wish one could have some faith in this argument, which invokes a very abstract premiss and makes it bear on a very concrete individual situation. The point about the past evolutionary process was that it could afford to make mistakes, even numerous mistakes.

1962

Note

1 T. A. Goudge, *The Ascent of Life*, London, 1961.

Chapter 17   Man's picture of his world

In one of Nigel Balchin's novels, a character reflects on the oddity of any moderate or modest attitude to the ideas of psychoanalysis: like the notion of God, these ideas, if true, make so enormous a difference that one can hardly escape making them the centre of one's thought and life. It also follows that the inquiry into their validity should be an important concern, and so should their falsehood if they turn out to be false.

In fact, however, the history of thought and indeed our own intellectual climate of opinion are full of ideas and ways of thought which *logically* have this overwhelming power, whose internal claims are such that they ought to force us into some supreme Pascalian wager and commitment about them one way or the other, but which in practice come to be used as small changes of the mind and to live in more or less peaceable coexistence with rival ideas (Marx, Freud, Wittgenstein . . .). At their inception, they may be treated with the seriousness their content calls for, but in the course of time they are somehow watered down and socialized, and learn to live and let live. This argues ill for human consistency and sincerity, but socially speaking it is a great blessing. For logically, Mao is probably right and Khrushchev wrong, and coexistence a heresy. But the survival of societies depends on such heresies being accepted. No society and no harmony without doublethink. (It is only through unavowed heresy, for instance, that Muslim states can subscribe to the United Nations charter and refrain from periodic Holy Wars.)

The ideas of Freud have gone through this process of domestication, though happily it is by no means complete or stable. This mellowing is due partly to sheer age, the acquisition of caution-engendering vested interests on one side and habituation and acceptance on the other, and in part it is deliberately fostered by some practitioners themselves, perhaps in the hope of avoiding criticism. One often hears protestations of modesty, such as that psychoanalysis should not be seen as a world-view, that it is but a technique with limited claims and powers, or that it cannot be expected to aid the psyche in difficulties which have an objective rather than neurotic basis—claims which, whether convenient or not, are I suspect in conflict with the inner logic of the ideas themselves.

The works of Mr Money-Kyrle are greatly welcome, for these are the reflections of a practising psychoanalyst who is also genuinely aware of the outer world, and attempts to explore the cross-implications with lucidity and candour. Mr Money-Kyrle does indeed see the world from the vantage-point of psychoanalysis, and a very strange world it turns out to be; and it is interesting to see the world from this perspective, its objects acquiring quite different proportions and positions from those they habitually possess. But at any rate it *is* our common world seen through a strange perspective, rather than a self-enclosed world of its own.

Mr Money-Kyrle's overt aim is not to explore the cross-implications of psychoanalytic and other thought, but to systematize the views of one segment of the psychoanalytic movement, the Kleinian, which he considers to be the most progressive. His conception of what such systematization involves, however, is so broad, including as it does views on ethics, aesthetics and politics, that in practice his discussions, whether one agrees with them or not, do have the effect of keeping the diverse fields sensitive and alive to each other, rather than insulated and coexisting into an insensitive eclecticism.

His approach in this book[1] is guided by a certain schema. One can see man in three ways: as an object, as the natural sciences see him, or dualistically, as common sense sees him, or finally as central and pivotal to the world which his mind had 'built', as he is seen by philosophers such as Hume and Mach. Though he also explores the first two visions, he explicitly commends the last 'as psychologists, we ought, perhaps, to reverse the order [of common sense] and think first of experience as that out of which each individual builds his world . . . and I suggest that psycho-analysis could make use of it also to construct a more comprehensive picture of man in relation to his world.' This is a truly amazing marriage of psychoanalytic and epistemological thought: the egocentric predicament of the empiricist picture of our knowledge is married to a Kleinian subjection to our infancy. This might seem a sad fate indeed, but Mr Money-Kyrle's book is not a pessimistic one.

I wonder, however, whether the psychoanalytic and epistemological approaches really will mix well: I had always supposed that what gave psychoanalytic thought its vitality was precisely that, unlike academic psychology, it did not originate from epistemological preoccupations. It was never a theory of knowledge driving itself into the laboratory from a sense of obligation to its own principles.

Mr Money-Kyrle's main reason for valuing the epistemological, subjective approach is that in seeing how the individual constructs his world, we at the same time see the general features of the world, of which the other sciences supply the detailed features. 'The task of psychology is to describe how world-models are constructed, that of other sciences is to extend and refine specific parts of them. . . .' Man being pivotal and the 'constructor' of his world, the study of man is also the study of the basic construction of that world: psychology is also an *ex officio* cosmology.

This has often been the aim of theories of knowledge: by as it were catching the world as it passes through the needle's eye of knowledge, to gain a short cut to its general features. What is novel in Mr Money-Kyrle's thought is that *three* (and not, as is more common, two) things are fused into one: a genetic account of the growth of our view of the world, a philosophical theory of knowledge which cannot but, at least tacitly, assess the validity of what we claim to know, and finally a synthesis of the findings of the sciences about the world. (One should add, in fairness to him, that he explicitly disclaims the ability to complete such a synthesis—but it is interesting to see that, on his view, a completion of a psychoanalytic system of thought would also be a unification of science: by knowing how our knowledge grows we would also know the general features of its content.) The problems which this triple identification raises are enormous, and whether solved or not, it is very interesting to see them raised. In practice, psychoanalytic thinkers do tend to see the world through their theories of what happens to the psyche, and it is good to see the problems inherent in this view brought into the open.

It is impossible to follow up all of Mr Money-Kyrle's applications of his programme, but it is worth commenting on some. He is familiar with the grave objections to psychoanalysis, best argued by Professor K. Popper, that a doctrine so elastic that *nothing* could falsify it is of no scientific value. Unlike some who are wedded to psychoanalysis, this point does not cause him to burst into a defensive anger. He argues with it earnestly, and his argument takes the form both of a theory of how in general we know about the thoughts and feelings of other people, and how in particular psychoanalytic interpretations come to be accepted and rejected.

Concerning knowledge of other minds in general, it is odd that he should not consider the theories of recent philosophers, who have devoted so much of their minute labours to this problem. 'Psychoanalytic reasoning', he says, 'is in essence very simple and of a type on which all our beliefs about other people are ultimately based. If we see two people embrace, we imagine them to be in love because we are acquainted with such feelings in ourselves.' Could we then never comprehend what we have not experienced? Or is it a part of his doctrine that in some sense we do experience all feelings our lan-

guage can describe? I can hardly be accused of being a wholly uncritical follower of Wittgenstein and Ryle, but I am surprised to see
him subscribe so flatly to the 'analogy with ourselves' theory of our
knowledge of others, without even attempting to answer those who
have claimed so firmly to have destroyed this theory.

The second part of his argument here, an account of the specifically psychoanalytic mode of choosing and rejecting interpretations of
the minds of others, is, if I understand rightly, open to other objections. His account of how the analyst comes to *reject* an interpretation—and this is crucial in answering a demand for falsifiability—is
in terms of the analyst's capacity to detect his own motivation which
had led him to see the situation falsely. He detects falsehood by un-
masking his own motives for embracing it. But this leads to a view
which I suspect is deeply embedded in psychoanalytic thinking,
namely, that error is always somehow motivated. Identify and
neutralize the motive, error will disappear, and truth is—the remaining residue. But is this so? Is truth manifest and simply available
even for a pure heart? I doubt it. Here Mr Money-Kyrle might well
consider another objection arising from Popper's thought—namely
that truth is *not* manifest, for anyone, not even for those who know
themselves.

Finally, a word about the author's views on society and history.
They are 'psychologistic' in the extreme: the crucial factor in social
changes appears to be the personality types (and their distribution in
various social classes) of the participants. Mr Money-Kyrle distinguishes between technical change, which he believes to be 'linear',
i.e. continuously progressive, and social change, which is sadly
'circular'. For one constellation of our psyches produces revolution,
which brings forth another constellation and reaction. And so on.
But is there no hope? May we not break out of this circle?

There is some. Psychological insight may soften and enlighten both
rebels and reactionaries. Mr Money-Kyrle feels diffident about
whether this cross-bench or cross-barricades diffusion of insight can
be attained, but confident about the beneficent consequences of its
achievement. Social change too would then become 'linear', though
he does not tell us in which direction the line would soar. The actual
description given of the happy post-insight period makes it sound
rather like a stable equilibrium, a balance between equality and its
absence. It appears that this balance would not be the same in all
places and circumstances. But what matters is that each side would
be 'fully conscious of the sources of tension between them, and
(would be) able to form true pictures of themselves in relation to the
other'. Thus an insightful class would be happy even with tensions:
or perhaps, a *very* insightful class with *very* mild tensions?

In connection with this, Mr Money-Kyrle comments on the

present international and ideological situation. Nowhere does his psycho-centrism come out more clearly. 'If . . . Communist autocracy had been allowed to dominate the world, most of the psychological knowledge we have so painfully acquired would have been lost. . . .' Thus the essence of the cold war is to preserve Freud for humanity. We are right to risk nuclear extinction in order to preserve those insights whose diffusion might eventually liberate us from 'cyclical' history. All this follows from the author's premisses, and it is good to see him have the courage of his convictions. But what if the Russians abjured Pavlov and embraced Freud? Would CND be vindicated?

This is not clear. Mr Money-Kyrle is sceptical of 'a desire for truth arising spontaneously at the pyramid of Communist power'. To believe in this 'might be to embrace [a] lethal delusion'. Would it reassure him (or perhaps he knows) that a cautious and partial rehabilitation of Freud has appeared in the Soviet Journal of Psychology? (Of the *young* and more materialist Freud, naturally. The East prefers its Freud young and Marx old, unlike our own metaphysical leftists who like their Freud old and Marx young.) Perhaps this would not reassure him much, for the valued insight 'can only partially be communicated by books and lectures'. More of it, but still not enough, was communicated by Freud to his disciples and by them to each other. 'Great difficulties will have to be overcome before this knowledge becomes deep enough and wide enough to have much effect on the . . . social cycles. . . .'

So, we must defend our society against the insightless barbarians, for they would destroy the knowledge which the Guardians amongst us communicate to each other, and we must hope that they multiply fast enough to be able in the end to save us from our own fatality.

1961

Note

1   R. E. Money-Kyrle, *Man's Picture of His World*, London, 1961.

Chapter 18 On Freud and Reich

In general, I subscribe to the sacred right of authors to write the book they wish to write, rather than a book which the reviewer would wish them to write instead. Nevertheless, certain terms of reference are on occasion dictated by time and circumstance. Freud's ideas were not born yesterday. In rough and possibly distorted outline, they are common property. Hence an author writing a short book on them, clearly aimed at an unspecialized audience, cannot content himself with a simple account of those ideas and their genesis. He must attempt to relate his hero to the intellectual climate which owes him so much, and offer some kind of stocktaking. It is just this which is so crucially lacking in Professor Wollheim's closely packed book on Freud's intellectual development.[1]

For instance: academic philosophy has in recent decades been preoccupied with the philosophy of mind. What was at issue was the standing of or normal conceptualization of our mental activities, and the question of the nature, need, possibility and desirability of supplementing this ordinary way of looking at ourselves by some other set of concepts, perhaps resembling, perhaps contrasted with those of natural science. Heaven knows that I am not an uncritical admirer of this tradition in philosophy (which postdates most of Freud), but the fact remains that it is hardly conceivable that if these two traditions are brought in contact, one or the other (probably both) will not require some modification. To find an author who is utterly familiar with both traditions, writing a book about one without referring to the other (Wittgenstein is mentioned only as a fellow-admirer of Lichtenberg), gives one an uncomfortable feeling that the author is badly scared of something. Are the allegedly razor-sharp tools of logical analysis used only on dead traditions, and not on current faiths? Does this lion prefer carrion? This is a suspicion I have long and, as some would say, unworthily entertained. I am genuinely sorry to find Wollheim's book providing it with encouragement.

Or again, it would be most interesting to have some discussion of whether the Freudian model is vulnerable to the kind of onslaught to which Chomsky subjected behaviourism. (Contrary to popular belief, that onslaught does not in any way hinge on the 'soulless' properties of behaviourism, but only on its explanatory poverty.) This question should be of special interest to Wollheim, for it is a distinctive feature of his exegesis that he takes very seriously Freud's rather physicalist *Project of a Scientific Psychology* of 1895, about which Freud himself became ambivalent and which he chose to leave as a torso, and which other analysts, as Wollheim observes, considered baneful. Wollheim himself rates its importance highly. Yet one wonders what would happen to this model and its variants, if one subjected it to the test of requiring it to provide genuine, non-circular explanations of human performances, instead of tolerating it as a para-mechanical just-so story, items within which cannot be independently described (let alone located), without tacitly invoking those very bits of behaviour which they are meant to explain. . . .

Or again, the most fundamental criticism to which psychoanalysis is open is that Freud unwittingly invented a system in which doctrine, concepts, technique and organization form an interlocking whole, so arranged that any difficulties or counter-examples are systematically evaded. No one should nowadays be able to write a general book about Freud without at least attempting to deal with this. Wollheim makes no effort in this direction. His account concentrates on doctrine. Therapeutic problems and their contribution to the genesis of doctrine are of course mentioned, but on the whole the tacit assumption seems to be that Freudian concepts and doctrines are capable of living a life of their own: 'The relation of therapy to theory in psychoanalysis is just a special instance of the way in which every empirical science permits of practical application.' He admits that special problems arise from the fact that the application consists of handing out explanations drawn from the very theory that is being applied, but does not seem to think this affects the general principle. The intriguing contrary possibility, that psychoanalytical concepts come to life only in the special milieu created for them by a therapeutic technique and its social organization, is not considered.

There is only one all too brief chapter, the final one concerned with Freud's social philosophy, in which the book really comes to life in terms imposed by its format and context. Here Wollheim concludes that there is no excuse for enlisting Freud, 'in the interest of this or that piety', as a 'recruit . . . to . . . optimism'. On the whole I agree, but Wollheim does not really dispose of the possibility that the facile optimism of some post-Freudians, indisputably in conflict with much of what Freud says, is nevertheless a perfectly logical development of other themes also genuinely present in Freud.

Why did Wollheim fail to make the connections, to ask the

questions which so clearly impose themselves? One can only suspect misplaced reverence. Though his dense style is not starry-eyed at all, there is a profoundly disturbing final sentence in the preface, which unambiguously implies that undergoing analysis is a *necessary* (*sic*, but italics mine) qualification for writing about Freud. A professor of philosophy does not use the term *necessary* lightly, and I fear Wollheim means what he says.

But if so, one can only hope that Wollheim will acquire the courage of his reverence and write that explicit defence of Freudianism which seems implicit in his extraordinary disregard of critics or even friendly commentators. (The book does not mention those numerous philosophers or philosophically oriented analysts who have attempted to relate this complex of ideas to other visions or external standards.)

Of course, there is also room for the kind of book of which this one seems a fragment—a meticulous account of the genesis of Freud's ideas, one which in philosophy goes no further back than Brentano, which stresses doctrine more than therapy, and within doctrine treats the rather physicalist early model as crucial, and which contents itself with raising problems internal to the outlook and its language, rather than fundamental and external. Such a book would of course have to be longer and addressed to specialists. The present book though it leans heavily towards this pole, is an unhappy compromise between it and the wider terms of reference imposed by the context.

Mr Charles Rycroft's book about Wilhelm Reich[2] is altogether admirable, and a model of what a book of this kind should be. For one thing, it is just right stylistically: without ever being superficial, it is extremely readable, and one is never obliged to retrace one's step in order to discern the structure of the argument. On a number of occasions, his dry but unmalicious humour made me laugh out aloud. For another thing, it is impossible to read this book without gaining in a kind of collective ideological self-knowledge: ideas which are very much in the air, whether or not one likes them, are convincingly traced to what clearly is one of their important sources, or at any rate one of their earliest articulations in a modern idiom.

Fate was cruel to Reich in a number of ways, but perhaps most of all in letting him live, or rather die, a decade or so too soon. It was he above all who forged the most characteristic items in the intellectual armoury of the *secessio iuventutis*. He forged that curious mixture of sexual mysticism, the blaming of ills on an oppressive social structure, and a passionate anthropodicy, which is so central to the movement. I suppose that in a world without god, it is essential that the earlier justification of the ways of god be replaced by a demonstration that, appearances notwithstanding, *man* is basically good. (If not, one is left with the discomfort of irreducible, inexplicable evil.) The only thing which prevents man from acceding to his rightful heritage of both virtue and happiness are distorted and distorting social and psychic structures, which, however, are contingent and not necessary evils. But where do they come from, given that they are not inherent in quintessential man? In this form, the problem of evil, exorcized at the first step of the argument, makes its reappearance, and not the least interesting part of Rycroft's book are the passages which describe Reich's struggles with this problem, struggles so arduous and demanding that they led even this otherwise most dogmatic of men into tentativeness and tolerance.

Reich believed himself to have burst through the conceptual fetters that have bound humanity for quite some millennia, and inferred logically enough that in consequence, his views could not be criticized by those who were still fettered. This logic, impeccable as far as it goes, has also been inherited by the protest movement. But, except for its extravagance, it is not inherently different from the practice of invoking *resistance* as supporting evidence for the justice and penetration of your views. Over and again, Rycroft shows how various of Reich's extravagances arise by pushing psychoanalytic ideas to their limit. It is not always clear that orthodoxy also possesses the logical, as opposed to prudential, means for not pushing on to some similar limits. This might lead one to adapt an eighteenth-century aphorism and reflect that if you really want to make it as a prophet, it is not enough to be outrageous—you need some social skills as well. These poor Reich on the whole lacked.

He was well placed in time to come in early on and attempt to fuse the messianic elements in Marx and Freud, and he was expelled from both movements for his pains. Rycroft shows the half-suppressed debt which orthodox analysis owes him, quite apart from the most manifest debt owed him by the more *freischwebend* gurus. Their gain is Reich's loss, for were he still with us they would have to share some of their glory.

Reich was, not to put too fine a point on it, as crazy as a coot. He believed he could isolate the life force chemically and consign it to boxes which were supplied to his followers. 'Orgone boxes . . . were constructed of alternating layers of steel wool and rock or glass wool . . . they were the shape of a telephone box or coffin . . . and I am told that one did indeed feel a bit strange after being encased in one, probably on account of their poor ventilation.' What makes Rycroft's book so admirable is that he takes this complex of ideas, which most of us would dismiss as far beyond the pale of reason and possible interest, and shows not merely its genesis and crystallization in the mind of a man, its intimate relation to the problems and conceptual equipments of an age, but also its elements of plausibility and the points at which it might contain something of merit. It is done with sympathy and not with derision, and in the end Rycroft converts the reader to a similar attitude. Given vitalism as a philosophical background, given the principle that psychic forces must in the end have a physical base, given a time in which both Freudianism and Marxism were making a powerful impact, given some therapeutic successes, the Reichian synthesis was not at all points absurd, and may have sinned by consistency rather than otherwise.

Rycroft's vision of him is as of a mystic who asserted insights which are within the Western mystical tradition commonplace rather than extravagant, who was led by a combination of scientism and scientific incompetence to formulate those insights in an inappropriate idiom, who responded to the problems of his age, borrowed from its visions and contributed to them, and within whose thought something of value might also be found alongside the absurdities. As an hermeneutic exercise, Rycroft's book is superb, for it converts one to sympathy without at any point abandoning sobriety and critical standards. Rycroft also compassionately observes that Reich was a central European and, as such, lacking in humour and incapable of formulating insights without wishing to anchor them to a System. He also had a central European trait which might have been a point of friction with his knowing or unknowing followers of today—he took academic titles and rank with utmost seriousness.

1971

Notes

1   Richard Wollheim, *Freud*, London, 1971.

2   Charles Rycroft, *Reich*, London, 1971.

Chapter 19 A genetic psychologist's confessions

'This book being something of a confession . . .', says Jean Piaget in a footnote of *Insights and Illusions*, in which he goes on to describe an encounter with 'the great Bergson'. The book is indeed an intensely personal one, and this, more even than its polemics with diverse philosophical psychologists (or psychologizing philosophers) is what gives it both its charm and its interest. It reminds one very strongly of R. G. Collingwood's *Autobiography*. A lady novelist once claimed that Russell told her that talking to her was more exciting than making love to other women. Whether or not we credit her story, there is no doubt that when a Piaget or a Collingwood confesses his doctrinal flirtations, the result is considerably more interesting than the accounts of other men's amours.

Piaget does not possess Collingwood's literary brilliance and elegance; on the contrary, his account of his intellectual adventures is a bit fumbling (rather like some old general in Anouilh dictating his memoirs), and he is not too well served by his English translation, which seems on occasion to follow the French word order to the detriment of both meaning and style. But this very artlessness gives one a sense that what one is given is close to the unadorned truth. Perhaps unfairly, a superb artist such as Collingwood puts one on one's guard, whereas Piaget's fumbling gives a strong impression of sincerity.

But they have one thing in common, which also explains why, despite the difference in degree of artistry, the intellectual confessions of both of them should be so interesting: their preoccupation with the philosophy of knowledge was deeply *engagé*, committed not in the absurd sense that they should refuse to look at rival views, but in the sense of being fed by a lifelong, haunting preoccupation, and one arising from genuine hard work in a substantive field. There are indeed striking parallels between the basic problems of method facing the archaeologist-historian and the genetic psychologist.

Like Collingwood, Piaget's work will be read not merely for its account of the development of one man, but also for its illuminating sketches of various intellectual climates. Some of his comments are devastating. Discussing the relationship between political irrational-ism, and anti-empiricism in the *Geisteswissenschaften* during the interwar period, Piaget describes a holder of a chair in Berne who 'taught a kind of Italian neo-Hegelianism under the name of psy-chology. Inspired by Gentile and adapted to his style, it was . . . a model of "autistic" philosophy.' 'Autistic philosophy' is a category we have long been in need of, and it is shameful that we should have had to wait for a Swiss psychologist to coin the phrase.

Or there is this splendid story about Spain: 'I read on the visiting card . . . Señor X. Catedrático de psicología superior. "Why higher?" I asked frankly. "Because it is not experimental. . . ."'

And there is also a footnote story about G. E. Moore, showing him at his characteristic and dreadful worst. Moore told Piaget that his, Piaget's, concern with the genesis of cognitive norms 'is of no interest at all . . . because the philosopher is concerned with true ideas, while the psychologist feels a sort of vicious and incomprehensible attrac-tion for the study of false ideas!' Piaget appositely referred Moore to history: 'How do you know . . . that your true ideas will not at a later date be judged to be inadequate?' Predictably, the extra-temporal Moore found this objection totally irrelevant.

Indeed, Piaget's opening chapter, 'An Account of and an Analysis of a Disenchantment', deserves to be read alongside Jean-François Revel's masterly *Pourquoi des philosophes?* as a succinct, witty, and perceptive account of an intellectual climate and its institutional underpinning. His splendid account of the structural bias of the French university towards intellectual conservatism contains the malicious observation that it is not for nothing that Durkheim's doctrine (of the social nature of truth) originated in France.

Piaget's account is no less valuable for the fact that the post-1968 reforms have now dated it. In this respect as in some others, the book bears marks of the fact that it was first published in France in 1965. For instance, it was evidently written before the work of Chomsky (whose themes are closely parallel to his) made an impact on Piaget. (Chomsky's name does not appear in this book, whereas it is frequently invoked in the other volume under discussion.)

Piaget's central problem in *Epistémologie des sciences de l'homme* is the question of method in the study of man and, more speci-fically, in the study of the genesis of our cognitive powers. He is fighting on a number of fronts. He dislikes being classed as a posi-tivist, for he uses this name to describe a theory concerning the manner in which we *acquire* knowledge, and of course a mistaken one. (This corresponds to Chomsky's modal use of the term 'empiricism'.) He might console himself by the reflection that there exists a Con-tinental usage according to which anyone not subscribing to autistic philosophy is automatically a positivist, and the two species are made to exhaust the universe.

At the same time, he is both appalled and perturbed by the apriorism, subjectivism and complacency of the philosophers, with their enthusiasm for sitting on their bottoms and laying down the law about the structure of the human mind, predicament, etc., and their new rationales for so doing. But it is important and interesting that Piaget is perturbed as well as appalled. He is not at all tempted to take the positivistic short-cut and proscribe all non-experimental thought as intellectually disreputable. He is acutely sensitive to the problem which arises for our intellectual world through the awkward relationship between Science and Something Else. It is altogether to his credit that he is not tempted by the two extremist solutions, either the brazen elevation to sovereignty of the Something Else (this might be called the Left Bank solution, though certain variants of it are very fashionable in Britain), or by its ruthless proscription.

The solution which he does offer is moderate and likable rather than high-powered. It consists of a division of labour between the experimental sciences, and a philosophy which does not presume to rival or condemn them, or have its own avenues to reality, but which confines itself to 'wisdom'. This does not really get us very far. Though Piaget is very observant when it comes to the specific social milieux and the way they encourage hostility to empirical psychology, he is not so perceptive when it comes to the general reasons which make for a tension between the world of science and of man, between (in Gaston Bachelard's phrase) the world in which we think and the one in which we live. To put this in another way, Kantian though he is in epistemology, Piaget has not learnt enough from Kant's ethics.

The largest part of *Insights and Illusions of Philosophy* is taken up with combating philosophical pretensions to a priori psychological knowledge and its modern rationalizations. But as Wolfe Mays observes in his insightful introduction, there are striking parallels between the Continental, predominantly phenomenological manner of doing this, which preoccupies Piaget, and Anglo-Saxon linguistic philosophy. Both do indeed spring from the same general situation, from the need to defend the *Lebenswelt* against the idiom of an abstract or experimental science. Thus they have a deeper root than the mere laziness of the non-experimentalist, though this factor is also important. The joke is that in the 'Anglo-Saxon' variant (whose most influential form was in fact invented by a Viennese), the attack on empiricism is carried out in the name of empiricism itself. The argument runs, roughly: our concepts are embodied in (or are tantamount to) the rules governing our use of language. What we say, however, is immediately accessible to us, because *we* say it, and thus an important realm is made available which we need not hand over to the experimentalists, and which, indeed, the experimentalist would travesty. And as, incidentally, our concepts define our world, we thereby find out a lot about that world—and reconfirm that the world is just as our traditional ways of thinking always led us to suppose. So everything is secure. A dispensation from the requirement to heed science could hardly go further, and, through the neat 'linguistic' twist, it is all done in the name of respect for empiricism, for fact, for language as it is actually spoken.

The so-called phenomenological method secures the land-deeds to virtually the same realm, but by a different route. Is it not legitimate, runs its argument, to examine our own concepts, whilst suspending the 'natural attitude', which is interested in the reality of the objects of those concepts? This procedure has a number of curious consequences, apart from handing over this realm of suspended concepts, in a kind of philosophical bonded warehouse, to the non-empirical contemplator. In at least two ways, it freezes and distorts that realm. The 'natural attitude' is not merely interested in the reality or otherwise of objects, it is also sensitive to the possible *in*validity of concepts. It is aware, in other words, of the possibility that things may turn out to be quite different from what we initially supposed, and hence that the concepts in terms of which they were seen in fact totally misdescribe them. The phenomenological attitude, by freeing our ideas of any such threat (for the natural attitude is 'suspended'), thereby also confers a kind of rigor mortis on them.

Secondly, it is part and parcel of at least our contemporary *Lebenswelt*, or commonsense, that there is built into it an uneasy sense of its own inadequacy. The notions of daily life are inadequate, they have a kind of *pis aller* or interim standing: we suspect that a true understanding of things requires some quite different idiom. In other words, tentativeness, insecurity, a kind of general *sursis* are already part of concepts in their normal daily life. We practise epoché as we speak prose, and we do not need Husserl to invent it for us. Thus phenomenology, in the name of suspending our concepts, does exactly the opposite. It confers on them a kind of rigidity and an unwarranted inner security. Thereby, it not merely issues a charter to bum-sitting apriorism (a small matter) but, through it, unjustifiably reconfirms the trustworthiness of our whole shaky *Lebenswelt*. It is by this kind of facile argument that Sartre, for instance, arrives so confidently at free will, at 'le self-service de sa conscience libre', in M. Revel's marvellous phrase. At this crucially important point, the parallel with linguistic philosophy is perfect. But in truth it is precisely a central feature of our condition, that the *Lebenswelt* (or world of ordinary language) is precarious and does not inspire confidence.

There is one further parallel at least. Phenomenology tends to be interesting only when applied to things human. In other spheres, its conclusions, its examination of 'suspended' concepts, tend naturally to have the form 'a rose is a rose is a rose'. But when applied to the structure of self-consciousness itself, there are at least suggestive things to be said. Similarly, the centre of gravity of linguistic philosophy tends to be in the philosophy of mind.

1972

Chapter 20   Eysenck: seeing emperors naked

Together with Skinner and Monod, Eysenck is perhaps the most influential of contemporary proponents of what might loosely and without prejudice be called scientism, and which is expounded and applied in his recent collection of essays.[1] Once upon a time this position might have been called materialism or even empiricism. Professor Eysenck is pleased to recognize Descartes on animals, and La Mettrie and Condillac on man, as intellectual ancestors, and speaks of 'the natural affinity of behaviourism and materialism'. Later on in the course of the same argument (a mere two pages later, in fact) he seems to change his mind and declares that 'metaphysical behaviourism . . . is of no interest to anyone . . . and . . . does not say anything sensible, and it is not specifically behaviouristic . . . because . . . behaviourism implies a completely empirical attitude, i.e. a denial that such *a priori* arguments can have any sense whatever'. For we had just been told that Descartes, La Mettrie and Condillac 'were philosophers and metaphysicians, primarily concerned with the mind-body problem', whereas *real* behaviourists such as Watson, Skinner and Thorndike 'did not care about this problem in the slightest, and never thought about it—they took it for granted that stimuli and their effects determine human conduct, and went on from there to elucidate the actual laws according to which this determination takes place'. Some might say that this does not amount to having no ideas about the mind–body problem, but on the contrary having rather rigid ones, 'not thinking' in a rather pejorative sense, and incidentally prejudging the interesting and plausible possibility that though human behaviour *is* law-bound, the laws *cannot* possibly be put into a stimulus–response form, or into any complex variant of that basic principle.

What has happened here is, of course, that Eysenck is a *modern* kind of behaviourist-materialist, trying eagerly to kick away the ladder by which he has ascended to his position. The intellectual ancestors knew they had a position to defend. Eysenck vacillates between hailing them as pioneers, and being embarrassed by the association, for he also wants to treat the position as something obvious for all men of goodwill and of sense—good but trivial, as something only talked about outside office hours (or lab hours): 'Behaviourism emerges as something really quite colourless and without any distinct doctrine. What it has to say is simply that psychology is a scientific discipline . . . and that like other scientific disciplines it has only one request to make of metaphysics—get off my back!' All this presupposes that there is no serious problem about what kind of world we are in and what is the proper way of investigating it. Contemporary philosophers have strongly encouraged this general attitude (though not necessarily on behalf of Eysenck's specific vision of things); and indeed Eysenck expounds these views of his in the context of a distinction borrowed with acknowledgements from one of them, between metaphysical, analytic and methodological behaviourism. It just so happens that the very unproblematical, obvious and unique worlds of Eysenck on the one hand, and of most of the philosophers from whom he has borrowed the idiom of epistemological complacency on the other, are not at all the *same* worlds. They are quite different. So the question as to which world we are in cannot have *quite* such an easy and obvious answer after all.

Eysenck differs from his metaphysically-tainted proto-behaviourist ancestors in another way, over and above wobbling between seeing his own position as a *position* amongst others, and as a kind of obvious null hypothesis which does not require defence. He also differs from them in that whereas they were contrasted with traditional religious or metaphysical views, Eysenck's battle, which brought him fame, was with a very contemporary and entirely living dragon. This is wholly to his credit, and shows that he can identify his enemy, without fear or favour. It is also in marked contrast to the fashionable *salon-positivismus* of yesteryear, which took up the posture of an intrepid knight when facing dragons long since dead, sheepishly looking around for applause and admiration for its daring, whilst remaining full of respectful deference, or worse, when facing any current, with-it superstitions. How tough-minded they were with superstitions that were out of date, yet how often they were incapable even of understanding a doubt concerning a current one! Eysenck certainly does not belong to that class of positivists *fainéants*. The position he holds, without finesse or logical depth, is held with sincerity and vigour.

His own very special dragon is of course psycho-analysis. He is not given to modesty, when describing his achievement in this field: 'I always saw my role in all this as being rather like that of the young boy in the fairy tale of the Emperor's New Clothes. . . .' Well, yes, there is no doubt but that he was in the forefront of this fight. But there were others too who felt that nothing is quite as superficial as depth psychology. It is an exaggeration to say that 'at one time nearly everyone thought that the Emperor did in fact have on the most gorgeous raiments'.

He tells us not merely that he was the brave child who disclosed the Emperor's nudity, but also that in consequence it is now generally recognized: 'Nowadays many young students take it more or less for granted that psychotherapy is pretty useless.' This, if true, is most interesting comment on changing intellectual fashions. What strikes me as interesting is that the time when psycho-analysis, with all its subjectivism, was taken most seriously, was also a period when ponderous scientism, the emulation of the supposed idiom and procedures of the natural scientist, was most rife in the social and human sciences. It was almost as if the hot intimacy of the one compensated for the cold impersonality affected by the other. It is curious that psycho-analysis should be on the wane at the time when objectivism is no longer fashionable, when leading social scientists try to write prose rather than tables, and when a large number of practitioners turn to schools which, in various styles, proclaim that truth is subjective and inward.

It is arguable that Popper's account, which is nowhere mentioned in this book, of how psycho-analysis fails precisely by not putting itself at risk at all, was as influential as Eysenck's insistence on how it fails. The absence of references to Popper or other philosophers of science is also symptomatic of something else: the trouble with Eysenck's position is not that it is scientistic, but that his scientism, though vigorous and sincere, is not very deep or perceptive.

Even so, this is not nearly so simple (let alone manifestly true) a position as he supposes. It contains a number of strands: a wholly admirable respect for the ascertainment of fact, and a contempt for those who would prejudge or ignore facts; a predilection for causal explanations; and a residual and very simple evolutionist social philosophy, which he supposes to be elicited from the facts. Like some of the materialists whom he so ambivalently claims as ancestors he has little understanding of the logical tension between the first two elements in this compound. (Behaviourism is in fact a case of logical miscegenation, of the application of criteria which make some sense when applied to *data*, to the quite different problem of the delimitation of possible *explanatory models*.) The third element, evolutionism, comes out in passages such as this: 'Opposed to the neo-cortex, which is the seat of reason, is the brain-stem . . . seat . . . of ancient, feelings and habits . . . derived from evolutionary developments no longer advantageous to us. . . . Science is the expression of reason in its highest form, and science therefore is our one and only hope for survival.' If this means that we have a better chance of survival, if we act in terms of facts rather than of illusions, then it is probably true; and that the system of activities known as 'science' is somehow related to the neo-cortex of individuals, is then an interesting side-remark. But if it means, as it appears to do, that there is somewhere a repository of saving precepts, which are sound *in virtue* of being the expression of something called Reason, which has higher and lower forms and can be graded by their physiological location . . . well, that sounds just like the kind of metaphysics which he says he wants to abjure, and a most muddled specimen of the genre to boot.

This conditional scientistic-evolutionist optimism is in curious and characteristic contrast to one of the opening passages of the book: 'Social science has been rather oversold; there is little that we can do, as scientists, about atomic war and its prevention, or about social unrest and upheaval, or about strikes and other confrontations.' Well, which is it to be? Related to this we find an old set of contradictions which pervade Enlightenment–type philosophy: a conviction that it is all really simple, provided you just attend to the facts as they really are (heed Nature, as they used to say); followed by exasperation at the way people will follow their irrational attitudes rather than heed facts; and this in turn tempered a little by a realization that this is precisely what, on one's own theories of human conduct, one should expect. Neo-cortex or not, rationality is more surprising than irrationality. . . .

1972

Note

1 H. J. Eysenck, *Psychology is about People*, London, 1972.

Chapter 21 On Chomsky

When Noam Chomsky came to give his Shearman Memorial lectures at University College, London, the enormous Collegiate Hall was packed and overflowed, and many had to be turned away. Yet the lectures that people had come to hear were not given by some entertainer-don. On the contrary, the lectures were on an abstract topic, by a lecturer who had contributed much, as some might complain, to make his subject much more abstract than it had ever been before.

Despite his effortless and almost diffident lucidity, the level of argument was such as to strain to the utmost the concentration, the logical powers, the sophistication and the range of the audience. Even if one were to suppose that some had come to hear Chomsky, the theoretician of language, only in order to see Chomsky, the prophet of peace in Vietnam and in the Middle East, this could account for only a small proportion of the audience, and does not explain the magic which this most abstract and unshowmanlike of theoreticians indisputably possesses.

There can be few, if any, intellectuals of his age who have already made as profound an impact on the intellectual scene as he has. There can hardly be another professor around the age of 40 who can calmly refer, without immodesty and with full justification, to his own work of a decade or so ago as 'classical' or 'standard', and contrast it with not one but two intellectual generations of subsequent revisionists of it. In the world of 'generative grammars', time appears to move fast, and scholarly generations succeed each other at a speed which leaves them quite out of phase with the slower pace of physical time: so these successive generations of linguists can build on the foundations laid by their intellectual grandfather who, in the physical world, is identical with quite a young man. He can, and apparently does, look at his own *alter ego* of two scholarly generations ago with detachment, calmly picking out what he keeps, what he rejects, or what he restores.

The concepts or terminology contributed by the grandfather of a decade ago have already entered and pervaded ordinary intellectual discourse. In the accumulating verbal strata of our intellectual life, 'deep structure' and 'generative grammar' are in a layer high above the paleolithic one of notions such as 'feedback' or 'information', and roughly contemporaneous with the debris of Lévi-Strauss. In other words, the fashion is well established. As far as one knows, it has not yet forced Chomsky to observe *moi, je ne suis pas Chomskien.*

The fashion is not merely well diffused, but also entirely justified. But how do ideas of this degree of abstractness and difficulty come to have so wide an appeal?

Part of the answer must be that Chomsky's ideas are only incidentally about language, in the sense which concerns primarily the professional linguist. They may be inspired or occasioned by language, and language may be their best, or most accessible, testing ground: but they are not specifically about language. What Chomsky explores is not so much the range, conditions, and mechanics of our *linguistic* competence, as of our linguistic *competence*.

What is really at issue is not our ability to acquire and use a language, but ability, competence, as such. Chomsky seems to be asking, and indeed in effect does ask, a kind of Kantian question about language: how is language as such possible? But his manner of finding an answer is such that it must tell us a good deal about abilities in general, linguistic and other, and must profoundly affect our picture of man, the possessor of surprising skills, and of the proper procedure of the study of man.

Chomsky is fully aware of this, and explicitly observes that language is only one among other cognitive structures. He is also aware of the philosophic dynamite packed into his theory of language. He is even open to the suspicion that he sometimes enjoys scaring philosophers and making it appear even more explosive than it really is. But it is explosive anyway, even when assessed soberly and formulated without unnecessary paradox. It is this philosophical explosive potential of Chomsky's ideas about language which must help explain some of the fascination which he exerts. There are *frissons* to be obtained from the manner in which he defies ideas that have been established truisms for so long.

What is the basis from which these erstwhile truisms are demolished? Though a linguist, Chomsky clearly does not seem tempted by the view that in the beginning was the word. Nor, one suspects, is he tempted by some form of the Faustian romanticism which maintains that in the beginning was the deed. The starting point, again, is *competence*: not the word, or the act, or even the speech-act, but the range of ability. Chomsky's favourite quotation seems to be one from von Humboldt, to the effect that language uses finite means for infinite ends. This remarkable capacity, and the manner in which it works, is what provides the problem. Faust should have said, perhaps: 'In the beginning was the competence.'

But this still is not quite correct. Competence is only the starting point in that, precisely, it sets a problem. It is not self-explanatory. On the contrary, it seems to be the very paradigm of what needs to be explained, and needs to be explained genuinely and rigorously, not nebulously, schematically and semi-vacuously. This is one of the points—and one not always noticed—at which Chomsky is in marked contrast to some recent philosophic fashions, which were inclined to take skill competence, 'know-how', 'practical knowledge', as somehow primary, ultimate and self-explanatory. Philosophers were inclined to think, for instance, that if some difficult concept could be shown to be rooted, not in some mysterious external reality, but in our linguistic competence, in what we do with words rather than in what words refer to—well then, that was the end of the matter. Language offered philosophic salvation to them precisely because linguistic competence was held to be in no need of explanation. This is the very antithesis of the Chomskian strategy.

This is the first, perhaps the most important, though not the most commonly noticed point at which Chomsky is in conflict with philosophic conventional wisdom. A very great deal in our view of man and the world—much more than is at first apparent—hinges on this question of whether or not our skills and competences are self-explanatory. The view that our competences are self-explanatory is closely connected with what may be called the 'humanist' vision: we are as we normally experience and conceptualize ourselves; the concepts we normally invoke, and which are easily accessible to us, are also sufficient for explaining our behaviour. Thus life and comprehension are not inimical, and true understanding remains within the same circle of ideas as those in terms of which we 'live'.

Chomsky's approach contains nothing to establish this conclusion. The implications of his position for the humanism/scientism battle may be complex and not fully explored: but they certainly involve no straightforward endorsement for such 'humanism'. His famous attack on behaviourism, the logic of which is also sometimes misunderstood, may have misled many people at this point.

This may become more obvious if one considers the next crucial step in the Chomskian approach. The first step was the insistence that competence is just what most requires and most deserves an explanation. The second step is the requirement that the explanation be offered in terms of structures and, ultimately, *deep* structures. Part, at least, of the force of saying this is that the elements and operations in terms of which this kind of structural explanation is to be offered, are not necessarily or generally accessible to consciousness.

For instance, he observes (in the first of the John Locke lectures which he has given at Oxford):

> Clearly, the rules and principles of . . . grammar are not accessible to consciousness in general, though some undoubtedly are . . . what we discover . . . is that those principles and rules that are accessible to consciousness are interspersed in some obscure and apparently chaotic way among others that are not, the whole complex . . . constituting a system of a very tight and intricate design. . . .

Freudian depth-psychology invokes elements which, admittedly, evade and flee consciousness with devilish guile, but which otherwise look and behave remarkably like the denizens of consciousness, except that perhaps they are weirder and wilder. They resemble the denizens of consciousness in that their connection with the behaviour they are meant to explain is even looser, more capricious and arbitrary, than is the nexus between consciousness and conduct, and their real explanatory power is correspondingly weak.

Chomskian depth-linguistics is quite different. The inhabitants of these linguistic nether regions do not evade consciousness with some fiendish Cunning of Unreason: they just seem indifferent to it. Their connection with the verbal behaviour, or rather competence, which they are meant to explain seems, on the other hand, rather more orderly and controlled.

The important point is that, on Chomsky's view, the structures which control our thought or our use of language are not readily available to consciousness simply because it is *our* thought or our language. What could be called the Vico tradition in human and social studies—what *we* make or do must therefore be intelligible to us—is mistaken. The explanation of our competence is only available to investigations which invoke elements and operations that are, in large part, unfamiliar and alien to our ordinary experience and consciousness.

Chomsky insists on this a great deal, and it is a point central to his much misunderstood attack on 'empiricism' and behaviourism. What he really holds against empiricism, in the sense in which he does object to it, is its restrictive regulations concerning what kind of explanatory concepts are to be allowed in human studies. Empiricism of this kind says that our mental life and powers must be explained in terms of elements found *within* our mental life. For instance, we are all familiar with 'association'—the way in which one image can call up another in our stream of consciousness. Hence empiricism attempted to construct a first-person model of the individual accumulation of knowledge in terms of this. Behaviourism, in an effort to be tough-minded, translated this notion of association of ideas into third-person language, refined it a bit, and tried to do the same.

Chomsky's two principal objections to this approach (sometimes not distinguished with sufficient emphasis) are:

1. The structures which emerge from this are too weak to account for the actually observed range and type of competence.

2. The concepts in which those structures are to be defined or designed are so nebulous that they give rise to no structures at all, only to a verbal make-believe substitute of one.

Chomsky's attack on behaviourism is aimed primarily at its genuine and tender-minded, not its spurious and tough-minded part: it is its restrictive use of explanatory principles, not its eagerness to look at man from the outside and willingness to disregard 'internal' evidence, which is under attack. (Chomsky is no fanatic, one way or the other, about the use of introspection, but clearly does not consider it either sufficient or exclusively privileged.)

All this is often misunderstood by those who welcome Chomsky's attack on behaviourism for reasons of their own, and miss the point that what is under attack is the camouflaged, residual but crucial 'internal' (*verstehende*) element in behaviourism, rather than its make-believe rugged husk. It is the crypto-'internal' element in associationism, or stimulus-and-response, which makes it yield such weak or spurious structures.

The misunderstanding is perhaps natural, and in some measure perhaps Chomsky must share the blame for it. It is not his fault if people seize on the negative results of his method—the demonstrations that certain ranges of competence cannot be accounted for by given crude structures—and pay less heed to his pervasive requirement that explanation should be in terms of structures and that these must be expected to contain unfamiliar elements. But he is less blameless of the charge of courting misunderstanding, if one considers the now famous philosophic battle over innate ideas.

Among philosophers, Chomsky is famous, or notorious, for his revival of the theory of innate ideas. A serious, non-frivolous revival of this hypothesis outrages the empiricist conscience. Are we to accept ideas or assertions because, allegedly, they are innate? Well, no: what in fact Chomsky asserted is that our capacity to use language simply cannot be explained by the empiricist model of how our knowledge and skills are acquired. This is quite another point: it amounts to saying that the genetic model associated with empiricism is grossly inadequate. This is almost certainly true. It has nothing much to do, at any rate directly, with the question of how ideas are *validated*; and above all it does not imply the outrageous view that there is a class of ideas that are true in virtue of being 'innate'.

The misunderstanding was not only natural, but it was also

avoidable. It hinges on the distinction between empiricism as a very crude model, or pseudo-model, of the acquisition of skills and information, and empiricism as a theory of how cognitive claims are, in the end, legitimated. One assumed that Chomsky could not be denying it in the latter sense. One of the reasons why his present courses of lectures are of interest is that one now need no longer assume that he *could not* mean this (because it would be too out-rageous), but one can show from his own words that he *does not* mean it. Commenting on a definition of behaviourism, which requires no more than that 'conjectures . . . must eventually be made sense of in terms of external observation', he observes (again in the John Locke lectures): 'This is, to be sure, a sense of "behaviourism" that would cover all reasonable men.' So, when certificates of rationality are to be issued, consistent transcendentalists need not apply! Here Chomsky goes too far—not in endorsing this form of empiricism, which is perfectly in order, but in treating it as so obvious as to be trivial, as to need no support; so obvious that all reasonable men can summarily be assumed to be in agreement with it.

This provides a convincing psychological clue for why Chomsky formulated the so-called 'innate ideas' hypothesis so very pro-vocatively. A man who takes 'weak' empiricism so absolutely for granted, and who, more significantly, cannot conceive of any reason-able man (in any society?) doubting it, will hardly take precautions against it. Nor did he. Yet it is perfectly natural, and historically plausible, to interpret the theory of innate ideas precisely in that manner, as a theory of what it is that legitimates ideas. Time was when not all 'reasonable men' treated weak empiricism as self-evident.

Chomsky seems to have noticed how unnecessarily provocative his formulation had been, and there are passages in the present sets of lectures which sound as if they were intended to mitigate the offence. Thus we find:

> Suppose one is willing to accept the characterisation of knowledge of a language in terms of possession . . . of a generative grammar. . . . Suppose that one is prepared to apply the notion 'knowledge' in this case . . . including [cases] that lie beyond awareness. Suppose that further investigation leads us to the conclusion that this knowledge is acquired on the basis of certain innate principles of . . . 'universal grammar'. . . . Would we want to say, as well, that the child 'knows' the principles of universal grammar?
>
> It seems to me that very little turns on the answer given to this question. It is also unclear to me whether the concept 'knowledge' is sufficiently clear to guide us in making a decision.

This all sounds as if Chomsky now saw how he had given offence by insisting on innate *knowledge*, and appreciated that what his thesis requires is certain innate *structures*, not 'knowledge'. But he is mistaken in supposing that 'very little turns' on this issue, and that it hinges simply on a decision concerning how we are to use the term 'knowledge'.

Something socially far, far more important does hinge on it: whether or not we accept the empiricist doctrine concerning what constitutes the final court of appeal for cognitive claims. It is possible to be an empiricist in this sense, and yet share Chomsky's contempt for the empiricist pseudo-models in psychology and linguistics. The talk about innate ideas failed to make this distinction, at any rate explicitly, even when its provocativeness became manifest.

What gives these rather abstract issues their philosophically exciting character, one which can easily be sensed even by non-specialists? What is at issue is really the uniqueness of man, or the uniqueness of thought, mind, language. The traditional, pre-modern, religious attitude assumed that man and mind were unique, and radically discontinuous with nature. A doctrine of innate ideas, though not necessarily implied by such views, had a natural affinity with them. Chomsky has openly embraced, or rather seemed to embrace, a doctrine of innate ideas. Many of his other views also open up and touch the raw, sensitive nerve of the question of what we are—of how like to nature and machines our thought is, and of whether, and what, uniqueness we may claim.

Consider the two approaches to the study of language which he frequently and joyfully attacks (for instance, in his first Shearman lecture): the behaviourist analysis of language, and the pursuit of analogies with animal systems of communication. Now these might seem matters of interest only to theoreticians of language. In fact, however, these two approaches correspond precisely to the two great paths that modern thought has taken in order to establish the unity of nature, the continuity of nature and man.

In the 18th century, empiricist philosophy did it in the first person, by endeavouring to show that thought was merely a kind of sensing, only perhaps feebler, and with its own principles of association. (The 20th-century behaviourist theories under Chomsky's attack are only refinements of this view, translated into a third-person idiom.) In the 19th century, Darwinism seemed to establish an inherently third-person continuity between man and specifically human skills, and nature: human skills could be seen as exemplifying, in a complex form, the same adaptive principles as all others.

Chomsky's work on language, if valid, destroys both these paths towards establishing continuity. Thus he encourages hopes of a fundamental, radical idiosyncrasy for man, and revives and feeds our ever latent anti-Copernicanism. When all is said and done, many of us would like to see man back at the centre of things and with a status placing us firmly above the rest of nature. All this cosmic equality, as a corollary to impartial styles of explanation, indifferently embracing men, brutes and machines under identical principles, does not please us too much. Many of us tend to be philosophical snobs, when thinking of the nature of existence: we'd rather fancy a special status; and we often look to modern philosophy as a kind of honours list that will gratify this craving. Chomsky offers titillation, if not outright encouragement, for such hopes and sentiments.

As far as I know, Chomsky does not really endorse such hopes, in the way in which he has endorsed the innateness hypothesis. The radical differences in principle between animal systems of communication and human language, which he firmly stresses, do not quite amount to a rejection of the unity of nature. But those who wish to read him in this way can do so.

My own guess is that the real implications and significance of his work are quite other. I do not think he is, philosophically, an arch-reactionary destined to reverse the whole empiricist and naturalist trend of modern thought. On the contrary: there is an old hope underlying human and social studies, of replacing the feeble and capricious explanations of conduct 'from inside' by stronger and more genuine explanations. (Ironically, behaviourist models, despite their spurious tough-minded exterior, belong to the inadequate 'insider' species, as Chomsky shows.)

The real significance of Chomsky's work is that he has taken this old hope and brought it much closer to reality and to precise, concrete research. He is of course perfectly capable, and willing, to carry out his own philosophical exegesis. But he might conceivably agree that a man's view of the philosophical implications of his own work are not necessarily privileged or final.

1969

Sources

The following are the original places and dates of publication of the chapters in this volume:

chapter 1: *Hibbert Journal*, **56**, April 1958, 251–5; chapter 2: J. H. Plumb, ed., *Crisis in the Humanities*, Harmondsworth, 1964, 45–81; chapter 3: *Worldview*, **16**, no. 6, June 1973, 49–53; chapter 4: *Rationalist Annual*, 1955, 74–81; chapter 5: *Hibbert Journal*, **56**, October 1957, 31–41; chapter 6: *Mind*, **60**, no. 3, July 1951, 383–93; chapter 7: *Proceedings of the Aristotelian Society*, **55**, no. 7, 14 March 1955, 157–78; chapter 8: *Analysis*, **12**, no. 2, December 1951, 25–35; chapter 9: *Analysis*, **16**, no. 5, April 1956, 97–103; chapter 10: D. J. O'Connor, ed., *A Critical History of Western Philosophy*, New York, 1964, 275–95; chapter 11: *The Times Literary Supplement*, no. 3708, 30 March 1973, 337–9; chapter 12: *New Statesman*, **78**, 28 November 1969, 774–6; chapter 13: *Ratio*, **5**, no. 2, December 1963, 168–80; chapter 14: *Question*, **5**, 1972, 81–9; chapter 15: *Spectator*, **227**, 28 August 1971, 307–8; chapter 16: *Inquiry*, **5**, no. 1, Spring 1962, 85–90; chapter 17: *Inquiry*, **4**, no. 3, Autumn 1961, 209–14; chapter 18: *Spectator*, **226**, 15 May 1971, 672–3; chapter 19: *The Times Literary Supplement*, no. 3666, 2 June 1972, 629; chapter 20: *Spectator*, **229**, 15 July 1972, 95–6; chapter 21: *New Society*, **13**, no. 348, 29 May 1969, 831–3.

Bibliography of Ernest Gellner

compiled by I. C. Jarvie

Those items which have been republished in the volumes of selected papers are marked by asterisks, as follows:

* = *Cause and meaning in the social sciences*
** = *Contemporary thought and politics*
*** = *The devil in modern philosophy*

1951

(a) 'Maxims', *Mind*, **60**, no. 3, July, 383–93.***
(b) 'Use and meaning', *Cambridge Journal*, **4**, no. 12, September, 753–61.
(c) 'Analysis and ontology', *Philosophical Quarterly*, **1**, no. 5, October, 408–15.
(d) 'Knowing how and validity', *Analysis*, **12**, no. 2, December, 25–35.***
(e) Review of Michael Polanyi, *The Logic of Liberty* in *British Journal of Sociology*, **2**, no. 4, December, 361–2.

1954

(a) 'The philosophy of Wittgenstein' (review of L. Wittgenstein, *Philosophical Investigations*), *The Tutor's Bulletin of Adult Education*, nos 95 and 96, June–September, 20–4.
(b) 'Reflections on violence' (review-article on Stanislaw Andrzejewski, *Military Organization and Society*), *British Journal of Sociology*, **5**, no. 3, September, 267–71.

1955

(a) 'On being wrong', *Rationalist Annual*, 74–81.***
(b) 'Ethics and logic', *Proceedings of the Aristotelian Society*, **55**, no. 7, 14 March, 157–78.***
(c) Review of Isaiah Berlin, *Historical Inevitability* in *British Journal of Sociology*, **6**, no. 4, December, 389; repeated (by mistake?) in **7**, no. 3, September 1956, 268.

1956

(a) 'The empty niche', *Truth*, 27 January, 94–5.
(b) 'Morality and *je ne sais quoi* concepts', *Analysis*, **16**, no. 5, April, 97–103.***
(c) 'Berbers of Morocco', *Quarterly Review*, **294**, no. 608, April, 218–23. Translated into French in Général P. J. André, *Confrèries Religieuses Musulmanes*, Alger: Editions La Maison des Livres, 345–50.
(d) 'Explanation in history', *Proceedings of the Aristotelian Society*, Supplementary vol. 30, *Dreams and Self-Knowledge*, July, 157–76. Reprinted (with additions) as 'Holism *versus* individualism in history and sociology', together with a Reply to J. W. N. Watkins's criticism in P. Gardiner, ed., *Theories of History*, Chicago: Free Press, 1959; and as 'Holism versus individualism', in M. Brodbeck, ed., *Readings in the Philosophy of the Social Sciences*, New York: Macmillan, 1968, 254–68.*
(e) Review of Margaret Hasluck, *The Unwritten Law in Albania* in *British Journal of Sociology*, **7**, no. 3, September, 271–2.
(f) 'The sheep and the saint', *Encounter*, **7**, November, 42–6.
(g) Review of Arthur F. Bentley, *Inquiry Into Inquiries* in *British Journal of Sociology*, **7**, no. 4, December, 357.

1957

(a) 'Determinism and validity', *Rationalist Annual*, 69–79.
(b) Review of Abraham Edel, *Ethical Judgement* in *British Journal for the Philosophy of Science*, **7**, no. 4, February, 360–2.
(c) 'Highlanders of Morocco', *The Times*, 25 March, 11.
(d) 'The summit of Azurki', *LSE Mountaineering Club Journal*, **4**, 7–12. (Also in *Humanist*, **74**, no. 1, January 1959, 16–19.)
(e) Review of D. Daiches Raphael, *Moral Judgement* in *British Journal of Sociology*, **8**, no. 2, June, 194.
(f) 'Independence in the Central High Atlas', *Middle East Journal*, **11**, no. 3, Summer, 236–52.
(g) 'Ideal language and kinship structure', *Philosophy of Science*, **24**, no. 2, July, 235–42.*
(h) 'Reflections on linguistic philosophy I and II', *Listener*, **58**, 8 and 15 August, 205–7, 237, and 240–1. (See also correspondence at 354, 439–40.)
(i) 'Logical positivism and after or: the spurious fox', *Universities Quarterly*, **11**, no. 4, August, 348–64. (*Also* in *Universities and Left Review*, Winter 1958, 67–73.)
(j) 'Professor Toulmin's return to Aristotle', *Universities Quarterly*, **11**, no. 4, August, 368–72. (Also in *Universities and Left Review*. Summer 1958, 73–4.)

(k) 'Beauty and the Berber', *Humanist*, **72**, no. 9, September, 15–18.
(l) 'Is belief really necessary?', *Hibbert Journal*, **56**, October, 31–41.***
(m) 'Contemporary thought and politics' (review of P. Laslett and W. G. Runciman, eds, *Philosophy, Politics and Society*), *Philosophy*, **32**, no. 123, October, 336–57.**
(n) Review of Morris Ginsberg, *On the Diversity of Morals* and *Reason and Unreason in Society* in *Universities Quarterly*, **12**, no. 1, November, 83–91.
(o) Review of J. Kraft, *Von Husserl zu Heidegger* in *British Journal of Sociology*, **8**, no. 4, December, 380.

1958

(a) 'Ernst Kolman: or communism and knowledge', *Soviet Survey*, no. 23, January–March, 66–71.**
(b) Review of P. H. Gulliver, *The Family Herds* in *British Journal of Sociology*, **9**, no. 1, March, 106–7; repeated in **10**, no. 2, June 1959, 165–6.
(c) 'The far West of Islam' (review-article on Jacques Berque, *Structures sociales du Haut-Atlas*), *British Journal of Sociology*, **9**, no. 1, March, 73–82.
(d) 'How to live in anarchy', *Listener*, **59**, 3 April, 579, 582–3.**
(e) 'Time and theory in social anthropology', *Mind*, n.s. **67**, no. 2, April, 182–202.*
(f) 'The devil in modern philosophy', *Hibbert Journal*, **56**, April, 251–5.***
(g) 'Reply to Mr. MacIntyre', *Universities and Left Review*, Summer, 73–4.
(h) Review of R. Firth, ed., *Man and Culture: An Evaluation of the Work of Bronislaw Malinowski* in *Universities Quarterly*, **13**, no. 1, November, 86–92.*
(i) 'The sociology of faith' (review of Werner Stark, *The Sociology of Knowledge*), *Inquiry*, **1**, no. 4, Winter, 247–52.*

1959

(a) 'Prepare to meet thy doom', *Listener*, **61**, 19 March, 510–11, 514.**
(b) 'The alchemists of sociology' (review of Pitrim Sorokin, *Fads and Foibles in Modern Sociology*), *Inquiry*, **2**, no. 2, Summer, 126–35.*
(c) 'Am Anfang war das Wort', *Studium Generale*, **12**, no. 9, September, 611–14.
(d) *Words and Things*, London: Gollancz; Boston: Beacon. (See also the correspondence in *The Times*, 5 November, 13 (Bertrand

Russell); 9 November, 11 (Gilbert Ryle); 10 November, 13 (Conrad Dehn, G. R. G. Mure); 11 November, 11 (Ernest Gellner, Leslie Farrer); 13 November, 13 (John Wisdom); 14 November, 7 (B. F. McGuiness); 16 November, 13 (J. N. Wright, Kevin Holland); 17 November, 13 (Joan Robinson, Arnold Kaufman); 18 November, 13 (T. P. Creed); 19 November, 13 (J. W. N. Watkins); 20 November, 13 (John G. Vance); 21 November, 7 (Alec Kassman, E. H. Thompson); 23 November, 13 (R. Meager, Alan Donagan); 24 November, 13 (Bertrand Russell and leading article.)

(e) 'Patterns of fact-and-choice' (review of A. J. Ayer, ed., *Logical Positivism*), *Guardian*, 4 December, 12.

1960

(a) 'The Middle East observed', *Political Studies*, **8**, no. 1, February, 66–70.

(b) Review of J. N. D. Anderson, *Islamic Law in the Modern World* in *British Journal of Sociology*, **11**, no. 1, March, 98–9.

(c) 'The concept of kinship', *Philosophy of Science*, **27**, no. 2, April, 187–204.*

(d) Review of Peter Winch, *The Idea of a Social Science* in *British Journal of Sociology*, **11**, no. 2, June, 170–2.*

(e) Review of F. Barth, *Political Leadership Among the Swat Pathans* in *British Journal of Sociology*, **11**, no. 2, June, 190.

(f) 'Allah and Caesar', *Hibbert Journal*, **59**, October, 54–8.

(g) 'Emergent sociology', *Spectator*, **205**, 2 December, 907–8.

1961

(a) Review of Robert K. Merton, *Social Theory and Social Structure* in *British Journal for the Philosophy of Science*, **11**, no. 4, February, 345–6.

(b) 'Time machines' (review of Raymond Aron, *Introduction to the Philosophy of History*), *Time and Tide*, **42**, 3 February, 176–7.

(c) *Parole e Cose* (Italian trans. of *Words and Things*), Milan: Il Baggiatore.

(d) 'The organization man', report of a conversation with W. H. Whyte, *Listener*, **66**, 7 September, 337–9.

(e) 'What makes Plato run?', *Humanist*, **76**, no. 9, September, 274–5.

(f) Review of R. E. Money-Kyrle, *Man's Picture of His World* in *Inquiry*, **4**, no. 3, Autumn, 209–14.***

(g) 'From Ibn Khaldun to Karl Marx' (review of Donald E. Ashford, *Political Change in Morocco*), *Political Quarterly*, **32**, no. 4, October/December, 385–92.

(h) 'The struggle for Morocco's past', *Middle East Journal*, **15**, no. 1, Winter, 79–90; reprinted in I. W. Zartman, ed., *Man, State and Society in the Contemporary Maghrib*, New York: Praeger, 1973.

(i) 'Morocco' in Colin Legum, ed., *Africa, A Handbook of the Continent*, London: Anthony Blond, pp. 43–60.

(j) Review of W. Montgomery Watt, *Islam and the Integration of Society* in *British Journal of Sociology*, **12**, no. 4, December, 392–3.

1962

(a) Review of T. A. Goudge, *The Ascent of Life* in *Inquiry*, **5**, no. 1, Spring, 85–90.***

(b) 'Concepts and society', *Transactions of the Fifth World Congress of Sociology* (*Washington*), Louvain, **1**, 153–83. Reprinted in B. Wilson, ed., *Rationality*, Oxford: Basil Blackwell, 1970, 18–49; and in D. Emmett and A. MacIntyre, eds, *Sociological Theory and Philosophical Analysis*, London: Macmillan, 1970, 115–49.*

(c) *Palabras y Cosas* (Spanish trans. of *Words and Things*), Madrid: Editorial Tecnos, S.A.

(d) *Slova i Vieshchi* (Russian trans. of *Words and Things*), Moscow: Publishing House of Foreign Literature.

(e) 'Patterns of rural rebellion in Morocco: tribes as minorities', *European Journal of Sociology*, **3**, no. 2, 297–311; reprinted in 1973(b), 361–74.

1963

(a) 'Going into Europe', *Encounter*, **20**, January, 54–5.

(b) 'A Tunisian visit', *New Society*, **1**, 3 January, 15–17.

(c) Review of Rom Landau, *Morocco Independent* in *Middle East Journal*, **17**, nos 1 and 2, Winter–Spring, 174–5.

(d) 'Sanctity, puritanism, secularisation and nationalism in North Africa', *Archives de sociologie des religions*, no. 15, 71–86. Also in J. G. Peristiany, ed., *Contributions to Mediterranean Sociology: Mediterranean Rural Communities and Social Change*. Acts of the Mediterranean Sociology Conference, July 1963, Paris: Mouton, 1965, 31–48.

(e) 'Thy neighbour's revolution', *New Society*, **1**, 16 May, 20–1.

(f) 'Nature and society in social anthropology', *Philosophy of Science*, **30**, no. 3, July, 236–51.*

(g) 'Saints of the Atlas', in Julian Pitt-Rivers, ed., *Mediterranean Countrymen*, Paris and the Hague: Mouton, 145–57.

(h) 'Ayer's epistle to the Russians', *Ratio*, **5**, no. 2, December, 168–80.***

1964

(a) 'Foreword' to I. C. Jarvie, *The Revolution in Anthropology*, London: Routledge & Kegan Paul, v–viii.
(b) Review of C. F. Gallagher, *The United States and North Africa* in *New Society*, **3**, 30 April, 28–9.
(c) 'The new blimpery', *Views*, no. 5, Summer, 105–10.
(d) 'Hume and North African Islam' in *Religion in Africa*, Centre of African Studies, University of Edinburgh, July, mimeographed.
(e) 'Political and religious organization of the Berbers of the Central High Atlas', *Proceedings of the Seventh International Congress of Anthropology, Moscow, August 1964*, **4**, 314–21; reprinted in 1973(b), 59–66.
(f) Definitions of 'Atomism', 'Concept', 'Determinism', 'Empiricism', 'Fact', 'Model', and 'Social Fact', in J. Gould and W. L. Kolb, eds, *A Dictionary of the Social Sciences*, London: Tavistock; New York: Free Press.
(g) 'French eighteenth-century materialism' in D. J. O'Connor, ed., *A Critical History of Western Philosophy*, New York: Free Press, 275–95.***
(h) 'The crisis in the humanities and the mainstream of philosophy' in J. H. Plumb, ed., *Crisis in the Humanities*, Harmondsworth: Penguin, 45–81.***

1965

(a) *Thought and Change*, London: Weidenfeld & Nicolson; University of Chicago Press (with the imprint 1964).
(b) 'The day the pendulum stood still' (review of Sylvia G. Haim, ed., *Arab Nationalism*), *New Society*, **5**, 15 April, 30–1.
(c) Review of E. E. Evans-Pritchard, *The Position of Women in Primitive Societies and Other Essays* in *Oxford Magazine*, n.s. **5**, 17 June, 417–19.*
(d) 'Tribalism and social change in North Africa' in W. H. Lewis, ed., *French-Speaking Africa, The Search for Identity*, New York: Walker, 107–18.
(e) Review of Abraham Kaplan, *The Conduct of Inquiry* in *British Journal of Sociology*, **16**, no. 3, September, 278.

1966

(a) 'On democracy in France' (review of Raymond Aron, *Essai sur les libertés*, and J.-F. Revel, *En France. La fin de l'opposition*) in *Government and Opposition*, **1**, no. 2, January, 255–64.**

(b) 'The shortage of generalisations' (review of Walter Goldschmidt, *Comparative Functionalism: An Essay in Anthropological Theory*), *New Society*, **8**, 11 August 239–40.
(c) 'Comments' on E. R. Leach, *The Founding Fathers, Current Anthropology*, **7**, no. 5, December, 571–4.

1967

(a) Review of *Asian and African Studies*, vol. 1 in *Middle Eastern Studies*, **3**, no. 2, January, 182–7.
(b) Review of I. M. Lewis, ed., *Islam in Tropical Africa* in *Cambridge Review*, **89**, no. 2138, 28 January, 180–1.
(c) 'Democracy and industrialisation', *European Journal of Sociology*, **8**, 47–70.**
(d) 'The concept of a story' (review of W. B. Gallie, *Philosophy and Historical Understanding*), *Ratio*, **9**, no. 1, June, 49–66.**
(e) Review of T. T. Segerstedt, *The Nature of Social Reality* in *Synthese*, **17**, 107–8.
(f) 'Sociology and social anthropology', *Transactions of the Sixth World Congress of Sociology (Evian) 1966*, Louvain, **2**, 49–83.*

1968

(a) 'The entry of the philosophers', *The Times Literary Supplement*, no. 3449, 5 April, 347–9. See also correspondence at 427, 457, 514.*
(b) Review of Ian Cunnison, *Baggara Arabs: Power and Lineage in a Sudanese Nomad Tribe* in *Middle Eastern Studies*, **4**, no. 3, April, 326–8.
(c) 'A Pendulum swing theory of Islam', *Annales marocaines de sociologie* (Institut de sociologie, Rabat), 5–14. Also in *Philosophical Forum*, **2**, Winter 1970–1, 234–44. Anthologized in Roland Robertson, ed., *Sociology of Religion*, Harmondsworth: Penguin, 1969, 127–38.
(d) 'The new idealism' in I. Lakatos and A. Musgrave, eds, *Problems in the Philosophy of Science*, Amsterdam: North Holland, 377–406 and 426–32; reprinted in Anthony Giddens, ed., *Positivism and Sociology*, London: Heinemann, 1974; in German in Hans Albert, ed., *Theorie und Realität*, 2nd ed., Tübingen: Mohr, 1972, 87–112.*

1969

(a) Ed. with Ghita Ionescu, *Populism: Its National Characteristics*, London: Weidenfeld & Nicolson; University of Chicago Press.
(b) 'Système tribal et changement social en Afrique du nord', *Annales marocaines de sociologie* (Institut de sociologie, Rabat), 3–19.

(c) 'The great Patron', *European Journal of Sociology*, **10**, 61–9.
(d) 'The panther and the dove: reflections on rebelliousness and its milieux' in D. Martin, ed., *Anarchy and Culture, The Problem of the Contemporary University*, London: Routledge & Kegan Paul, 129–47.**
(e) 'On Chomsky', *New Society*, **13**, no. 348, 29 May, 831–3.***
(f) 'Far West and Wild West' (review of André Adain, *Histoire de Casablanca des origines à 1914*), *New Society*, **14**, 17 July, 102–3.
(g) 'Behind the barricades at L.S.E.' (review of H. Kidd, *The Trouble at L.S.E.*), *The Times Educational Supplement*, 12 September, 33.**
(h) 'Poker player' (review of K. T. Fann, ed., *Symposium on J. L. Austin*), *New Statesman*, **78**, 28 November, 774–6.***
(i) 'Myth, ideology and revolution', *Political Quarterly*, **40**, no. 4, October–December, 472–84; reprinted in B. Crick and W. A. Robson, eds, *Protest and Discontent*, Harmondsworth: Penguin, 1970, 204–20.**
(j) *Saints of the Atlas*, London: Weidenfeld & Nicolson; University of Chicago Press.

1970

(a) 'The aims and criteria of development', in K. B. Madhava, ed., *International Development 1969*, Society for International Development, Washington; New Delhi: Oceana, 50–3.
(b) 'Erkenntnis als Ernüchterung' in Willy Hochkeppel, ed., *Soziologie zwischen Theorie und Empirei*, Munich: Nymphenburger Verlagshandlung, 51–9.
(c) 'Pouvoir politique et fonction religieuse dans l'Islam marocain', *Annales: économies—sociétés—civilisations*, **25**, no. 2, mars–avril, 699–713.
(d) Review of Gavin Maxwell, *Lords of the Atlas* in *Middle Eastern Studies*, **6**, no. 2, May, 224–7.
(e) 'Structuralism' (review of Michael Lane, ed., *Structuralism: A Reader*), *Beaver*, 12 November, 6.*

1971

(a) Review of Talal Asad, *The Kababish Arabs: Power, Authority and Consent in a Nomadic Tribe* in *British Journal of Sociology*, **22**, no. 1, March, 110–11.
(b) 'The dangers of tolerance', *Government and Opposition*, **6**, no. 2, Spring, 211–18.**
(c) Review of Robert E. Fernea, *Shaykh and Effendi: Changing Patterns of Authority Among the El Shabana of Southern Iraq* in *Sociology*, **5**, no. 2, 267–8.

(d) 'Ernest Gellner on Freud and Reich' (review of Richard Woll-heim, *Freud*; Penelope Balogh, *Freud: A Biographical Intro-duction*; Charles Rycroft, *Reich*; Sigmund Freud, *The Complete Introductory Lectures on Psychoanalysis*), *Spectator*, **226**, 15 May, 672–3.***

(e) 'Our current sense of history', *European Journal of Sociology*, **12**, 159–79; also in *Survey*, **17**, no. 3, Summer, 13–30; reprinted in English and in French in J. Dumoulin and D. Moisi, eds, *L'Histoire entre l'Ethnologie et la Futurologie* (*History between Ethnology and Futurology*), postface par Raymond Aron, Paris and The Hague: Mouton, 1972, 9–37, discussion 38–72.**

(f) 'Going into Europe—again?', *Encounter*, **37**, August, 40–1.

(g) 'The anti-levellers of Prague', *New Society*, **18**, 5 August, 232–4.

(h) 'Ernest Gellner on the belief machine' (review of Alasdair MacIntyre, *Against the Self-Images of the Age: Essays on Ideology and Philosophy*), *Spectator*, **227**, 28 August, 307–8.***

(i) 'Stratification with a human face', *The Times Literary Supplement*, no. 3633, 15 October, 1275–6.

(j) 'The pluralist anti-levellers of Prague', *European Journal of Sociology*, **12**, 312–25; also in *Dissent*, Summer 1972, 471–82.**

(k) 'The sacred word' (review of Bryan Magee, ed., *Modern British Philosophy*), *Spectator*, **227**, 18 December, 888–9.

1972

(a) 'Ayer on Moore and Russell', *Question*, **5**, 81–9.***

(b) Review of Elie Kedourie, *Nationalism in Asia and Africa* in *British Journal of Sociology*, **23**, no. 1, March, 120–3.

(c) 'A genetic psychologist's confessions' (review of J. Piaget, *Insights and Illusions of Philosophy* and *Epistémologie des sciences de l'homme*), *The Times Literary Supplement*, no. 3666, 2 June, 629.***

(d) Review of Vladimir V. Kusin, *The Intellectual Origins of the Prague Spring* in *British Journal of Sociology*, **23**, no. 2, June, 258–60.

(e) 'Eysenck: seeing emperors naked' (review of H. J. Eysenck, *Psychology is About People*), *Spectator*, **229**, 15 July, 95–6.***

(f) 'Doctor and saint' in Nikki R. Keddie, ed., *Scholars, Saints, and Sufis*, Berkeley and Los Angeles: University of California Press, 307–26.

(g) Contribution to 'The achievement of Sir Karl Popper', *Listener*, **88**, no. 2265, 24 August, 228.

(h) 'A cheerful philosopher of social science' (review of I. C. Jarvie, *Concepts and Society*), *The Times Literary Supplement*, no. 3679, 1 September, 1026.

(i) 'The Savage and the Modern Mind', in Robin Horton and Ruth Finnegan, eds, *Modes of Thought*, London: Faber, 162–81.

1973

(a) 'Post-traditional forms in Islam: the turf and trade, and votes and peanuts', *Daedalus*, **102**, no. 1, Winter, 191–206.
(b) Ed. with Charles Micaud, *Arabs and Berbers*, London: Duckworth. Contains an introduction and reprints of 1962(e) and 1964(e).
(c) Preface to the English trans. of Robert Montagne, *The Berbers*, London: Frank Cass.
(d) 'Thought and time, or the reluctant relativist' (review of Michael Krausz, ed., *Critical Essays on the Philosophy of Collingwood*), *The Times Literary Supplement*, no. 3708, 30 March, 337–9.***
(e) 'Reflections on philosophy, especially in America', *Worldview*, **16**, no. 6, June, 49–53.***
(f) *The Legitimation of Belief*, Cambridge University Press.
(g) *Cause and Meaning in the Social Sciences*, ed. I. C. Jarvie and J. Agassi, London: Routledge & Kegan Paul.
(h) Review of Peter Laslett, W. G. Runciman and Quentin Skinner, eds, *Philosophy, Politics and Society*, 4th Series, in *The Times Literary Supplement*, no. 3694, 22 December, 1552.
(i) 'Scale and Nation', *Philosophy of the Social Sciences*, **3**, no. 1, March, 1–17.
(j) Introduction to Cynthia Nelson, ed., *The Desert and the Town. Nomads in Wider Society*, Research Series no. 21, Institute of International Studies, University of California, Berkeley.
(k) *Populismo, Suo Significago y Caracteristicas Nacionales* (Spanish trans. of 1969(a)), Buenos Aires: Amorortu Editores.
(l) Review of Yu. V. Maretin and D. A. Olderogge, eds, *Stranyi i Narody Vostoka* (Countries and Peoples of the East), in *Man*, n.s. **8**, no. 3, September, 505.
(m) Review of G. V. Osipov, ed., *Town, Country and People*, in *Man*, n.s. **8**, no. 3, September, 506–8.
(n) 'Primitive Communism' (review article on *Ochotniki, Sobirateli, Rybolovi (Hunters, Gatherers, Fishermen)*), *Man*, n.s. **8**, no. 4, December, 536–42.
(o) Review of John H. Barnsley, *The Social Reality of Ethics*, in *Man*, n.s. **8**, no. 4, December, 645–6.

1974 and forthcoming

(a) Review of Magali Morsy, *Les Ahansala*, in *L'Annuaire de l'Afrique du Nord*, Aix en Provence.
(b) Review of Harvey E. Goldberg, *Cave Dwellers and Citrus Growers*, in *Middle Eastern Studies*.

(c) *Contemporary Thought and Politics*, ed. I. C. Jarvie and Joseph Agassi, London: Routledge & Kegan Paul.
(d) 'The Re-Enchantment Industry or the Californian Way of Subjectivity', in a volume edited by Robert Wilson.
(e) Review of H. T. Morris, *Saharan Myth and Saga*, in *Man*.
(f) *Legitimation of Belief*, London: Cambridge University Press.
(g) Review of Michael Gilsenan, *Saint and Sufi in Modern Egypt*, in *Religious Studies*.
(h) Review of Vincent Crapanzano, *The Hamadsha: A Study in Moroccan Ethnopsychiatry*, in *Africa*.
(i) *The Devil in Modern Philosophy*, ed. I. C. Jarvie and Joseph Agassi, London: Routledge & Kegan Paul.
(j) 'The Unknown Apollo of Biskra', *Government and Opposition*.
(k) Translation of Yu. I. Semenov, 'Theoretical Problems of "Economic Anthropology" ', *Philosophy of the Social Sciences*, **4**, September 1974.

Index of names

In these indexes italic numerals indicate an important reference, *n* indicates the reference is in a note, and *q* indicates a quotation.

Index of subjects

absolute, the, 20
absolute idealism, 51, 165
absolute presuppositions, 158–60
absolutism, 136
abstract, abstractness, 4; general metaphysics, 10–11, 24–6, 28; levels of, 67, 76, 83, 89
absurd, 54–6, 81–2, 91, 98
academic titles, 215
Acceleration Principle, 26, 35–6n
Achilles and the tortoise, 98–100
act, action, 67–8, 70–1, 74–8, 83–4, 92, 134, 138; justification of, 71–4, 78, 83–4, 91–2, 104, 197
acte gratuit, 84, 90
ad hoc, 107
adaptation, 205
aesthetics, 95–7, 207
Africa, 53
ahistorism, 161; *see also* timelessness
alienation, 33, 194
America, 37–44, 56, 60
analysis, 178–9, 181, 183–4, 189, 191, 195, 197; *see also* language analysis
Anglo-Saxon philosophical tradition, 124, 218
angry cult, 30
anguish, 196
animal language, 231
animism, 71, 132
anthropodicy, 213
anthropology, philosophical, 131–3, 166, 226–7, 231–2
anthropology, social, 35, 55, 61, 105

anthropomorphism, 128–31, 133, 138, 145–6
anti-clericalism, anti-revelationism, 54, 113–17, 124; absence of in Britain, 124
anxiety, intellectual, 18–19, 163; *see also* complacency, cognitive
anything goes, 54, 219
apartheid, 180–1, 201
appearance, 7, 16, 28; *see also* explanation; realism
applied science, 182, 212
approximations, 13
a priori, apriorism, *see* rationalism; *see also* Cartesianism; intuition
arbitrariness, arbitrary, 54–5, 81, 90, 92, 99, 102, 109
archaism, 182
argument, *see* critical debate
artisans, 29
arts, 29–30, 53
associationism, 228–9
atheism, 33, 57, 121, 144–5, 148
atomism, 13, 15, 34; logical, 156
attitudes, outlooks, 61, 80–1, 90, 92, 108, 114–22, 124, 160; *see also* world-picture
Austria, 23
authority, 54–5, 113, 135–6, 143, 145, 166, 177
autism, philosophical, 158, 217; *see also* anxiety, intellectual; complacency, cognitive
Autobiography, R. G. Collingwood's, 34n, 151–3, 156, 163–4, 216